Death until Resurrection

Death until Resurrection
—— An Unconscious Sleep According to Luther ——

Joseph Saligoe

WIPF & STOCK · Eugene, Oregon

DEATH UNTIL RESURRECTION
An Unconscious Sleep According to Luther

Copyright © 2020 Joseph Saligoe. All rights reserved. Except for brief quotations in critical publications or reviews, no part of this book may be reproduced in any manner without prior written permission from the publisher. Write: Permissions, Wipf and Stock Publishers, 199 W. 8th Ave., Suite 3, Eugene, OR 97401.

Wipf & Stock
An Imprint of Wipf and Stock Publishers
199 W. 8th Ave., Suite 3
Eugene, OR 97401

www.wipfandstock.com

PAPERBACK ISBN: 978-1-7252-5339-1
HARDCOVER ISBN: 978-1-7252-5340-7
EBOOK ISBN: 978-1-7252-5341-4

Manufactured in the U.S.A.   03/02/20

This book is dedicated to my mother, Wanda, and to my father, Joe (d. 1986).

Won't somebody tell me . . . what is the soul of a man? . . .
As far as I can understand, a man is more than his mind.

—Steven Stern and George Krikes, "Soul of a Man," in *Son of God*,
Original Motion Picture Soundtrack (2014)

Contents

List of Tables and Outlines | xi
Acknowledgments | xiii
Abbreviations | xiv

1: What Happens When People Die? | 1
    Resolving the confusion on what Luther thought   1

2: Was It Really Just for a While? | 10
    An overview   10
    My purpose and disagreement among the experts   16
    Anthony Thiselton and his analysis of death   27

3: Luther Lore versus the Truth | 30
    Let's start at the beginning   30
    The Luther paradox   34
    Five hundred years of confusion is long enough   42
    Luther from 1505 to 1518   47

4: Unraveling the Issue with This Study on Luther | 51
    Luther is an ocean   51
    Assessment of similar studies   53
    My analysis begins in the winter of 1515–1516   56
    Luther in 1517   62
    Luther in 1519   64
    Luther in 1521   67

5: An Investigation of Luther's Early Period | 80
  Luther in 1522 80
  Luther in 1523 to 1525 94

6: An Investigation of Luther's Middle Period | 106
  Luther in 1526 to 1531 106
  Luther in 1532 to 1535 111

7: An Investigation of Luther's Later Period | 120
  Luther in 1536 to mid-1540 120
  Luther in mid-1540 to 1546 128

8: The Where and How of Death and Resurrection | 141
  Luther's descriptions of where the deceased go 141
  My claim about death and resurrection 151
  Letting Luther speak more on death 158
  Returning to my claim 163

9: Was Luther a Physicalist Regarding the Soul? | 168
  Did Luther use sleep *literally or symbolically in the sense of mortality?* 168
  Which top theologians knew what Luther believed about soul immortality? 185

Conclusion | 191
Epilogue | 198
Appendix: Analysis Tables and Outlines | 201
Bibliography | 211

THE RIETSCHEL LUTHER

Ernst F.A. Rietschel (1804–1861) designed, in 1859, the celebrated Luther Monument in Worms, Germany (which consists of twelve bronze statues), and who also completed the 11-foot tall statue of Luther (as well as one other, Wycliff) shortly before his death, leaving Hus, Calvin, Zwingli, etc. to his pupils (with an unveiling in an 1868 ceremony attended by some 20,000 people).

Tables and Outlines

Tables: Each of the following tables was created from the author's original research and forms part of the basis of the book's conclusion.

> Table 1. Comparison of periods that Luther discussed death as unconsciousness | 201
>
> Table 2. Relevant works by type and number of distinct daily events (producing 61 days) | 202
>
> Table 3. Genesis chapters with the most instances in the Genesis lecture series | 202
>
> Table 4. Most instances ranked by type of work | 203
>
> Table 5. Sermons and lectures on books of the Bible with death as unconsciousness | 203
>
> Table 6. Years ranked by highest incidence of "death as unconscious sleep" mentions | 203
>
> Table 7. Measuring Luther's emphasis in his works containing "death as sleep" (210 instances) | 204

Outlines: The following three outlines concisely summarize Luther's discussions of death during three stages of his life where the first two outlines are preliminary and thus are excluded from the count of 210 instances using strict criteria where he had mentioned literal death being like natural sleep over the last twenty-four years of his life (excluding his quotes of Scripture and of its commentators).

> Outline 1. The very first mention of "death as sleep" during a university lecture on Romans 6 in the winter of 1515–1516. | 206

Outline 2. Further ambiguous mentions of the subject are seen in five writings from 1517 to 1521. | 207

Outline 3. The count begins in January 1522 with a personal letter from Luther responding to a friend's question and contains several unambiguous mentions of literal death as being unconscious sleep, and this outline presents an annualized summary from 1522 to 1546, the year of Luther's death, and it includes several quotes in 1522 and in 1545 from his translated writings. | 207

Acknowledgments

I want to thank the following individuals for reading and commenting on the draft chapters of the manuscript: Dr. Scott Seay (history professor, etc. at Christian Theological Seminary) who has particular expertise in Luther studies and who has continued to be helpful to me; Dr. James Lewis (former dean of the seminary at Anderson University) who has continued to provide great encouragement to me ever since the beginning of this long project and after his own retirement from teaching there; and Dr. Gregory Robertson (theology professor at AU). I also want to thank the present dean of the AU seminary, Dr. MaryAnn Hawkins. If it wasn't for her input one day, this book may not have been written. Additionally, I want to thank the following people: Jonathan Stemerick for providing extensive comments on the draft chapters of the manuscript (who also recently obtained an MTS degree from AU); Dr. Janet Brewer (library director at AU); and Nicholas Stanton-Roark (library archivist at AU) who also provided invaluable assistance as a most knowledgeable writing tutor.

I appreciate the support and academic instruction from them in improving my writing and research techniques, and in maximizing my potential as a student of Scripture. I would like to express special gratitude to Caleb Shupe, copy editor at Wipf and Stock Publishers, for providing many helpful suggestions and corrections to the manuscript. For the final product, however, I take full responsibility. Sincere appreciation goes to the editorial, copyediting, and production team. I also want to especially thank my wife, Novalea Saligoe, for her patience and abiding care throughout these last eight years of near full-time study and writing (Master of Theological Studies, and presently, I'm working on a PhD in Theology). This preparation has culminated in this book (my first of hopefully several books on the biblical topics of rethinking the nature of the soul, the nature of death and of resurrection, and as a consequence of this, the rethinking of the nature and duration of hell).

Abbreviations

E The Erlangen edition of the works of Luther (in their original language); contains over 100 volumes; published in 1826–1857 plus later revisions; and is also referred to as "Luthers Samtliche Werke," "Erlangener Ausgabe," or "EA."

LW *Luther's Works* is an English translation; first published in 1955 with about 68 volumes so far (a few more are expected); and is also referred to as the "American Edition." There were at least two other series consisting of an English translation that preceded *LW* (in the nineteenth and twentieth centuries).

StL The Saint Louis edition of the works of Luther (in Luther's original language, either German or Latin) was revised in 1885–1910; first published in 1740–1753; contains 24 volumes; and is also referred to as the "Walch Edition," "St. Louis-Walch," or the "Halle Edition."

WA The Weimar edition is the most complete set of Luther's works (in their original language); published in 1883–2009; contains 136 volumes; and is also referred to as "Martin Luthers Werke" or "Weimarer Ausgabe."

── CHAPTER 1 ──

What Happens When People Die?

Resolving the confusion on what Luther thought

What happens to the soul when people die? What really happens to the invisible aspect of us—that which provides our identity and uniqueness—shortly after the moment of death according to Scripture? One good way to approach this question about the literal, constitutional nature of a human being is to start by asking the following three questions:

1. Since there are so many references to *sleep* in the context of literal death throughout the Bible, could this repetition be valuable as an important part of the message of God? I have found fifteen passages in the New Testament (NT) and forty-one passages in the Old Testament (OT) that are indicating perhaps (with its use of the words *sleep, slept, sleeper,* etc.) that death may be similar to the unconsciousness of natural sleep.[1] There are a plethora of other scriptural verses (that don't use these words) that by direct inference or indirect implication are probably saying that the mind of the deceased person is no longer conscious anywhere until the time of resurrection.

    Over a very long period of time, this group of fifty-six sleep verses that refer to literal death, or more likely, that describe the nature of death as being similar to sleep is more than enough repetition throughout Scripture to be considered meaningful, and not just an unnecessary addition, based on a variety of good reasons. This amount of repetition must be considered intentional both on an individual level (and Paul is

---

1. NT verses: Matt 9:24; 27:52; John 11:11; Acts 7:60; 13:36; 1 Cor 11:30; 15:6, 18, 20, 51; Eph 5:14; 1 Thess 4:13–15; 5:10. OT verses: Jer 51:39, 57; Dan 12:2; Pss 13:3; 90:5; 1 Kgs 11:43; plus another thirty-five verses in the OT very similar to the one that says, "Solomon slept with his fathers, and was buried."

the best example) as well as on a divine level that included the prophets and the apostles (since it is the inspired word of God).

It is particularly relevant to remember that included in this long list are quotations of Jesus Christ (as seen in three verses in the Gospels). Furthermore, also included in this list are quotations of the Lord God as written by the prophets (such as Jeremiah). It is not the case, as some people have asserted (based on published books) that the apostle Paul used the word *sleep* only a small number of times when referring to literal death. When an electronic search is conducted on just 1 Corinthians and 1 Thessalonians, for example, the results show there are nine legitimate uses of *sleep* and its directly related forms such as *slept*. Maybe there's a tenth sleep verse in these particular letters that I have overlooked.

The *sleeper* designation may itself suggest that Paul saw it as a *description* of the nature of death and was probably not just *referring* to death euphemistically given the context of how Jesus used *sleep* and *awaken* in John 11:11 to describe the situation to his disciples that their friend, Lazarus, was not naturally asleep, but had actually died. The common explanation of death as *a sleep* as being just a meaningless euphemism will be challenged in this book.

2. Since there have been many leaders of the church—following its reformation in the sixteenth century—who have urged followers of Christ in their writings about death as a sleep to refocus on the nature of death, could these many scriptural passages on death be important?

3. If it is both important and relevant today (as this book intends to show) that curious Christians rethink the nature of death, our resurrection, and the basic nature of the soul, then why not include in it a life-long preacher and professor, who was a most influential Reformer—Martin Luther? He had a lot to say about this matter, and he kept bringing it up *all the time* until he died, as this book will clearly demonstrate.

Death until Resurrection represents a first step, or is a preliminary and helpful place to begin, regarding a whole multitude of issues that eventually can become indirectly related to the question of what happens when people die. A subsequent step—which is beyond the scope of this book's primary goal—would then be to determine how Luther's interpretations match up with various passages throughout Scripture. This book on Luther devotes very little space to showing the reader why a verse in the Bible can be legitimately interpreted the way Luther did. Therefore, I encourage you to check out my new website, WhenPeopleDie.com, for in-depth assistance on what all Scripture says about the nature of death.² Additionally, I should refer you to another website of mine (that is finished, unlike this other website mentioned here that will eventually be much bigger) which introduces the topics of death and resurrection: John-3-16.org.

The following online conversation within a Facebook group named "Eschatology—the Intermediate State Before the Resurrection" shows there is a need for *Death until Resurrection* regarding an examination of Luther's views on the nature of death. One member named Bob wrote the following in December 2018: "I think you are right about Luther speaking out of both sides of his mouth on this issue. . . . I wish that someone would do a definite study (perhaps a doctoral dissertation or master's thesis) on Luther's changing views on the intermediate state. So far I have only seen conflicting statements from Luther and different opinions as to what exactly he believed." Doug (an administrator for this group) replied, "I won't dispute Luther's wavering" which was then liked by Donna and Bob. Michael (who knew about my expertise on Luther and death) responded by just tagging my name (to pull me into the discussion). I responded by posting (in part), "Bob, your Christmas wish may have been granted."

One of the primary goals of this book is to demonstrate, characterize, and evaluate Luther's then-unique view of the nature of death, and his still-novel understanding of the soul's nature, by emphasizing what he said (as dispersed throughout many of his books) rather than quoting him only sporadically. Two of the reasons this book on Luther is relevant today include:

1. The likely fact that many people have been either misled on Luther's beliefs about death, or are uncertain just how sure Luther was on this subject of death as an unconscious sleep; (e.g., didn't he change his mind on it?). For other Christians who are unaware what Luther may have said about death, they probably already know something about the greatness of Luther. So for them, this book is relevant because it is common knowledge that he improved on some church doctrines and significant teachings of the Bible. Therefore, due to the very large amount of his own writings that have survived, it would not be too surprising that Luther could be potentially helpful in other areas too.

2. The fact that although Luther gave several explanations in his attempt to resolve the confusion on what he really believed, an extremely small number of authors over the centuries have attempted to explain them

---

2. Unfortunately, this website is presently in an early stage of construction (although much of the research has been completed). Eventually, it will explain—with the help of many expert commentators of the Bible—a very large number of relevant passages beyond the fifty-six verses mentioned previously.

(or just refer to them) such that the "Luther paradox on death" is resolved. This rarity is understandable given the fact these explanatory quotes of Luther are widely dispersed in various works of Luther that are immensely voluminous (i.e., tens of thousands of pages).

Luther himself inadvertently created a paradox of contradictions on death by making a few statements (usually at big funerals) that appears to many people today to be confusing given his more numerous comments that are apparently inconsistent with his funeral speeches. I describe this situation as an apparent inconsistency because several people have taken their Luther quotes out of context (including from Luther's funeral sermon for Duke John of Saxony). His repetitious explanatory efforts to resolve this confusion have proven to be insufficient and entirely ineffective mainly because these clarifications themselves are also dispersed throughout Luther's writings. *Death until Resurrection* shows that Luther did potentially resolve the tension between two apparently contradictory stances, and that his explanations make sense and can be understandable with some additional help. This book provides that extra assistance in the following three ways:

1. It shows in a very comprehensive way that the "tug-of-war" between the two views of death that Luther described is not even close to being balanced, regarding the number of times throughout his life that he discussed each viewpoint. This ratio, seen in this book, is much more lopsided, numerically, than anyone has identified before in any publication. See chapters 5, 6, 7, and the appendix.

2. It shows in a comprehensive way how to digest Luther's explanation for reconciling the apparent inconsistencies, and how it all can be possibly understood. See chapter 8 for my description of many of Luther's quotes that discuss the "how and where" of death which provide the basis for seeing why Luther said what he did at the funerals.

3. It shows in a somewhat comprehensive way, in chapter 9 (the last chapter), that there were many occasions where Luther provided comments on a related issue that, when taken together, establishes the grounds for asserting that there never was any tension or actual contradiction in Luther's mind. Although a skeptic, or non-theological type of author, may say it is irreconcilable to claim that "death is like a sleep" while saying that "death is also not like a sleep," the oxymoron method of discourse was not an uncommon tactic Luther used in other, non-related matters in his teaching and preaching. He seemed to love creating a conundrum on this or that, and then show people how to exit it logically, using Scripture, while making a larger theological point.

Chapter 2 of this book demonstrates the failure or inadequacy of Luther's efforts to resolve the confusion of a general and simultaneous characterization of death *is/is not* a sleep. There are several authors who have described Luther's beliefs about death in a way that are inconsistent with the evidence shown in this book. On one side, there are three authors quoted in chapter 2 who unequivocally wrote that Luther believed that death is like sleep. On the other side, there are nine mostly contemporary authors who say, in different ways from each other, that the characterization of Luther seen in, for example, these three authors, is incorrect. That is, they contend Luther did not go to his grave actually believing that death is like unconsciousness.

Even a pair of top Luther experts, Paul Althaus and Bernhard Lohse, disagreed regarding what Luther basically believed about unconsciousness in death. This book, *Death until Resurrection*, shows in a comprehensive way who was right (Althaus) and who was wrong (Lohse) that is easily verifiable within its own text (and thus minimizes the need to look them up in primary sources). For those today who follow Lohse on this point (and there probably are many), my intention is to present the results of my research (and electronic word searches) for your consideration. My search results, which produced numerous quotes of Luther, have the potential of changing some minds on the question of what Luther believed.

Too many historians and scholars of Luther have repeated erroneous claims such as: Luther changed his mind on the mysterious subject of death as he became older. On the contrary, he did not do this. Those experts on Luther today who insist he changed his mind on death have taken it out of context by ignoring his many explanations he had made earlier in life. This professor of forty years discussed it with his students in the classroom several times during the last year of his life—some two-and-a-half decades after Luther first promoted the idea of death being like an unconscious sleep.

What does it really matter how this leader of the Protestant branch of Christianity understood death? Who cares if the dead are awake or asleep? The answer to these two questions involves the implications of this starting point. Its ramifications are where this topic becomes more and more interesting the further various questions are pursued, such as:

1. What exactly is the soul? Scripture's many hints can lead to a shocking answer.
2. Where does it go at death? Luther has a good explanation for his surprising answer.

3. What does the soul actually do between the points of death and resurrection, or what is done to it?

4. What is the spirit, and how does it literally differ from the soul, according to the Bible?

5. What actually happens at the resurrection of the dead, and what are its scriptural warrants?

6. What is God's plan for those who finally reject his love and grace?

7. Does a person go to heaven or to hell immediately after dying according to Scripture, and if not, what happens to them until their bodily resurrection?

It is likely the reader already has an answer for some of these questions. However, this book follows the example of Luther, who was an ordained priest when he examined the suspicious teachings of his Catholic church, and who embraced only those beliefs that he verified in his reading of the Bible. One consequence for addressing your curiosity about death and any question in the list above is the realization that the Bible, together with helpful commentary on it, can provide further understanding. It is good advice to follow the example described at Acts 17:11 regarding "the Berean Jews who were of more noble character . . . and who examined the Scriptures every day to see if what Paul said was true."

This book investigates Luther's claims and why it may be appropriate and biblical to say the minds of deceased persons, in general, are in heaven now with Christ even though they may not be in a normal, conscious state. Some of the practical benefits of pursuing this examination of Luther (in addition to continuing it beyond this Reformer) include the following:

1. Significantly reducing our natural fear of death by learning the details in God's word.

2. Getting to know God better and possibly revising one's perception of God's character—and perhaps even loving God more (which Jesus identified as being the most important commandment). One way to do this is to rethink the nature and duration of hell while relying on a close inspection of many parts of Scripture. A good way for some people to approach a rethinking of hell is to consider that which some biblical scholars and theologians have said about the nature of the soul (i.e., the literal makeup of a person). Luther can be included in this group, and this book shows how he could be helpful on this point.

3. Seeing that the age-long philosophical endeavor to describe the soul and its capabilities (e.g., what is man?) will always fall short, whenever God's word to the prophets and apostles is minimized, because these biblical writers have already given us a surprising answer—if only we remove our philosophical and neoplatonic bias.

4. Holding a better understanding of essential doctrines such as the importance of the resurrection of the dead, and also the basic meaning of the divinely promised gift of eternal life. That is, it may not be just a better life, but it probably was intended as being a *literal* gift of life.

5. Having a better understanding of confusing passages in Scripture due to an adjustment of certain presumptions, in addition to well-known verses that may or may not be directly related to any of the questions above. A review of some of these old assumptions (e.g., related to the soul) that may have little basis in Scripture can help you in grasping a clearer understanding of the more common passages like John 3:16.[3]

The reality of hell, with its biblical promise of severe punishment due to unforgiven sin, directly affects the perceived character of our God when Christian groups believe that God's torture of a person held in confinement could never end. It can seem so medieval and unlike how a most loving Jesus described his loving Father, and how the apostle John described the creator of light and life (i.e., "God is love"). Rethinking the traditional portrayal of hell means allowing the possibility that people may have misinterpreted and, before that, had mistranslated Scripture, and that many parts of it have been overlooked that may support another view of hell that fits better with Scripture.

Rethinking the nature of death and the theological anthropology of the Bible means allowing the possibility that its writers did not promote the belief, nor did they presuppose the notion, that the human soul/mind is born with the characteristic of immortality or deathlessness. Rather, it is possible that Scripture informs us that a person, as a whole, is mortal. The good news of the NT may also be understood as being a *literal* gift of life for those persons who are divinely judged to be saved from actual destruction and consequently, from a complete death involving the entirety of the person. It may not just be the body that dies, but also that part of us that made the mental decision to repeatedly sin against God. Another main purpose of my book is to evaluate the grounds—directly using the writings of Luther—for

---

3. Question: Why did Jesus refer to people "perishing" in this most famous verse, and what is it that perishes? If you are interested in the Bible's most quoted passage, check out my website, John-3-16.org.

claiming that Luther rejected the neoplatonic or the traditionally dualistic view of innate immortality of the soul for everyone born.[4]

Luther outlined an interesting, alternative option very few people have discussed in print probably because they have never heard of it. Luther's historical contributions to scholarship is unquestioned, yet his impact on the topics of death and the nature of the soul have been limited thus far. It is my intention with this book to contribute to the discussion and maybe even correct the situation and show that Luther's sophisticated, yet undeveloped, claim about the heavenly location and unusual status of the souls of the deceased is relevant and important. Chapter 8 will attempt to provide support for Luther's exploratory statements beyond "death as sleep" that are still based on the Bible yet remain unexplored to this day.

If someone were to extrapolate upon a collection of Luther's comments on this subject of the soul (which are dispersed widely in his voluminous writings), it is possible to detect in Luther a sort of dualism-monism combination. He definitely set aside the traditional dualism ideas of body and soul, yet he modified the dualistic soul such that it existed very differently during death compared to normal life. Other labels that have pushed back against various iterations of "dualism," "platonism," and "innate immortality of the soul" have been historically known as Christian mortalism, materialism, monism, multi-aspect monism, physicalism, non-reductive physicalism, and conditional immortalism (in the context of the nature of the soul around the time of one's birth).

Recognizing that the church and its leaders have carried Plato's teaching for only the last 1,600 years, instead of since the first century, may cause some curious Christians to consider whether Plato's student, Aristotle, may have been closer to the truth about the soul's nature. Many scriptural clues can lead the reader towards a different view—different from Plato's dualism (where the spirit/soul within a person is independent of the brain's neurons). Instead, God may have created humanity such that everyone is completely dependent—both the body and the soul/mind—on God's literal, life-giving spirit (i.e., the "breath of God") as seen in its animation of our bodily cells. When this power of the Creator (i.e., the spirit) exits the body and returns to God, a physicalist understanding of the biblical "soul" can be differentiated from this literal "spirit" that gives motion to the microscopic cells of our body and subsequently to various systems of the human body. There are many scriptural passages that support this understanding that when this

---

4. If you are interested in discussions of this theological subject (e.g., physicalism or mortalism), perhaps you may want to check out the Facebook group named "Biblical Anthropology."

spirit-force of the Creator is withdrawn from a person's body, it necessarily takes with it the life of that body.

Paul urged his listeners and readers to accept the resurrection of Jesus at Easter as being a historical fact that is central to the faith. One of the implications of taking an interest in this Luther study is to realize that the Gospel message emphasizes the importance of *our* resurrection from the dead as well (e.g., having the gift of eternal life). Both the NT and the OT state that both the righteous and the wicked will be resurrected out of death (see Dan 12:2 and Acts 24:15). The preliminary purpose of being brought back to life is for everyone to know the power of God and to learn of their divine judgment in the context of forgiven sin.

The next chapter further explains the misconception loosely held today by many people, including experts and readers of books about Luther, regarding what he actually believed, and what he taught people in his sermons, lectures, and private letters to friends and family about the nature of death. In the epilogue of this book, Luther is quoted near the end of his life as telling his friends and family that they should comfort themselves against their own death, and "be not afraid." One of the purposes of this book is to provide the reader information (especially in the last two chapters, 8 and 9) on how this can be done, why it should be done, and why Luther's assertions should be believed rather than assuming his critics are correct in describing this pastor/professor as having significantly changed his mind about death.

The last thing Luther told his students as he concluded his years-long series on Genesis regarding the last verse of the last chapter of Genesis on his last day before retirement was, "He [Joseph] wants that tomb to be before the eyes of all his descendants, in order that his children and grandchildren . . . may persevere in the same faith and promise in which he had *fallen asleep* with his fathers." One of the purposes of chapters 5, 6, and 7 (the "investigation" chapters) is to show that this quote of Luther three months before he died should be interpreted as Luther believing that death is like an *unconscious* sleep to be consistent with its twenty-four-year context where he further described what he meant. As a consequence of facing our mortality, and hearing what all the Scriptures say about death and, especially, about our resurrection back to life—even an everlasting life—we can become unafraid of that which will eventually happen to everyone.

---- CHAPTER 2 ----

Was It Really Just for a While?

An overview

In Luther's theology, fear of death stands at the center and is a constant presence throughout much of his voluminous writings. Modern scholars have generally overlooked his horror before death and his unusual claims about the nature of death. One of the main purposes of this book is to show Luther's assertion—that death is an unconscious sleep until resurrection—is much more prevalent in his work than previously claimed, and thereby can provide clarification for the confusion that exists on Luther's actual belief about the soul during death. A second primary purpose of this book is to demonstrate, using many quotes of Luther, how he surprisingly described the period between death and resurrection (in the second-to-last chapter). And, the third primary purpose of this book (in the last chapter) is to show what Luther meant by "sleep." That is, it explains how one can say that Luther clearly disagreed with the church teaching on innate immortality of the soul (and that the wage for sin [i.e., death] applies to the mind since that is what chooses to disobey).

The competing interpretations of Luther among various experts—e.g., Bernhard Lohse and George H. Williams versus Paul Althaus and Anthony Thiselton—and the contention that Luther made contradictory statements repeatedly (i.e., death is not a sleep versus its opposite) may be resolved in this book by theological explanation based directly on Luther's own words. Also, the analysis in this book provides a numerical accounting of his repetition (and development of the concept over time) summarized by a period-based characterization of Luther from its year-by-year presentation. Although five previous general anthologies over the last two centuries have shown some quotes of Luther on death, they provided no explanation for this particular conundrum and little or no social-historical context for his quotes. Only one study (from 1946) has attempted over the last five centuries to assess just *how often* Luther explicitly mentioned death as a sleep. Unfortunately, this unpublished thesis included very little context, analysis, or explanation of the supposedly contradictory statements Luther had made. The 1946 paper claimed there are 125 instances of this repetition, but that the main bulk of his teaching indicates that he believed in the conscious state of the dead.

Thiselton disagrees with this view (based on his characterization of Luther), and he writes in *Life after Death* (2012) that during the intermediate state deceased Christians are safely with Christ, and yet they cannot be conscious of being with Christ. Thiselton is often described as a world-renowned specialist in biblical interpretation. In support of Thiselton's view of Luther, this new study demonstrates there exists over 200 legitimate instances that meet strict criteria—and not a little over 100 instances (as some authors have portrayed this 1946 study). My original research has discovered 210 occurrences on sixty-one days during his last twenty-four years where Luther mentioned literal death as being an unconscious sleep (excluding quotes of commentators and of Scripture). Its method includes sufficient social-historical and literary context (for easy verification) of nearly all his quotes on the nature of death according to Luther's interpretation of Scripture. This widely sourced study of mine (that has specifically cited over 160 books and articles as seen in my bibliography of about 200 entries) endeavors to persuade the reader that Luther clearly did not change his mind at any time, or show unsteadiness, on the subject of unconsciousness right after death and regarding Luther's particular meaning of "sleep" during death. That is, this book provides the grounds for believing that Luther actually used "*sleep*" metaphorically (in the sense of mortality) instead of Luther describing death as being literal *sleep* (in the sense of a napping ghost).

The claim that Luther did not ever change his mind about death being like sleep is clearly contrary to, at least, eight authors—with half of them being published since 1996 and the most recently published of this group include two authors in 2008 (separately). Four others were published subsequent to the fatally flawed study from 1946 (mentioned above). Two writers of this group of eight specifically referenced the conclusion of this 1946 study to support their positions, with one of them from 2008. Interestingly, a ninth scholar also used the numerical findings of this same faulty study to support his own position, although he entirely disagreed with the other nine writers on this topic. Due to the internal inconsistency of the 1946 unpublished study and its incorrect conclusion on what Luther believed about death—which is probably the only work available to attempt an accounting of each of Luther's mentions of "death as sleep"—and due to its grossly inaccurate total of these instances, it is being suggested that this new study replace it. *Death until Resurrection* shows why the issue of "death as unconscious sleep" matters, as well as the importance of understanding the nature of the soul and death as described in Scripture.

It would have been helpful to readers and scholars of Martin Luther if this monk, professor, preacher, Bible translator, and Reformer had made some time to write a systematic summary of his theology. Because Luther did not combine his thoughts on death into a single book, references to his understanding of the nature of death and what occurs to the human soul when a person dies are scattered throughout his tens of thousands of pages. The method he preferred was to tell his students, or the assembled church, what he believed some particular passage of Scripture meant. One of the very top Luther scholars, Paul Althaus (1888–1966), described Luther's unique style of theology as follows: "His theology is nothing more than an attempt to interpret the Scripture. Its form is basically exegesis."[1]

Therefore, the writings of Luther—as they relate to what happens to the soul/mind at death—have been assembled here with some social/historical context for the purpose of describing Luther on it. There is one other work in addition to the 1946 study, from 1959, that collected some quotes of Luther on death, but its goal was not to show *how* prevalent "death as sleep" is in his extant writings. It is a great improvement on the earlier study. However, it also has little historical context, and there is no explanation of these apparent contradictions that would enable the reader to reach an appropriate judgment on Luther's actual belief.

The conclusion seen within the flawed study from 1946 contradicts itself on a major question it set out to address, in addition to being inconsistent with its tabulation table without any explanation. The analysis by Toivo Ketola is seriously deficient, and it should not be used anymore by authors. Although it provided a number of instances to represent Luther's emphasis on the nature of death over his lifetime, it presented only very limited means for the reader to verify the judgment of the author. In comparison, the method used in this book shows the reader that, in fact, only legitimate uses of particular keywords (e.g., death, sleep, etc.) have been included. For example, "sleep" as meaning slothfulness is excluded.

Two or three phrases typically will be provided in this book around the keyword for context as this emphasis is calculated by a running total. Since there are many dozens of these instances, the sum after reading this book of

---

1. Althaus, *Theology of Martin Luther*, 3. This is a translation of *Die Theologie Martin Luthers*, 2nd ed., published in 1963.

these various phrases and sentences drawn from Luther's writings amounts to more than just a small number of Luther's unusual thoughts about death, as this previous research sought to imply. In the sixteenth century, Luther's assertions on this specific topic were very unusual and even shocking, just as they are today for some (perhaps many) Christians.

Although other books have presented excerpts of Luther on the topic of death, they placed much less emphasis on context and analysis of the often-perceived paradox seen in Luther on death. "Probably the best-known comprehensive anthology is entitled *Geist aus Luthers Schriften* . . . 1827 to 1831 . . . in four volumes. . . . Unfortunately . . . no description of the context [of the 10,301 items] is given."[2] Another book titled *So Spricht Dr. Martin Luther* (1903) "enjoyed considerable popularity" at the time with its three hundred pages, but "this little volume, too, offers no contextual information."[3] Then in 1943, Hugh Kerr published *A Compend of Luther's Theology*, "a 250-page book [that] also presents its selections without dates and context."[4] The chapter titled "eschatology" presents excerpts of twenty-two works of Luther in fifteen pages. However, only two of them are relevant to the subject of this book.[5]

The 1959 work referenced above, *What Luther Says: An Anthology* (in three volumes) by Ewald Plass, was published under the direction of the Committee for Scholarly Research, which was created by the Lutheran Church–Missouri Synod in 1947.[6] Over 5,000 quotes for nearly 200 wide-ranging subjects within its 1,627 pages make it comprehensive, but the entry on death consists of only twenty-six pages. Regarding this section on death and its principal purpose (including the Luther paradox), "it is not at all the intention of this work to present a critical discussion and evaluation . . .

2. Plass, *What Luther Says*, xviii.
3. Plass, *What Luther Says*, xx.
4. Plass, *What Luther Says*, xx.
5. The preface to Klug's Hymnal and a fantastic sermon titled "Twenty-fourth Sunday after Trinity" are the two examples referenced. Regardless, this book by Kerr is one of my top favorites of all Luther books for purely personal reasons. This is related to my sudden realization in August 2013 that I needed to change my mind about going to seminary. Consequently, I began attending classes in January 2014 at age fifty-three and graduated at age fifty-seven with a master's degree in theological studies. I am presently on track to obtain a PhD in theology (ABD) in 2021.
6. I attended a Lutheran Church–Missouri Synod while enrolled in its Lutheran grade school for eight years (St. John in Indianapolis). However, the three denominations I have mainly been associated with as an adult include the Church of God (Anderson, Indiana) and independent Christian churches of various locations, and I am presently employed by the Free Methodist Church as Assistant Director of Ministerial Development and Credentialing. This denomination was established in 1860 in New York and now has 1.2 million members in ninety countries.

[since] an anthology . . . is hardly the place for scholarly analysis."[7] However, among the various problems related to the interpretation of Luther, "the reader will find that the footnotes do briefly examine some of the problems, both the real ones and those due to a superficial knowledge of the Reformer's writings or to some preconceived notion."[8]

The entry on death addresses the issue by providing some very brief context for each quote. However, there is no discussion of the "rather paradoxical . . . conclusions . . . [of the] mystery . . . of what sort of life [the intermediate state] may be . . . [and] how the soul is resting [between death and resurrection]" as is appropriate for the type of book it is.[9] Another difference between the 1946 thesis and the 1959 work by Plass is the emphasis on the repetition, or the number of times Luther mentions death as being like sleep. The earlier work provides a total number of these instances that amounts to over a hundred occurrences, while the later one does not do this. However, if one were to scrutinize the contents of Plass, which includes a citation for each quote, then a total number can be produced. My count of this material by Plass shows that Luther mentioned literal death as being similar to sleep only about twenty-seven times.[10]

Death until Resurrection is probably the first published book anywhere that (1) characterizes Luther on the nature of death by presenting original research that quantifies his repetition of the topic over his lifetime (to show its dominance over the apparently contradictory view of his that death is *not* an unconscious sleep), and (2) explains Luther's clarifications of his paradox on death in a way that makes them understandable potentially. The last chapter in it expands the scope of the original seminary thesis by answering the following question: what did Luther mean by *sleep*? Did he describe it as meaning *literal sleep* of the soul, or rather, did he make repeated assertions that clearly show he meant *sleep* as being metaphorical? My book also goes a step beyond these previously identified anthologies of Luther by presenting his quotes in their social-historical context with dates of composition of the specifically identified work. Finally, it also analyzes the data, presents the results in a set of tables, and summarizes my conclusions of what it all means.

7. Plass, *What Luther Says*, xx.
8. Plass, *What Luther Says*, xx.
9. Plass, *What Luther Says*, 385.
10. The breakdown of these twenty-seven instances in about a dozen sections by keyword is as follows: (1) sleep (including asleep, sleeps, sleeping): twenty-one instances; (2) wake (including awake, awakened, woke, woken): 3 instances; slept: two instances; and slumber: one instance. Care was taken to exclude those instances of keywords whose context shows they are illegitimate examples (e.g., *sleep* as apathy).

While there are some books on the Reformer that offer to briefly interpret his position on the human soul and death, occasionally it is necessary to hear the voice of Luther beyond a small amount, or a paragraph here and there. I intend to demonstrate Luther's view on this subject using his own words through a comprehensive approach. As Althaus once wrote in his preface, "I have as much as possible permitted Luther to speak for himself."[11] He is still considered one of the foremost experts on Luther's theology, so he will be referred to on occasion throughout this book. Althaus was a Lutheran theologian and professor of practical and systematic theology at the University of Erlangen, in Germany, who was moderately critical of Lutheran orthodoxy.

Regarding the reputation and influence of Althaus, Robert Ericksen, who is the Kurt Mayer Chair in Holocaust Studies at Pacific Lutheran University, stated in a 2013 lecture that Althaus "was probably the most significant Luther scholar in the world in the 1930s and 1940s, and he also served as President of the International Luther Society from the mid-1920s to the mid-1950s. Many of his books were translated into English and his work remained a significant foundation for theological study until long after . . . [WW2], both in Germany and abroad."[12] The importance of seeing sufficient primary sources of Luther, in addition to books about him, is based on preventing scholarly gridlock as described next by Plass: "Too many persons depend on interpretations (if not misinterpretations) of Luther's words. They accept as the Reformer's view what they get at second hand. Especially some modern 'interpretations' of Luther are found to turn contrasts into contradictions and Luther's paradoxes into doctrinal impasses."[13] The importance of an updated study that is primarily based directly on Luther's own words such as my book can be appreciated by those who are not avid readers of Luther, but know of his relevancy today to the church.

One of my main claims in this book is the following: in *Life after Death: A New Approach to the Last Things* (2012), Anthony Thiselton (in addition to others such as Althaus) accurately characterizes Luther's belief that the deceased remain unconscious between the point of death and the point of bodily resurrection on the last day, generally, instead of the often-repeated assertion that the best portrayal of Luther on the nature of death is one of ambivalence or revocation of this view as he became older.

---

11. Althaus, *Theology of Martin Luther*, vi. This book has been considered as a standard work. The fourth printing of it in 1979 indicates the popularity of the English translation.

12. Ericksen, *German Churches and the Holocaust*, 4.

13. Plass, *What Luther Says*, xxi.

Thiselton addressed a broad range of issues in his book on life and death. Therefore, little space was available—actually only one-half of one chapter—for explaining his most unusual statement about the nature of death and what happens to someone then. Thiselton chose to describe Luther's view on death without casting it as a tentative opinion of the Reformer. It is the goal of my book to provide the grounds (1) for other writers to imitate Thiselton's unequivocal characterization of Luther on the nature of death, (2) for readers of Luther to be able to appropriately reach their own conclusions on what the Reformer really believed, and (3) for curious followers of Christ to see how Luther's biblical interpretations can be beneficial in practical ways.

My purpose and disagreement among the experts

The basic purpose of this book is to show an analysis of the life and writings of Luther regarding his widely dispersed comments that death should be seen as unconscious sleep. Luther's often repeated claim was based on his close reading of Scripture and was in obvious contrast to the widely accepted belief five hundred years ago that most deceased Christians need first to agonize after dying in a state or place called purgatory, so as to suffer the appropriate temporal penalty and thus be purified before ascending to God's presence in heaven. These assertions regarding death as a sleep and a rest were first made (somewhat successfully) at a time when the Western Church was just beginning to split into various groups in Europe. Luther had launched his lifelong crusade on a new view of death and resurrection about four years into his struggle with the pope's defenders, and shortly after revealing his decision before the emperor and the Diet assembly at Worms in Germany that he would not recant his charges against the leadership of Rome concerning forgiveness of sins and being pardoned from purgatory through monetary purchase.

The sixteenth-century Roman Catholics widely believed in the reality of purgatory and many people demonstrated this belief with cash payments to the church in Rome using indulgences for a promised early exit from purgatorial pain. It was this church doctrine and the subsequent local issuing of indulgences that sparked the posting of, and sending to Archbishop Albert of Brandenburg, Luther's famous ninety-five theses in late October 1517. "Luther issued no ultimatum . . . but if nothing changed, he warned, somebody less respectful than Luther would . . . insult the Archbishop openly."[14] In a fantastic 2015 book on Luther, Scott Hendrix writes

14. Hendrix, *Martin Luther: Visionary Reformer*, 60. A "richly detailed" and

that Luther also reminded Archbishop Albert, who was about five years younger than him, that "a pope had never clarified the theology behind indulgences. . . . To remedy that, he [Luther] was calling for a debate. . . . His assertions did not merely question the poor judgment of popes, they also placed limits on papal power."[15]

Consequently, Albert asked the scholars at Mainz and his own advisors to appraise Luther's deductions. They decided to ignore Luther's critique of indulgences and, instead, clenched onto a more confrontational dispute: the charge that he challenged the pope's authority to outline the benefits of an indulgence to the laity. Rather than conducting a theological debate on how to reform the church from within (without immediately attracting the attention of Rome, as Luther preferred), Albert forwarded the ninety-five theses and an attached essay on indulgences to Pope Leo X and the Roman curia in Italy. "That action by Albert, more so than a posting of the ninety-five theses on church doors, launched the conflict between Luther and the Roman hierarchy."[16] Luther probably forgave his staunch, lifelong adversary for it (based on a statement by Luther shortly before they died—only five months apart—Albert in late 1545 and Luther in early 1546).[17]

The motivation for my analysis of Luther's writings, which contends that the mysterious subject of death should be seen as unconscious sleep, stems partly from a claim made in Thiselton's well-received book, *Life after Death: A New Approach to the Last Things*. Four of the following five book reviews (from Jackson, Plantinga, Dunnett, Wilkinson, and Cocksworth) gave it an unqualified excellent rating. However, none of them mentioned Thiselton's claim regarding being with Christ after death, but not really being with Christ after death (i.e., in a conscious state). Thiselton's assertion that death must be seen as a sleep, to be consistent with Scripture, was apparently based in part on his characterization of Luther's view of the matter. However, many other scholars, both recently and over decades, have suggested instead that Luther did not really hold tightly to this contention on death and the afterlife. Some of them have even proposed that Luther changed his mind toward the end of his life, using phrases such as "for a while" and the more common general descriptor, "young Luther."[18]

"definitive biography [that] provides a fresh, bold, and insightful perspective. . . . No recent biography in English explores as fully the life and work of Martin Luther"—from the book description (not reviews) on the Amazon website.

15. Hendrix, *Martin Luther: Visionary Reformer*, 60, 63.
16. Hendrix, *Martin Luther: Visionary Reformer*, 60.
17. Hendrix, *Martin Luther: Visionary Reformer*, 23.
18. For example, from a 1974 book that focuses on a Hebrews lecture series early in Luther's career, notice the title of Hagen's book: *A Theology of Testament in the Young*

Since my book presents his relevant writings in chronological order, a detailed characterization can be made of Luther's claim (that consciousness is temporarily forfeited at death). For example, did the trend for this teaching gradually dissipate over the decades until late in life when he just revoked his earlier statements? Did Luther consistently over time, and at the end of his life, hold to this understanding? It is beyond the scope of this book to explain a perceived contradiction between Luther's view and a particular passage of Scripture.[19]

There is a wide variety of characterizations of Luther on this subject in the literature as seen in the following list of eight examples from somewhat recent authors. The first example of these eight groups contains quotes from three writers which are very different from most of the others in this list. In these following quotes by Thiselton, Althaus, and Nancey Murphy, there is no hedging seen in them; they all were probably intentionally non-ambiguous in their portrayals. That which separates them from those who, in some cases, were rather unsure of Luther's actual set of beliefs on this topic, is their preference to not equivocate.

The following assortment of eight Luther characterizations, which contain fifteen quotes from published materials on Luther's understanding of "death as being similar to natural sleep" is as follows:

1. Luther believed death consists of unconsciousness. Several instances in the literature can be seen where a qualification to this observation is not included (i.e., no equivocation needed). Three examples of this description follow (written by Thiselton, Althaus, and Murphy):

    a. "Luther imagined the state of the dead as a sleep, in which a person remains so deeply asleep that this state is dreamless, unconscious."[20]

    b. "Christ awakens a . . . [person]—not only . . . [their] body—from the sleep of death . . . which comes only with the resurrection on the Last Day. . . . Luther therefore says . . . they sleep in 'the peace of Christ' . . . [Those who have died in Christ] 'rest' and 'sleep' in the bosom of Christ. This is Luther's definitive statement about the condition of the departed."[21]

Luther.

19. This comprehensive task regarding basic biblical interpretation of a plethora of passages on the topics of death and resurrection will be eventually posted at my new website, WhenPeopleDie.com.

20. Thiselton, *Life after Death*, 69.

21. Althaus, *Theology of Martin Luther*, 413–15. There are several other writers who have described Luther in the same way. "Some followed the soul-sleeping ideas that Luther had found in Scripture, but most sprang from Anabaptist seed blown over from

c. "Luther and some of the Radical Reformers argued that the soul either dies with the body or 'sleeps' until the general resurrection."[22]

2. Luther may have said it repeatedly, but he held to it tentatively and was not certain about it many times. One example follows:

   a. "How sleep is to be conceived, whether unconscious or in some way consciously expectant, remains vague in his [Luther's] writings; likewise, it is not clear whether the souls of the pious sleep in the grave with the body or whether carried aloft by angels they already rest in the bosom of God in heaven."[23]

3. Although a large number of statements may have seemed unambiguous, he alternated back and forth between holding a dogmatic understanding of it versus a less certain, or even contradictory, view during much of his life. Four examples follow (which include the Luther expert, Lohse, and a writer, Secker, whose article was published in *Concordia Theological Monthly*, which is a theological journal of the Lutheran Church–Missouri Synod):

   a. "It is fundamentally irreconcilable with it. . . . This utterance renders it doubtful [that Luther believed in death as sleep]."[24]

   b. "Luther was less than wholly consistent in his teaching about the state of the dead."[25]

   c. "Luther's teaching about the sleep of death and the state of the departed is by no means consistent."[26]

   d. There existed "moments of hesitation and occasional ambiguities, even contradictions."[27]

4. Luther may have been convinced about the afterlife consisting of sleep—however, he changed his mind as he became older. Four examples follow (which include an expert on the Protestant Reformation,

---

the Continent." Burns, *Christian Mortalism from Tyndale to Milton*, 8.

22. Murphy, "Human Nature," 19; and Murphy, "Introduction," v. Both of these sources contain identical quotes.

23. Quistorp, *Calvin's Doctrine*, 100.

24. Lohse, *Martin Luther's Theology*, 328.

25. Secker, "Martin Luther's Views on the Dead," 434.

26. Quistorp, *Calvin's Doctrine*, 100.

27. Ball, *Soul Sleepers*, 30. Based on its context, it is obvious that Ball is closer to Thiselton, Althaus, Murphy, and Moltmann on his overall judgment of "death as sleep" in Luther, rather than to most of the others in this list (i.e., Lohse, Williams, George, Quistorp, Rathel, Secker, Morey, and Ketola) who reached a different judgment.

Williams, who contributed to a highly acclaimed encyclopedia on the Reformation, and another prolific author, George, who has written a textbook on Reformation theology that is used in many seminaries):

    a. "He [G. Williams] has written at length on psychopannychism, the doctrine of soul sleep, widely held in the sixteenth century by such diverse figures as Camillo Renato, Michael Sattler, and *for a while*, Martin Luther."[28]

However, the question must be skeptically asked: was it really just for a while? I doubt that Luther held to death as unconscious sleep for only a while based on the research presented in this book. Regarding the use of the soul-sleeper label on Luther at some point in his life, I doubt Luther ever used the term "soul sleep" (as translated) even once based on my research. Instead he described it more generally as the person being unconscious during death with sleep being used metaphorically. This distinction relates to the traditional view of body-soul dualism and neoplatonic assumptions regarding Luther's rejection of this view (i.e., a literal sleeping soul) that a ghost-like spirit falls into a deep sleep until resurrection. The following three quotes are further examples of this erroneous claim that Luther changed his mind as he became older.

    b. "At the beginning of the Reformation, even Luther himself toyed with the idea of soul sleep as a quick and clean answer to the Catholic teaching of purgatory. But later writings reveal that he changed his mind."[29]

    c. "In church history, adherents of soul-sleep have included orthodox believers such as Martin Luther (at one stage in his life) and many Anabaptists."[30]

    d. "Like the young Luther, most radicals (and even a Lutheran like Tyndale) were Christian mortalists."[31] ("Generally known during the sixteenth and seventeenth centuries as 'mortalism' or 'soul

---

28. George, "George Huntston Williams," 33. George has served as founding dean and professor of divinity at Samford University's Beeson Divinity School in Birmingham, Alabama since 1988. George retired from Beeson last year (effective in June 2019). He is the author of over twenty books, including *Theology of the Reformers*, which is "the standard textbook on Reformation theology in many schools and seminaries" as quoted from the Samford website, https://www.beesondivinity.com/directory/George-Timothy.

29. Morey, *Death and the Afterlife*, 201.

30. Rathel, "Theories of Death," 166.

31. Williams, "Radical Reformation," 376.

WAS IT REALLY JUST FOR A WHILE? 21

sleep,' advocates of these views held that after death the soul either slept in an unconscious state, or ceased to exist as a separate entity apart from the body."[32])

5. It was only at the beginning that Luther was unsure, but afterward he was certain about death being an unconscious sleep. The following quote by Moltmann (who has written over forty books) can be placed in the same category as the quote above by Ball (see footnote 27) since they reached a different judgment on this compared to the eight others who are named on this list.

   a. "After some initial wavering, Luther imagined the state of the dead as a deep, dreamless sleep, removed from space and time, without consciousness and without feeling. . . . If the dead are no longer in the time of the living but in God's time, then they exist in his eternal present. So how long is it from a person's death in time to the End-time raising of the dead? The answer is: just an instant!"[33]

6. The "death as sleep" idea was not what Luther ever actually believed. One example follows:

   a. Regarding "the idea of soul sleep in Luther . . . we should not attempt to regard the one or the other idea as his true opinion."[34]

7. An analysis of the frequency of discourses on "death is not a sleep" exceed the number of times he mentioned "death is a sleep." One example follows:

   a. Luther wrote about unconsciousness in death "sometimes" but "the main bulk of his teaching indicates that he believed in the conscious state of the dead."[35]

8. Nothing can be said definitively on this, so it should just be ignored and perhaps forgotten. A large number of examples can be seen in many books on Luther's theology that are silent on the topic of his repeated assertions during the last twenty-four years of his life that death should be seen very differently compared to the common view. See footnote 36 and the bibliography for the identification of fifty books on Luther that have passed on this topic of "death as sleep" that was so dear to him.[36]

---

32. Ball, *Great Expectation*, 244.
33. Moltmann, *Coming of God*, 101–2.
34. Lohse, *Martin Luther's Theology*, 328.
35. Ketola, "Study of Martin Luther's Teaching," 35.
36. The following list of authors of books that describe Luther at some length (usually with *Luther* in the book title) are provided for verification (see bibliography for

It would seem to be a mistake, henceforth, for authors to silence Luther on this subject he cared about so deeply.

There are dozens of authors on Luther's theology that remain in the middle, and are probably unable to pick one side or the other regarding what Luther believed about death. I have quoted eight authors (within five different negative variations describing Luther) who put themselves on the side that would oppose the conclusion seen in my book (as represented by Lohse, to pick a more explicit leader in his assertions). However, there are other well known scholars who disagree and have instead sided with Althaus, who is another recognized expert on Luther's theology.

There is a ninth category that can be added to the above list of eight and is unique in that I have only a record of a few emails and a Facebook post, rather than a quote that appeared in an article or book (which was the case for all the quotes in the eight categories). It involves two examples with both individuals being in the Lutheran Church–Missouri Synod, and both being from 2019. The value of including these two informal discussions here is to show this is, in fact, an ongoing issue and a present dialectic that deserves further investigation. I believe there are, unfortunately, many people today who would probably agree with the following characterization as being the best fit of these nine options regarding their own view of Luther's understanding about death.

First, in a conversation between an ordained Lutheran pastor and a Facebook friend of mine named Bob, my friend asked the pastor about Luther's view of death. The pastor responded to Bob's assertion that Luther believed death to be an unconscious sleep by saying that Luther instead believed that "death is a conscious sleep." Bob told me this is quite confusing in itself.

The second example involved another person who I have had a conversation with by email, and who has requested anonymity. I will grant him that to a certain extent. He occupies a position of leadership and prominence, is well-educated, and claims to have "deeply" studied Luther's writings throughout his life specifically on the topic of death, including a focus on Luther's Genesis lecture series (which was his last before retiring from the university). Furthermore, he wrote in an email that those who disagree with him are "dead wrong." In his first email response to me, this ordained Lutheran pastor also said he had recently conferred with close "Luther

---

titles): Althaus, Baker, H. Barth, Bayer, Blackburne, Boehmer, Bornkamm, Brecht (3), Canright, Childs, Ericksen, Froom, George, Gritsch, Hagen, Heinz, Hendrix, Holder, Hsia, Kolb et al., Kolb/Trueman, Kostlin, Lohse (2), Lull, Marius, Marty, Matheson, Maxfield, McGrath, McKim, Michelet, Noll, Oberman, O'Reggio, Paulson, Pelikan, Piper, Rosin, Selderhuis, Schwarz, Secker, Smith, Tavard, Thielicke, Thiselton, Whitford, and Williams.

scholars" who agreed with him on the question of what Luther believed about the nature of death.

In his second email to me (subsequent to his July 9, 2019 email), he wrote the following (in part): "You are dead wrong when you describe Luther's view of the intermediate state as a dreamless sleep . . . it is easily documented that, in fact, he believed quite the opposite."[37] Moltmann wrote in his 1996 book that based on Althaus and his interpretation of Luther, among others, Moltmann judged that Luther conceived death to be a "dreamless sleep."[38] Recall that the first person quoted in the above list was Thiselton who wrote the following in his 2012 book on the afterlife: "Luther imagined the state of the dead as a sleep, in which a person remains so deeply asleep that this state is dreamless, unconscious."[39] Both Moltmann and Thiselton included the "dreamless" description of Luther's view. You may also recall that I had characterized Thiselton as being often described as a world-renowned specialist in biblical interpretation. It would seem appropriate that I further describe the credentials and accomplishments of the man who used the word *dreamless* when Thiselton described his own understanding of Luther's view of death (since I refer to his recent book in one of my main claims here).

Thiselton (b. 1937 in the United Kingdom) is a theologian, academic, and Anglican priest in the Church of England who has written at least twenty-three books, with sixteen of them published between 2005 and 2017. Thiselton is a former head of theology at the University of Nottingham, and he has served several commissions and committees on theological education and doctrine. His main published work has been in the area of hermeneutical theory and biblical interpretation having written two substantial commentaries on 1 Corinthians: one on the Greek text and a shorter pastoral commentary. Thiselton has also written on Christian doctrine including eschatology and pneumatology. St. John's College, Nottingham, inaugurated a series of "Thiselton lectures" in 2013 to honor his work in hermeneutics.

However, Thiselton's claim about Luther's belief (in addition to Moltmann's identical claim) that death is dreamless could still be wrong, of course, since the boldly stated assertion by the unnamed Lutheran is that Luther saw the period between death and resurrection as "the opposite" of a dreamless sleep. Therefore, I need to quote one more person: Luther himself. Luther said the following in a speech at a well-attended funeral for the Elector, Duke John of Saxony, on August 18, 1532: "Therefore, they should not be called

---

37. Email to author on August 19, 2019.
38. Moltmann, *Coming of God*, 101.
39. Thiselton, *Life after Death*, 69.

dead people but sleeping and henceforth death should not be called death but a sleep, and such a deep sleep that one *will not even dream*; as without doubt our beloved lord and prince lies in a sweet sleep and has become one of the holy sleepers."[40] This proclamation occurred ten years after Luther first went public with his claim that death is like a deep and unconscious sleep with the publication of a book in 1522 (in addition to his sermons on the topic that same year).

When Luther scholars within the Lutheran Church contend in the present day that the "will not even dream" quote here by Luther is *not* the same as "dreamless," even saying it is "quite the opposite," then, we have just witnessed another Luther conundrum. Additionally, when Bob's Lutheran pastor promotes Luther's view of death (e.g., a "deep sleep" from the above quote of Luther) is instead to be understood as being a "conscious sleep," then, the Luther paradox becomes the elephant in the room that few people want to acknowledge, let alone even discuss. This disagreement between people of prominence (consisting of several on each side) begs for some explanation for the apparent inconsistencies seen in Luther and for further research into the primary writings of Luther. Therefore, I submit my evidence and research conclusions for your consideration and your evaluation of nearly everything Luther wrote on the subject (contained herein) regarding whether or not Luther has sufficiently explained himself.

To put the above quote by Luther in context, volume 51 of *Luther's Works* also shows that Luther had repeated his "death as unconscious sleep" claim fifteen times that day in the same sermon to those attending this big funeral. The key to realizing that Luther meant *unconscious* sleep, rather than "conscious sleep," in this funeral sermon is to *not* take it out of context. The key is to examine his usage of *death as sleep* throughout the Genesis lecture (volumes 1 through 8 in *Luther's Works*) and especially throughout the fourteen years prior to the start of this lecture series. The key is to investigate what all he said in the beginning and in the middle of this period of twenty-four years (chapters 5 and 6), and then compare these two subsets to the last period of his life (chapter 7). This comparison is one of the methods this book uses to demonstrate that Luther was consistent throughout. Regarding the Luther paradox on death, and the "lively sleep" description some have used, another method this book uses to resolve it is to try to gather together everything Luther said and wrote about the conundrum and its related subject and then explain them (chapters 8 and 9). The consequence of a comprehensive and in-depth examination is that the reader may notice

---

40. Lehmann and Doberstein, *LW*, 51:242. *LW* is the common abbreviation for the English-language *Luther's Works* series.

that Luther owned a viewpoint that was more nuanced than, for example, someone today placing a confusing label about death such as, Luther saw it as "a dreamless but conscious sleep." For those who are curious, I have found a way out of this mess.

Regarding the email reply to my quotes of Thiselton, Althaus, and Luther (but only one quote from each of these three scholars), and my respectful request for an email address of one of the "Luther scholars" (as they were described in his first email), the implication of his discourteous response was rather astounding. I never received an email address nor a person's name. Perhaps his particular synod of the Lutheran denomination is hesitant in pursuing Luther's explanation of his paradox on death that I have assembled from widely dispersed snippets discovered in the enormity of Luther's works. I hope I'm wrong about this initial impression and their terse hesitancy within this Lutheran synod. Those who are presumably closer to the thought of Luther (compared to a non-Lutheran) are seemingly comfortable with the confusing ideas of "conscious sleep" and "dreamless—but still dreaming—sleep" when describing the nature of death, as Luther taught it.

To summarize: I know of ten people (with eight of them named here) who would disagree with my conclusion on Luther and death (Lohse, Williams, George, Quistorp, Rathel, Secker, Morey, and Ketola). However, there are six different ways these people have described Luther's view of death over his own lifetime. This means that due to some internal inconsistency within this group of ten, most of them must be wrong, if not all of them. These six negative statements on what Luther believed about the nature of death (i.e., it is like unconscious sleep) are as follows: (1) His explanations are "vague" and "not clear" (2) Rather, they are actually "inconsistent" and "contradictory" (3) No, Luther just changed his mind as he got older, so it was only "for a while" or only when he was "young" that he "toyed with soul sleep" (4) No, this was never "his true opinion" (5) Wrong, Luther believed it and wrote it "sometimes" through his life, but the "main bulk" of his writings on this topic was the opposite view that death is not like sleep (6) It is certainly true that Luther believed whole heartedly that "death is a conscious sleep" and that it was "the opposite of a dreamless sleep." There you have it; confused?

Thus, the need for my book is quite evident since I claim that Luther tried to resolve the inconsistencies for his students and church members in a way that is potentially not confusing. Let's give Luther another chance to solve the mysterious puzzle of what the man actually believed. Although he seemed on rare occasion to struggle to articulate his thoughts, my hunch (based on his quotes seen in this book) is that had Luther lived in the computer age with the helpful analogies of information technology and biology, the direction he roughly described five centuries ago (related to what happens to the soul when people die, and specifically the nature of the soul there) would be cutting-edge biblical theology today that would be surprisingly understandable. My opinion is that Luther was five or six centuries ahead of his time when the subject is theological anthropology of the Bible (i.e., beyond the basic "death as sleep" descriptor). I have been searching for several years for a published theologian who has somewhat developed the advanced ideas that Luther had expressed to his theology students, and have yet to identify that person, other than the great "visionary Reformer." The last two chapters of this book explain Luther's novel and "out-on-a-limb" exploration of this topic, and I have provided a suggestion on what he may have been pointing toward.

In the early sixteenth century it was quite common for people throughout Europe and beyond to believe that which the Roman Church had been teaching about death for many centuries. This social/historical context of Luther's statements on death and afterlife easily shows the dramatic contrast recognizable by many at that time. One of the main aims of this book is to demonstrate that the gang of eight published writers (Lohse, Williams, George, Morey, Quistorp, Rathel, Secker, and Ketola) is mistaken with these claims of inconsistencies and contradictions on this topic by repeatedly showing different quotes of Luther that dispute these assertions of him being "vague," "not clear," and that it was only "for a while" for "the young Luther." However, none of these eight scholars, nor anyone else who repeats their assertions about Luther and death, should be blamed, in my opinion. Everyone (up until now) is allowed to resort to the legitimate excuse which relates to the tens of thousands of pages of the works of Luther, combined with the fact that Luther never summarized his thoughts on "death as sleep" into a book or article.

Regarding the tendency of some scholars to develop their knowledge and understanding such that on occasion they change their mind as they become older, there is a group of Luther scholars who take a different general view of the "young Luther" portrayals. "So far as Luther's major writings are concerned, our studies have inclined us to agree with the judgment of Hugh Kerr, who, in his *A Compend of Luther's Theology*, says that the difference between the earlier Luther and the later Luther has often been greatly exaggerated."[41] Consequently, the ultimate question on this matter for both writers and readers of books about Luther would be as follows: Should this historical trend of confusion and equivocation and the impasse seen today regarding this subject come to an end? And for everyone else: I suppose that a

---

41. Plass, *What Luther Says*, xviii.

majority of people could agree that if anyone would read these Luther quotes on death, and my analysis and explanation of them, then it could become understandable for some people on what Luther actually believed.

On the subject of what happens when people die, Luther also repeatedly offered his interpretation of biblical passages that he extrapolated towards a unique understanding of the soul's situation prior to the last day. Another aim of my book is to ask (i.e., within the context of only Scripture) the following: Where do the souls of the deceased go and how does God preserve them? My claim in chapter 8 will be based directly on several sophisticated comments made by Luther and extends them a bit towards some twenty-first-century specificity on these two questions above. It is that discussion which could potentially help the reader to accept Luther's assertions on the nature of death consisting of not having any consciousness.

Following my explanation of what Luther meant regarding the where and how of death and resurrection, chapter 9 will then describe what exactly Luther meant by saying that death is like unconscious sleep (i.e., relating to innate immortality of the soul). Although this area has been explored very little in the literature on Luther's theology, it is where Luther's "death as sleep" mantra becomes relevant and even important. The ramifications of following a study on the "constitutional nature of a person and their soul" includes the nature of hell. As a consequence of rethinking hell while using Scripture in its original languages, a person can ask about how we should see God and characterize our God regarding how God treats those who have finally rejected God's love and grace.

Anthony Thiselton and his analysis of death

Thiselton was selected for inclusion in the primary claim of *Death until Resurrection* because of the relatively recent publication of his book that highlights an unusual assertion about the nature of death. Also, Thiselton's long-established proficiency in the techniques of biblical interpretation and, consequently, his often-described expertise in hermeneutical principles is appealing. This example of extraordinary scholarship may relate to Thiselton's assessment of Luther's conclusion about death, and consequently, it is possible that Luther's techniques of biblical interpretation are appropriate in this case. Because Thiselton agrees with Luther's unusual view of this topic and since Thiselton is widely recognized as a leader in principles of interpretation, it seems likely that Luther's understanding of death may not be contrary to Scripture.

Obviously, determining whether their view on this topic is appropriate requires an extensive amount of widespread exegesis throughout Scripture. However, since this is mostly a historical book, and again, not the type of book that would explore the biblical meaning of several passages, it is beyond the scope here to assess their congruence with the Bible. However, the next book in the series aims to answer this question since it examines many scriptural passages on this subject.

In *Life after Death*, Thiselton opens chapter 5 by writing, "We have already examined 'a new approach' to the concept of *expecting* [emphasis original]. This was achieved with the help of the philosopher Wittgenstein's clarification of the term 'to expect.' It cohered fully with the biblical witness."[42] What can a biblical theologian or a curious follower of Jesus Christ *expect* to happen at death based on Scripture primarily? Thiselton then employs the reasoning of another philosopher to help formulate "a similar new approach" for answering the following question about the basic nature of death:[43] "Do the dead enter Christ's presence immediately, or are they to await the general resurrection after an interval that is usually called the intermediate state? In this case we shall argue that the researches of the secular philosopher Gilbert Ryle suggest an approach which not only allows, but necessitates, a positive answer to both alternatives without contradiction. Both ways of approaching human destiny are thoroughly biblical."[44]

Thiselton then quotes four scriptural passages before quoting Oscar Cullmann and Luther.[45] First, Cullmann's quote: "The transformation of the body does not take place until the End, when the whole creation will be made new by the Holy Spirit, when there will be no death and no corruption."[46] Thiselton summarized Luther by writing that he "imagined the state of the dead as a sleep, in which a person remains so deeply asleep that this state is dreamless, unconscious, without any feeling."[47] As Thiselton observes, "Luther points out that, according to Paul, Christ is 'the firstfruits of those who have fallen asleep' (1 Cor 15:20–21)."[48]

He then quotes Luther and his interpretation of this passage of Scripture by writing that, for Christians, it means that "this remnant of death is to

---

42. Thiselton, *Life after Death*, 68.
43. Thiselton, *Life after Death*, 68.
44. Thiselton, *Life after Death*, 68.
45. The passages identified are as follows: Phil 1:23, 2 Cor 5:6, 1 Cor 15:52, and 1 Thess 4:16–17.
46. Cullmann, *Immortality of the Soul or Resurrection of the Dead?*, 37.
47. Thiselton, *Life after Death*, 69.
48. Thiselton, *Life after Death*, 69.

be regarded as no more than a deep sleep, and that the future resurrection of our body will not differ from suddenly awaking from such a sleep. . . . Scripture applies the term 'sleep' to those who are placed into the coffin and grave. These people, however . . . will simply be transformed, or changed."[49] Such is the extent of his references to him; Thiselton uses a snippet of Luther to support his claim about death. My book provides the grounds for saying that Thiselton correctly characterized Luther on this subject, although other respected scholars on the Protestant Reformation would disagree.

Perhaps this book leads a reader to ask themselves whether Scripture, as a whole, should cause a follower of Christ to believe that the mind of a departed person is conscious right after dying, or not. One response is to concur with that which Thiselton wrote in his conclusion within chapter 5 of *Life after Death*: deceased Christians "are safely 'with Christ,' and yet they cannot be conscious of being with Christ."[50] Thiselton's suggestion that even a Christian loses their consciousness at the moment of death while also being with Christ, in some sense, is remarkable.

This particular Thiselton claim acts as the impetus for evaluating this similar claim by Luther. Should it be a concern that a widely respected scholar from five hundred years ago and this quote above by another highly respected theologian from less than ten years ago have both written that although a deceased Christian is, in fact, with Jesus now, that person is not aware of being with Jesus until the general resurrection?

---

49. Oswald, *LW*, 28:110, 200.
50. Thiselton, *Life after Death*, 70.

———— CHAPTER 3 ————

Luther Lore versus the Truth

Let's start at the beginning

Martin Luther was born on November 10, and according to his mother, it happened just one hour *before* midnight. However, he was not named after St. Leo the Great, the pope of the fifth century, who is celebrated today on November 10 by Roman Catholics, which is the day this highly regarded pope died. Rather, he was named after someone else who is commemorated on November 11. A thousand years earlier, Pope Leo I "worked to suppress heresy, which he regarded as the cause of corruption and disunity."[1] The famous Council of Chalcedon in 451 was held under his direction. As the pope, he personally persuaded the Huns and later, the Vandals, who had both invaded Italy, to give up the fight and turn back. He is described as a "master exponent of papal supremacy."[2]

The oldest documentary evidence for Luther's life consists of three ledger entries at the university in Erfurt, which remains as the oldest public institution of higher learning in Germany. In all three entries, "he was identified as Martinus Luder from Mansfeld."[3] It was a "top-level university . . . [located in] a high-powered academic town . . . [that had bestowed] upon it the nickname 'Rome of the North.'"[4] Naturally, he would identify Mansfeld as his home at the time, having spent his childhood there until his fourteenth year. However, it is rather clear now that Eisleben was probably the place of his birth instead of Mansfeld. A 1908 book containing the letters of Luther show that he referred to Eisleben as his "native town" in a May 29, 1531 letter

---

1. "Saint Leo I."
2. "Saint Leo I."
3. Hendrix, *Martin Luther: Visionary Reformer*, 28.
4. Hendrix, *Martin Luther: Visionary Reformer*, 28, 30.

to Conrad Cordatus.⁵ Hans Luder, who died in 1530, was a leaseholder for mining and smelter operations, and Margaret, who died in 1531, was an ex-nun and became an expert in brewing beer. The Luders were not to become the parents of Leo Luder, but instead, they "named him after Saint Martin of Tours, whose feast day was November 11."⁶

Saint Martin was the bishop of Tours, France who founded a monastery near there, and his tomb had become a pilgrimage site that "was once the most important after Rome, Jerusalem, and St. James of Compostela" in Spain.⁷ This "amazing and paradoxical" Martin traveled around France preaching and baptizing for many years, making numerous converts to Christ, and became widely known as a humble servant of the common man as well as the nobility.⁸ Saint Martin is presently one of only four patron saints of France. "We most ordinarily think of him as the young soldier, cutting his cloak in two with his sword to give a part to the shivering beggar he met upon his way."⁹ He left a successful military career to become a monk, and the other half of his "cape, or *cappella*, was preserved . . . [and had become] so popular that it gave rise to a term that is now commonly used in French: *chapelle*, meaning 'chapel.'"¹⁰

One of the most basic questions about Martin Luther, but rarely asked, is the following: Was the Protestant Reformer born in 1482, 1483, or 1484? It is the year of Luther's birth that Scott Hendrix describes as having shakier evidence compared to the day of his birth.¹¹ There are seemingly good reasons for each of these options; however, only one of them can be the truth, obviously. The grounds for 1482 (rather than the more common designation of 1483) include the following: (1) Martin Luther's grave marker in the Castle Church in Wittenberg, Germany, says he was born in 1482 (although it also includes December for his birth); (2) In 1542, when Luther and Philip Melanchthon (1497–1560), his chief co-reformer for

5. Currie, *Letters of Martin Luther*, 266.
6. Currie, *Letters of Martin Luther*, 18.
7. Pernoud, *Martin of Tours*, 11.
8. Pernoud, *Martin of Tours*, 11.
9. "Ordinary Time: November 11th."
10. Pernoud, *Martin of Tours*, 161.
11. See Hendrix, *Martin Luther: Visionary Reformer*, 17. This is not a trick question related to the sixteenth-century calendar change from the Julian to Gregorian style (e.g., in 1583, 1700, or 1752 for different countries), nor the difference in the timing of this change within the Holy Roman Empire (i.e., Catholic states and Protestant states held to each of these calendars separately during different decades), nor is it related to calendar changes a few decades before this to make January 1 the start of the new year (in 1544 in the Catholic states and in 1559 in the Protestant states of the Holy Roman Empire).

decades, were arguing over his age, Luther said he was sixty and thus born in 1482; and (3) a setting of 1482 would remove definite difficulties in the chronology of Luther's youth.

The basis for 1483 includes the following: (1) Melanchthon published the first ever biography of the reformer soon after Luther died, and a 1483 birth date has prevailed since then; and (2) Martin's brother, Jacob Luder, told Melanchthon that the family [i.e., a part of it] believes his birth year was in 1483. The evidence for 1484 is the following: (1) according to a brief chronology of his life written by Luther himself, he was born in 1484, and on one occasion he claimed "for certain" he was born at Mansfeld in 1484; (2) for as long as Luther was alive, Melanchthon himself adhered to 1484, and once reported that the horoscope cast by a famous Italian astrologer confirmed 1484; and (3) during the argument (above) with Luther in 1542, Melanchthon claimed that Luther's mother told him her son was fifty-eight and that placed his birth in 1484. The final answer for Hendrix is that it is not personally objectionable to identify more than one possibility (i.e., either 1483 or 1484). Notice the dates in the following subtitle by Hendrix, "Chapter Two: All That I Am and Have, 1483/84–1501." My point here is that in my book a truthful characterization of some matter carries a higher priority than being left with making an inconvenient or an ambiguous statement about it.

What may be even more difficult (as seen in the works written by Reformation scholars) is determining the most appropriate way to settle a paradox of a philosophical/theological nature. Regarding the question of what really happens when people die, the follow-up question could be, who should receive primacy on this theological/anthropological matter: biblical theologians, secular philosophers, or (as a middle ground) philosophical theologians? It is beyond the scope of this book to review leading theories on the issue from Plato, Aristotle, Augustine, Aquinas, or others.

Having certainty on basic matters in life and in death is desirable, of course, but not knowing something for certain can serve a purpose. "It cautions us against accepting too quickly other assumptions about his early life that have become part of Luther lore."[12] It can also serve the purpose of this book on Luther's view of death as sleep by cautioning us against accepting too quickly the views of those who suggest that his writings on the topic amount to ambiguity and even a clear reversal of Luther's opinion. Turning to Luther now to hear him speak: "How I astonished everybody when I turned monk [after studying law briefly] and again, when I exchanged the brown cap for another [to become a professor] . . . [Then] after that, I got

---

12. Hendrix, *Martin Luther: Visionary Reformer*, 17.

[around to] pulling the pope about by the hair of his head . . . Who saw these things in the stars?"[13]

Luther's reference to astrology takes the form of a sarcastic question since "Luther makes quite clear that superstitious elements (that is, astrological predictions) . . . do not hold weight with him . . . Unlike Luther, Melanchthon took astrology very seriously."[14] Luther told his class in 1535 at the beginning of his great Genesis lecture series that he "shall never be convinced that astrology should be numbered among the sciences. And I shall adhere to this opinion because astrology is entirely without proof. The appeal to experience has no effect on me."[15]

What if Luther had continued to follow his father's wishes to stay in law school and pursue a successful judicial career? In the public letter to his father written in late 1521, he admitted that "his father was right: he, Martin, should have complied with the fourth commandment to honor and obey his parents."[16] On the other hand, what if Luther had stayed a monk and remained in the monastery rather than becoming a professor? Regardless of his career path, what if his parents had named him after the famous Pope Leo I? Could Luther have settled for following the traditions of the popes, and therefore not publicly ridicule Pope Leo X over his 1513 papal bull on the nature of the soul?

How different would everything had been if there was not to be a visionary reformer like Luther for a very long time? In Jules Michelet's 1835 biography of Luther, he wrote that "it is not, therefore, inexact to say that Luther was, in point of fact, the restorer of liberty to the ages which followed his era. He denied it theoretically, indeed, but he established it in practice. If he did not absolutely create, he at least courageously signed his name to the great revolution which legalized in Europe the right of free examination."[17]

In Kerr's topical collection from 1943 of short excerpts of Luther's writings, he characterizes Luther as follows: "Surely, he is one of the pivotal personalities of history, and he has always been acknowledged as such. His appeal is universal . . . he grows in importance with the passing years."[18] In Timothy Lull's book on Luther's theological writings (in which Jaroslav Pelikan wrote the foreword), Lull "seeks to bring his [Luther's] voice more fully into both the

13. Michelet, *Life of Luther*, 1.

14. Maxfield, *Luther's Lectures on Genesis*, 44.

15. Pelikan, *LW*, 1:45.

16. Hendrix, *Martin Luther: Visionary Reformer*, 114. See Lehmann and Krodel, *LW* 48, 334–35.

17. Michelet, *Life of Luther*, xii. Michelet was the first historian to use and define the word *Renaissance* in his nineteen-volume masterpiece, *History of France* (1855).

18. Kerr, *Compend of Luther's Theology*, v.

study of theology and our current debates" and Lull suggests that "Luther deserves to be read rather than read about."[19] Even though some Catholic leaders today still despise him for what he did, Joseph Lortz (1887–1975), a Roman Catholic, frankly said in his best-known work the following (as translated in Plass): "One may stand before Luther with reverence. . . . Of all presentations of Luther here and abroad ought to agree. Above all other qualities which may characterize him he was a religious man."[20]

It is well known, of course, that Luther spoke quite harshly about Jewish people; but this probably was primarily done towards the end of his life, after a series of unsuccessful attempts to persuade some of them to convert. As Timothy George observes, Luther and others should not be marginalized for this sin because they had other important things to say to Christians: "Luther's invective against the Jews, [Huldrych] Zwingli's complicity in the drowning of Anabaptists, and [John] Calvin's in the burning [death] of [Michael] Servetus, are all the more tragic because one senses that these, of all people, should have known better. However, what is remarkable about the reformers is that, despite their foibles and sins and blind spots, they were able to grasp with such perspicuity the paradoxical character of the human condition and the great possibility of human redemption through Jesus Christ."[21]

How relevant and helpful is it to reading Luther nowadays? Martin Brecht put it this way in 1991 in the foreword to the third volume of his biography of Luther: "People who have read very much in Luther know that they constantly find new insights that are rich and surprising, even in contexts that they know well."[22]

The Luther paradox

The main method employed here for answering the question of Luther's beliefs is to first determine *how* prevalent the "death as unconscious sleep" idea actually is throughout the enormous collections of Luther's writings. A comprehensive yet critical method of search and analysis would be fair and reliable. If only a dozen quotes were selected for a judgment on Luther over

19. Lull, "Introduction," 6.

20. Lortz, *Die Reformation in Deutschland*, 382. Lortz was a member of the Catholic academic fraternity "K.D.St.V. Teutonia" in Freiburg/Uechtland.

21. George, *Theology of the Reformers*, 8.

22. Brecht, *Luther: 1532–1546*, xii. Following the acclaim of Brecht's second volume in the series, Mark U. Edwards Jr. asserted that "Brecht now replaces as the standard biographical reference Kostlin and Kawrau as well as . . . Boehmer . . . and . . . Bornkamm." Brecht, *Luther: 1532–1546*, back cover endorsement.

his entire career, instead of many dozens that are available, then someone's interpretation of him is liable to be erroneous. Next, by highlighting the year of composition of each example, one goal of this book is to characterize them over his lifetime using additional criteria.

For example, this includes the measurement of the intensity of Luther's claim, and not just the number of books and articles in which it appears. Intensity means the following: while discussing the meaning of some passage in Scripture, does Luther mention the "death as sleep" idea just once and then address something else shortly afterwards? Or does he dwell on it, and does the idea get discussed repeatedly on the same page? Does the conception appear on page after page consecutively? The question of the longer time span is also important within the measurement of how common it was for Luther. Did Luther bring up this matter for only a decade of his life, or did he constantly talk about it over the last three decades of his life? Naturally, an enigmatic topic that someone may find interesting develops over time such that specific details are understood better later on.

My plan is to assess the various writings of Luther chronologically, beginning with his second lecture series at the University of Wittenberg (the book of Romans), through each relevant year of his life, and then ending with his long lecture series on Genesis. Luther concluded it with the last chapter, Genesis 50, just a few months before he died. Upon evaluating just these two starting and ending lecture series, it would be obvious that there is a difference between them regarding his specificity on Scripture's use of terms related to death and the afterlife. Consequently, an examination of Luther's works between these starting and ending points is necessary to fully characterize his view on death and resurrection, and the pervasiveness of his raising the issue. It would not be a surprise that he had much to say about death and its related eschatological topics. Because "in his own life as well as in all his theology, the idea of death and the last judgment was Luther's constant companion. . . . For both his biography and his theology, Luther's attitude toward death and judgment is the touchstone for the truth and authenticity of everything said or written. A theology that does not reflect on this horizon of the end time misses both the truth of the gospel and the reality of human existence."[23] The reader would be wise to remember this observation made by one of the recognized experts on Luther's life and his theology.

Carl Stange began his powerful little book released in 1932 in German on Luther's fear of death with the sentence (as translated in Marius), "In

---

23. Lohse, *Martin Luther's Theology*, 325.

Luther's theology his thought on the fear of death stands at the center."[24] In Richard Marius's book on Luther, he observes that modern scholars have generally overlooked Luther's basic motivation, or his response to this natural fear of death seen throughout much of his writings, as follows: "Luther's horror before death is a continual presence in his work—a presence seldom noticed by modern scholars, almost ignored by biographers, even by those who have seen the melancholy in him that was so common to the age. One exception is Werner Elert, who wrote of a 'melody of death' resounding through Luther's work."[25] You may notice in footnote 25 the full subtitle of Marius's book which shows the importance of death to Luther. As a consequence of these astute reflections by Lohse, Stange, Marius, and Elert that scholarship over the decades and centuries on Luther has usually completely disregarded a very important aspect of his thought, *Death until Resurrection* intends to fill this need.

In this struggle to resolve a tough issue for Luther himself within this inescapabilty of death, notice how he adopts freedom of will, in the context of love, as the bigger temptation over the natural fear of death, as follows: "What man does not shudder, does not despair, in the face of death? Who does not flee it? And yet because God wishes that we endure it, is apparent that we by nature love our will more than the will of God."[26] Luther correlates God's reaction to sin, not with the punishment of hell, but instead, Luther focused more on death in his 1518 defense of his views. Marius writes: "Throughout the Heidelberg disputation, Luther equates the wrath of God against sin with death and not with a hell beyond Judgment Day. . . . This seems to be a clear definition by Luther of his *Anfechtungen*. One's relation to God is defined by one's relation to death. . . . Hell does not concern him; death devours his mind."[27] *Anfechtungen* has been used by Luther in the sense of dark temptations at night that, although being an unpleasant trial, eventually can benefit a believer. The importance of seeing Luther's lifelong emphasis on understanding death, and the reader's grasping of his main point, is directly related to one's relation to God, Marius asserts. This may be a key observation when evaluating whether or not Luther saw the punishment for sin as consisting of literal death of the body and the mind. According to a collection of letters in a 1913 book I found, Luther made a great impression at Heidelberg. In a letter written shortly afterwards by Martin Bucer, the friar who also turned into

---

24. Stange, *Luther's Gedanken über die Todesfurcht*, 7.

25. Marius, *Martin Luther: The Christian between God and Death*, 60. Marius (1933–99) was widely praised for his biographies of Thomas More and Martin Luther.

26. Lehmann and Grimm, *LW*, 31:39.

27. Marius, *Martin Luther: The Christian between God and Death*, 153–54.

a leading reformer at Strassburg, we see that he was enthralled with Luther's "sweetness . . . patience . . . [and he was] so brief, so wise . . . [Luther] easily made all his hearers his admirers . . . [even though the] chief men refuted him with all their might."[28]

This book intends to establish the basis Luther himself proffered for accepting the possibility that "death as unconscious sleep" may be a legitimate and truthful interpretation of Scripture. Based on the objections described in the previous chapter, one may have the feeling that a generalization similar to Thiselton's brief description of Luther on death is erroneous, misleading, and should be avoided by writing, instead, that Luther held to the sleep of the soul for only a period of time.

To resolve this situation once and for all, four of the primary inquiries of this book are the following: (1) Did Luther really alternate back and forth with ambiguity or was he certain and clear? (2) Did he change his mind late in life and hold to this belief only "for a while"?[29] (3) Did Luther advocate "death as sleep" as being an unconscious or a conscious state? (4) Did he mean *sleep* in the literal sense, or instead in a metaphorical sense as it relates to innate soul immortality? There are enough comments in the writings of Luther to suggest he had developed a metaphorical understanding of "death as sleep," rather than a soul that literally sleeps, although he usually left it unspecified even when lecturing to his students. A clear metaphorical use of *sleep* in the context of literal death would indicate a likely belief in physicalism, or mortalism, for the soul/mind. See chapter 9 for this analysis.

It is recognized here that any summarized characterization of Luther's stance on the "death as sleep" subject must address his seemingly contradictory comments on it. A handling of Luther's comments about the dead having life, in some sense, will be addressed now. Chapter 8 picks up on the following discussion for further elaboration.

Consider the following hypothetical condolence: "the departed is surely with God now, enjoying her absence of pain and disease, and is now relishing a beautiful life in heaven." When Luther makes a similar, sympathetic consolation that is appropriate for times around a funeral, it must be evaluated in its proper context. This would include the literary context of Luther's other writings and the social/historical context of a funeral speech, for example. The late-Medieval fascination with death and dying, as well as the widely observed pastoral role of having a "good death," impacted Luther's choice of words to the general public. We have ample evidence from the lecture hall and the church pulpit over the decades that the professor/pastor decided to

28. Bucer, "Martin Bucer to Beatus Rhenanus," 80.
29. George, "George Huntston Williams," 33.

not capitulate, when not speaking at a well-attended funeral, and to not continue with his loving, soothing words about the suddenness of death while speaking in front of his divinity students.

It is as if Dr. Luther was saying: "As a university student of the Bible, this professor will not be talking about death as though we are at a big funeral. As a member of a Protestant church, this pastor expects the congregation to be able to handle the truth, and not talk as though we are at a Catholic church discussing indulgences and purgatory." To make a judgment on Luther, it is necessary to fully evaluate the context of additional comments on death Luther made. When faced with a contradictory quote by him on death, it must be determined what else he said, how often he said it, and how intense and repetitive Luther was when he brought up the idea. Then, a resolution to the puzzle can probably be found based on a theological explanation that draws freely from Scripture.

"Nearing the last years of his life, Luther was recorded as making statements which would seem to indicate that all the souls (not just the few exceptions) are completely awake, conscious and rejoicing in heaven. Incidentally, such statements were frequently recorded during the funeral speeches in which Luther presided."[30] There exists a letter Luther wrote in 1542 to Justus Jonas in which Luther offers the following condolence: "After mourning for a season, we shall enter into joy unspeakable, where your Cathy and my Magdalene, together with many others, have preceded us and daily call, admonish, and beckon us to follow."[31] Beyond this private letter, Luther also shared the following surprising thoughts in public in a 1542 preface related to the 1541 death of Urbanus Rhegius, who was a prominent Protestant reformer who promoted unity of Lutherans throughout the regions later to become known as Germany: "We know that he is blessed and has life and eternal joy in fellowship with Christ and the heavenly church, in which he now personally learns, sees, and hears of those things which he proclaimed here in the church in accordance with the Word of God."[32] Other examples similar to these are presented chronologically throughout this book.

Markus Wriedt observes that "through these few sentences runs a basic pattern, which is typical for Luther's theology: Since positive statements often turn out to seem quite unclear or even contradictory, he makes conscious

30. O'Reggio, "Re-examination of Luther's View," 165.

31. O'Reggio, "Re-examination of Luther's View," 165.

32. O'Reggio, "Re-examination of Luther's View," 165–66. See WA 53:400. This preface is in the book titled *Prophetiae veteris testamenti de Christo*. The common abbreviation for the Weimar edition of the works of Luther is "WA" for Weimarer Ausgabe of *Martin Luthers Werke* (in German and Latin).

use of the style of opposites or paradox. Speaking in opposites or word pairs is very much preferred by Luther . . . the space of tension related between the two extremes or even contradictions is the content of his theological concept."[33] Additionally, Hans-Martin Barth submits that Luther "was a skilled dialectician with a joy in paradox . . . In a sense dialectic constitutes the constructive principle of his theology, which developed in a polar tension between alternatives and complementarities."[34]

Furthermore, Timothy Lull writes that "the deepest obstacle to hearing Luther in today's theological discussions is that his theology is so rich, complex, and dialectical that he seems unreliable both as an opponent and as an ally. There is always with Luther the element of surprise. . . . which . . . leads many people to distrust this element in Luther as a sign of muddled thinking or evasive paradox."[35] And finally, Gerhard Ebeling suggests that it is "*how* these two apparently opposed points of view can be reconciled is the heart of the problem with which Luther's thought confronts us. The situation is at first sight confused, but there is no doubt . . . that the dominant point of view in Luther is that of the conflict, which he makes as acute as possible, treating it, as one might almost think, with a delight in paradox."[36] Whenever someone enjoys being ironic or confusing, it usually is because they believe they can explain their way out of the box through clear logic and thereby enlighten their accuser from the dark, obvious contradiction.

So, how can we begin to make sense of the paradox on death that Luther deliberately set before the public, such as at funerals? If I may offer the view that it appears Luther sees the oxymoron of "asleep in death while also being awake in some sense" as the combination of (1) the difference between the deceased having actual versus potential consciousness, and (2) their having an actual promise of salvation from Scripture prior to dying. Luther has gone into lengthy discussions of how God sees time differently to address this particular conundrum. Althaus has succinctly described Luther's view of the confusion this way: "If God introduces himself to you as your God, then you are alive to God even when you die."[37] So Luther might put it this way: he meant it in the sense of "having the potential to enjoy an abundant life upon the resurrection of the dead, but until then, remains in an unconscious state with God and with already having the promise of life

---

33. Wriedt, "Luther's Theology," 103.
34. Barth, *Theology of Martin Luther*, 26.
35. Lull, "Introduction," 2.
36. Ebeling, *Luther*, 89.
37. Althaus, *Theology of Martin Luther*, 411.

through evident faith in Jesus Christ."[38] Althaus also observes that "holding these two views beside each other creates no difficulty for Luther. . . . Thus the 'intermediate state' is compressed together into a very short period of time. For those who have died, the Last Day comes very soon after their death—even immediately when they die."[39]

Further explanation of this "contradiction in Luther here" would be needed for a reader who has thought for a while that Luther held to soul-sleep only for a while. People could correctly see the present condition of a deceased person as not just having hope for their own salvation, but also having a certain hope, a certainty, and thus, the perception in this world is that the deceased are already being joyful in heaven. However, Luther is pointing out, to those willing to listen to him, that a dead person cannot actually enjoy heaven when they are without consciousness. From the divine perspective, though, God may see the same holy person differently. (It should be noted that chapter 8 addresses and tries to resolve a particular nuance of this point about an unconscious soul in heaven still being able to interact with God in another sense of "having life" that Luther repeatedly described as well.)

On occasion, Luther speaks from this divine perspective that God sees King David, for example, as someone who will certainly become conscious again at resurrection. Consequently, this certainty becomes an actuality, when from a human perspective for a Christian mortalist, or for someone who just believes the soul is literally asleep, it is still a potentiality. Although the joy is certain to come, a period intervenes, similar somewhat to natural sleep, between life in this world and the heavenly life. Luther tried to clarify this enigma for his university students in his Genesis lecture as follows: "Nevertheless, the life is one hoped for rather than one already possessed. . . . And because of Christ, when we die we keep this hope . . . yet we who believe in Christ have the hope that on the Last Day we shall be revived for eternal life."[40]

When Luther speaks at a funeral and describes the current condition of a famous, important, and loved person who has just passed away, he would use this alternative mindset at times knowing that someone in the crowd has heard him describe "death as unconscious sleep" a hundred times. Therefore, after going through Luther's theological explanations of this enigma as dispersed throughout his writings, a different conclusion

---

38. This summarized, consolidated quote is directly based on actual quotes seen in this book.

39. Althaus, *Theology of Martin Luther*, 416.

40. Pelikan, *LW*, 1:196–97.

can be reached compared to those who cry foul and throw their hands up. Anyone can notice a supposed contradiction by Luther given, in the same month, at both a funeral of a famous person and at a lecture hall filled with divinity students interested in theology.

A legitimate identification of the paradox within the works of Luther is obviously appropriate in any study. However, a sufficient number of quotes by Luther on both sides of this matter is included in this book to show that this apparent inconsistency can be resolved. This may be done primarily by removing the philosopher's hat, or the historian's hat, and then delving into it using the biblical theologian's way of comprehensively reading Scripture. If a church historian is presenting Luther's contradictions on death and is unable to sufficiently contemplate theologically to assess whether the contradiction stands, then their conclusion could be in error. Obviously, the traditional view of the dead remaining conscious is quite strong today, and for centuries people have presumed it to be the case whether it was supplication to the saints, concerns about purgatory, or desires to comfort the grieving over the passing away of a loved one. This pull today of persistent tradition, natural intuition, and personal preference can affect someone's interpretation of various passages of Scripture, and it can rout a minority view (e.g., Luther's view on death). Due to this combination of factors, Luther's "death as unconscious sleep" teaching can be hard to accept even for a well-intentioned pastor, or a biblical theologian who knows the NT very well.

Luther, an ordained Catholic priest, certainly was a visionary Reformer who imagined a more biblically focused church, who had an instinct and far-sightedness that could dispense with his praying to every saint or holding to a costly purgatory. During an extraordinary lecture on Genesis 25:8 in 1540, Luther told his students that "Purgatory is the greatest falsehood, because it is based on ungodliness and unbelief; for they deny that faith saves."[41] Luther's dogmatic certainty on unconsciousness during death until resurrection extended to writing a popular hymn on this topic which was republished many years later within a smaller collection of hymns Luther had written. This Reformer urged people to set aside the tradition of talking to hundreds of unconscious dead people, i.e., those honored as saints, who may or may not be intermediaries for us, in addition to rejecting purgatory and its indulgence payments. He said it was better to refrain from any supplication to the saints since the practice is not mentioned in Scripture.

In Julius Kostlin's highly regarded 1897 book on Luther's theology, he wrote that "Luther was at a later day content to restrict himself to a simple rejection and condemnation of the traditional conception of purgatory . . .

---

41. Pelikan and Hansen, *LW*, 4:315.

in regard to which divine revelation is silent."[42] Luther "takes up the passages of Scripture . . . in order to prove that . . . the former [Scripture] have no reference at all to purgatory."[43] When we consider the social and religious context of Luther's period, the difficulties that Luther had with the public over purgatory or stopping the practice of prayer to the saints can be appreciated easier. His environment and close associates contributed to his decision to spend more time on death being an unconscious sleep rather than emphasizing all the time a more complicated topic: the death of the soul/mind when the body dies. The deadly, cultural environment back then placed a heavy emphasis on the value of tradition, especially in the church, which is seen in Marius as follows:

> By the sixteenth century, churchmen knew that the only persuasive proof for church doctrine lay in tradition, the continuation of belief for hundreds of years. As Thomas More and battalions of other Catholic foes of Luther would say, Christ had promised to be with his people the church until the end of the world. If the church erred in any particular and if the error continued for a long period without being eradicated by divine intervention, Christ had broken his promise, and the world would be plunged into a chaos of meaninglessness. . . . The assumption that tradition defined faith was to the Catholic Church of the sixteenth century what the theorem that parallel lines never meet was to Euclid.[44]

Five hundred years of confusion is long enough

Consider the Luther characterization that George H. Williams (1914–2000) provided in *The Radical Reformation*. This historian and ordained minister "expertly inquires into the doctrines of the Radical Reformers [such as Menno Simons]."[45] Williams wrote that "in 1524 he [Luther] declared in a sermon that the soul sleeps until God at the Last Judgment awakens both soul and body. . . . In another sermon, in 1533, he declared, 'We shall sleep until He comes, and knocks on the grave and says, "Dr. Martin, arise!"'"[46] Nevertheless, he occasionally lapsed into his inherited

---

42. Kostlin, *Theology of Luther*, 473.
43. Kostlin, *Theology of Luther*, 473–74.
44. Marius, *Martin Luther: The Christian between God and Death*, 144.
45. Szczucki, "George H. Williams' Studies," 130.
46. See Althaus, *Theology of Martin Luther*, 415, which reads, "We are to sleep until he comes and knocks on the grave and says, 'Dr. Martin, get up.' Then I will arise in a moment and will be eternally happy with him." See WA 37:151 and also Luther's earlier

Catholic view of the afterlife, with the consequence that little by little within Lutheranism the doctrine of the sleep of the soul was replaced by the idea of a natural immortality."[47]

Did Luther ever really "lapse" back into the view that the dead are generally awake? No, he never once did. Did Luther ever say that the "soul sleeps"? No—it is probably extremely rare, and it is quite likely he never once put these two words together in the same phrase in either German or Latin as Calvin did in his book (published in 1534). In Calvin's refutation of soul-sleep, he wrote the following at the beginning of the preface: "At first, some only vaguely alleged that the soul sleeps, without defining what they wished to be understood by 'sleep.'"[48]

However, the interesting observation that Williams has articulated well regarding Lutheranism's lapse back to the traditional view of innate immortality of the soul in this same quote is instructional. The question of whether or not Luther held to an understanding of the nature of the soul (i.e., mortalism or physicalism) that is different from what came after his life as well as before it (i.e., platonic dualism or natural immortality) can be informed by Williams here. Chapter 9 of my book identifies an extensive list of quotes of Luther that support this particular view seen in Williams that Luther's "sleep of the soul" was not meant literally, but rather metaphorically, as it relates to the soul/mind being mortal and, thus, dying with the body.

How relevant is this book by Williams which my book is attempting to refute on the staying power of Luther's belief about death that he took to his grave? Consider how George has characterized the importance of Williams's book: "By pointing to interweaving themes and commonly held assumptions among the Radicals (e.g. believer's baptism, the doctrine of soul sleep, disavowal of the sword), he [Williams] emphasized the hitherto unrecognized coherence and continuity of the Radical Reformation."[49] Another author in the same collection of essays backs up his opinion by asserting that "*The Radical Reformation* [is] a book which was soon to occupy an eminent place. It would be no overstatement to say that Williams was the first to introduce into Western scholarly writings the problems of the

---

sermon titled "Sixteenth Sunday after Trinity on Luke 7:11–17" which includes in the middle of it this "knocks at the grave and we arise from a quiet sleep" line.

47. Williams, *Radical Reformation*, 197n65. Williams's footnote adds the following: "See Paul Althaus, *Die letzten Dinge: Lehrbuch der Eschatologie* (Gutersloh: Bertelsmann, 1956), 146–47."

48. Calvin, "Preface by John Calvin to a Friend," 414.

49. George, "George Huntston Williams," 30.

Radical Reformation in Central Europe [e.g., to use just one region in his wide-ranging book]."[50]

When assessing the standing of Williams in the context of this study in *Death until Resurrection*, consider the worldwide impact of the sterling reputation of the Oxford University Press as seen in *The Oxford Encyclopedia of the Reformation*. It is "the world's largest university press with the widest global presence."[51] Published in 1996 (and published online in 2005), the Oxford University Press description says this particular set of four volumes "is the first major reference to cover the immense subject of the Reformation in its entirety. . . . it is the most authoritative reference available on early modern European society as a whole. . . . This is the ultimate reference . . . the first source scholars, students, and general readers in any discipline will reach for when studying the Reformation."[52]

Under the entry "Radical Reformation," contributor George H. Williams said the following at the fourth paragraph in this article of ten pages: "Not until the Fifth Lateran Council (1517) had the church authoritatively defined the human soul as naturally immortal, and most of the radicals embraced a primitive and scriptural eschatology, believing in the sleep of the soul until the general resurrection of the dead. Like the young Luther, most radicals (and even a Lutheran like William Tyndale) were Christian mortalists."[53] It is debatable whether or not Luther changed his mind on this subject of "death as sleep" as he grew older, regardless of the sense of *sleep* used. "Generally known during the sixteenth and seventeenth centuries as 'mortalism' or 'soul sleep', advocates of these views held that after death the soul either slept in an unconscious state, or ceased to exist as a separate entity apart from the body."[54]

Authors are not to be blamed, in my opinion, for repeating a judgment on this from someone they trust, such as that found in "the magnum opus, *The Radical Reformation*. It is remarkable not only that a book of such

---

50. Szczucki, "George H. Williams' Studies," 130.

51. Oxford University Press, "About Us."

52. Oxford University Press, "Oxford Encyclopedia of the Reformation."

53. Williams, "Radical Reformation," in *Oxford Encyclopedia of the Reformation*, 375–76. The 1517 papal bull reads: "We condemn and reject all those who insist that the intellectual soul is mortal. . . . For the soul not only truly exists of itself and essentially as the form of the human body, as is said in the canon of our predecessor of happy memory, pope Clement V . . . but it is also immortal . . . This is clearly established from the gospel when the Lord says, They cannot kill the soul; and in another place, Whoever hates his life in this world, will keep it for eternal life." Roman Catholic Church, *Decrees of the Ecumenical Councils*, 605. See also Papal Encyclicals Online, "Fifth Lateran Council 1512–17 A.D." (esp. session eight).

54. Ball, *Great Expectation*, 244.

comprehension in so fluid an area of scholarship should have remained in print for nearly twenty years, but also that it continued to be cited in all of the relevant literature as the standard study in the field."[55] The reason for this opinion of mine is due to the sheer volume of primary sources of Luther, not to mention the incredible number of secondary sources about the great Reformer.

Given the momentum of the traditional belief that the deceased remain conscious after death within various churches worldwide, as well as a perceived lack of sufficient books on this particular subject, it is to be expected that many authors would attach to their conclusion about Luther on "death as sleep" some qualifier just to cover themselves. What about those Luther scholars who are expected to know better, though? Perhaps an author on Luther's theology, instead of a respected historian on the radical reformation, could be trusted to save a writer much time from doing their own research of *many* primary sources. Next, we turn to Lohse.

Bernhard Lohse (1928–97) provides an even more detailed example of a Luther scholar who clearly casts doubt that Luther was certain on the sleep of the soul. Following Lohse's 1980 book on Luther's life and his work (translated in 1986), he then wrote *Martin Luther's Theology: Its Historical and Systematic Development* (1995 in German, 1999 in English).[56] After quoting at length Luther's remark on the 1541 death of Urban Rhegius (referenced above), Lohse opines that "this significant statement about fellowship with Christ immediately after death is in considerable tension with the assertion of soul sleep. It is fundamentally irreconcilable with it. . . . This utterance renders it doubtful that words concerning soul sleep, which are certainly more numerous, can really be promoted to the rank of a 'doctrine of Luther.' . . . We should not attempt to regard the one or the other idea as his true opinion."[57]

Is that correct that Luther's talk about "death as sleep" was not his actual attitude on what Scripture says? The appendix and the conclusion within *Death until Resurrection* contain the reasons why Luther's numerous mentions of "death as unconscious sleep" throughout his life can be promoted to the rank of his true opinion. It should be noted that in the book just quoted, Lohse repeated a questionable theological viewpoint on Luther's view of death, related to innate immortality of the soul, which could act as a warning sign. The reason it is especially relevant to Lohse's critical view of Luther

---

55. George, "George Huntston Williams," 29.

56. Lohse's first Luther book is a comprehensive and wide-ranging introduction to Luther and includes over eight pages in the table of contents.

57. Lohse, *Martin Luther's Theology*, 328.

regarding "death as sleep" is due to both assessments being of a theological nature. In both cases a biblical/theological application is appropriate which could resolve Luther's presumed contradictions on "death as sleep." It is not surprising that Lohse did not sufficiently apply this method to relieve its "considerable tension" on "death is sleep/death is not sleep" due to his questionable judgment on this related topic of natural immortality.

Lohse's explanation is insufficient for why he believes the following conclusion: "This leaves no doubt that Luther held to the immortality of the soul"[58]—from Thiede's 1993 article in *Luther*. Based on several Luther quotes that take a step beyond "death as sleep" into the area of theological anthropology (i.e., physicalism or mortalism), this "no doubt" from Lohse can be seriously challenged. See chapter 9 for a brief description of sixteen quotes of Luther (the vast majority of which I discovered in primary sources of Luther) regarding immortality of the soul that, taken together, refute Lohse's conclusion. The opposite of innate soul immortality is the view that the soul/mind is mortal and subject to perishing or disappearing when the body dies (except in God's memory for resurrection).

Lohse's statement that Luther should not be characterized as holding this "death as sleep" claim dogmatically because it is inappropriate to conclude that it was his "true opinion," clearly allows a reader to repeat in their own work that Luther's position amounts to ambiguity and uncertainty. However, there are other Luther scholars who have specifically disputed this view. Additionally, there are a number of books written by those whose specialty is other-than-Luther that characterize Luther as holding an unambiguous and dogmatic belief on "death as unconscious sleep."

One of the top Luther scholars, Althaus, summarized Luther's view on the basic topic the following way: "Luther generally understands the condition between death and the resurrection as a deep and dreamless sleep without consciousness and feeling."[59] The context around this quote (over several pages) contains no equivocation and does not even hint toward an actual contradiction since a reasonable explanation is provided by Althaus.[60] Chapters 5, 6, and 7 of this book will examine Luther's works themselves to provide the full range of evidence necessary to then determine whether Lohse's judgment on this Luther subject is accurate or not. But first, some relevant background.

58. Lohse, *Martin Luther's Theology*, 326.
59. Althaus, *Theology of Martin Luther*, 414.
60. Because Althaus wrote this book in 1963 in German (released in 1966 in English), which is many years prior to Lohse's first of two books on Luther (i.e., 1980 in German and 1986 in English), further examination of the primary sources of Luther is especially warranted to test Lohse's findings.

Luther from 1505 to 1518

Luther entered the monastery in 1505 after studying law for only a few weeks that year. "In later times there are surprisingly axiomatic statements from him that may possibly date back to his deliberations in the summer of 1505. . . . All his life Luther had a critical relationship toward lawyers and their discipline."[61] This particular opinion towards the sixteenth-century vocation of attorneys is relevant to understanding Luther today and the main claim of this book. Although he certainly can be perplexing, Luther was not a person, when faced with a difficult theological issue, to settle for ambiguity, uncertainty, and brevity. In addition to his writings in general, consider the following observation made within the "impeccable scholarship" of Brecht's biography.[62] "In the context of criticizing the continual use by rabbis, scholastic theologians, and jurists of ambiguous rather than unequivocal concepts, he mentions his previous reading of Accursius, the glossator of Roman law. Accursius had introduced various possibilities of interpreting a passage and openly acknowledged that he did not know which one was correct. Luther took offense at this uncertainty. He considered jurisprudence a discipline of evasion, or divisibility."[63]

Luther began lecturing on Aristotle at Wittenberg in 1508 and on Peter Lombard's *Sentences* at Erfurt in 1509, which was the standard theological work of that time period. In 1517, Luther said "that it is exceedingly doubtful whether Western theologians have rightly understood Aristotle at all."[64] Luther had been recalled to the monastery in Erfurt after graduating with a bachelor's degree in biblical studies in March 1509. He mentioned his surprise (in a letter dated May 18, 1517 to John Lang, an eventual reformer in Erfurt) that the lectures on the *Sentences* were despised. This may be an indication that Luther's students responded more positively to Luther's style of teaching. Consequently, the standard of excellence Professor Luther likely portrayed in the classroom may have some amount of relevancy when determining whether a modern critic's judgement is plausible in the context of my book. If it is true that Luther's unusual interpretation of the Bible on death was not his true opinion, as Lohse contends, then some of his divinity students would likely have experienced some discord and uneasiness in this situation. So, examining Luther's lectures and sermons on this subject given later would be very useful. The appendix and its several tables in *Death until*

---

61. Brecht, *Luther: 1483–1521*, 44.

62. Lotz, back cover of Brecht, *Luther: 1532–1546*. Brecht's biography won the 1991 *Choice* Magazine Outstanding Academic Book Selection.

63. Brecht, *Luther: 1483–1521*, 44.

64. Ebeling, *Luther*, 89. See WA 1:226.

Resurrection characterizes the longevity and intensity of Luther's unequivocal assertions about death, which included both numerous sermons and many university lectures.

Luther was encouraged to complete the steps leading to the doctorate in Biblical Theology after being transferred to Wittenberg in 1511. Luther's forty-year teaching career first "came into full bloom especially after he turned specifically to theology."[65] Before taking that assignment though, Brother Martin took the trip of a lifetime to visit headquarters in Rome with another friar.[66] After conferring with the general of the Augustinian order there, as they were directed to do, and seeing Pope Julius II from a distance, they set out on their long return over the Alps. They departed Vatican City as the year 1511 ended (i.e., the visit was probably not in 1510 as many today suppose).[67] "The date and purpose of that trip have recently been revised by a persuasive piece of detective work and puzzle solving" by Hans Schneider in 2011.[68]

Then, upon receiving his doctorate degree in theology in October 1512 (at age twenty-eight or so), Luther became a lecturer on the Bible at the University of Wittenberg. He held the position there as Doctor of Bible for the rest of his career, ending in late 1545. For years, Luther had already participated in disputations, which he enjoyed doing, and "as Professor Luther in Wittenberg he was still doing both [delivering classroom lectures plus disputations] until shortly before he died."[69] With his days as a monk in the monastery ending, Luther chose to teach the Psalms first, through a long series of lectures beginning with the summer semester of 1513 and lasting until 1515. Perhaps Luther felt more comfortable with this book since he "had taken seriously the prescription of his monastic order to read in the Psalter daily."[70]

Dr. Luther "had become increasingly popular with the students. Many men were coming to Wittenberg for the express purpose of hearing Luther. Townspeople were also attracted to this young professor of the Bible."[71] Lang wrote to George Spalatin, the secretary and chaplain to Elector Frederick, the Wise (1463–1525), on March 10, 1516, saying that

---

65. Oswald, "Introduction to Volume 25," ix.

66. It has been said that Luther actually walked the 800 miles from Erfurt to Rome (taking roughly 260 hours one way) at age twenty-seven or so.

67. See Hendrix, *Martin Luther: Visionary Reformer*, 6.

68. Hendrix, *Martin Luther: Visionary Reformer*, 6.

69. Hendrix, *Martin Luther: Visionary Reformer*, 6.

70. Oswald, *LW*, 25:ix.

71. Hagen, *Theology of the Young Luther*, 5.

the young Luther's lectures "in Wittenberg were being well received."[72] We now know that "very many students [were] all excited and enthusiastic about the lectures on the Bible and the early Fathers."[73] Brevard Childs (1923–2007) believed Luther's brand of exposition of the Psalms ranks among the top ten, and he identified the others.[74] The trend continued the next year as evidenced by Luther's letter to Lang on May 18, 1517, which was just five months before his famous ninety-five theses began to be distributed on October 31, 1517, and which then sparked the very beginning of the Protestant Reformation.

Luther told Archbishop Albert that "he could keep quiet no longer" regarding the widespread payment of indulgences to the Church in return for the false assurance under Albert's name of being saved from purgatory and brought into heaven.[75] With that as his starting point for debating church doctrines versus Scripture, Luther decided to urge people to look at death differently following his most public refusal to recant. The pressure to repudiate his assertions on indulgences and forgiveness was enormous in 1518. Cardinal Thomas Cajetan, a man of "good will and mildness," responded to Luther's defense "that faith brought certainty of forgiveness," by saying to him that "papal authority was superior to the authority of scripture and of church councils."[76] On the last day of the October 1518, hearing at Augsburg, Germany (rather than at Rome as originally ordered), Cardinal Cajetan responded to Luther's written defense "with the ultimatum: 'Either recant or do not show your face again.'"[77]

The next chapter sets the stage for how Luther went from uncertainty to certainty, and from "death as sleep" in an unspecified sense to "death as an unconscious sleep." It describes the beginning of a lifelong crusade to talk about this subject again and again, whether it was in a sermon, university lecture, funeral speech, private letter, book preface, hymnal preface, hymn,

72. Hagen, *Theology of the Young Luther*, 5. Frederick the Wise was the Elector from 1486 to 1525, succeeded by his brother, John (between 1525 to 1532), who was then succeeded by his son, John (between 1532 to 1547). Although Frederick the Wise was Catholic, his brother (the Steadfast) and his nephew (the Magnanimous) were both Lutherans. There were seven electors at any point in time throughout the lands of the Holy Roman Empire that selected the emperor (which did not include Rome or Vatican City in its territory at the time). Charles (1500–1558) became Emperor of Spain at sixteen years of age, and was the Holy Roman Emperor from 1519 to 1556.

73. Hagen, "Addition to the Letters of John Lang," 31. This article is quoted in Hagen, *Theology of the Young Luther*, 5.

74. See Childs, *Introduction to the OT*, 523.

75. Hendrix, *Martin Luther: Visionary Reformer*, 59.

76. Hendrix, *Martin Luther: Visionary Reformer*, 73–74.

77. Hendrix, *Martin Luther: Visionary Reformer*, 74.

table talk, academic disputation, treatise, or written commentary on Scripture. Each of these categories is represented here as showing Luther's belief that death is very similar to a nice, deep sleep (i.e., "RIP"), and our resurrection is like suddenly awakening from a good night's rest in peace.

―――― CHAPTER 4 ――――

Unraveling the Issue with This Study on Luther

Luther is an ocean

The contribution of this book on Luther's beliefs serves to unravel various opinions and misunderstandings that have accumulated over the last five centuries. The main reason this has happened is because Luther is an ocean, and also because electronic word-search had not been available for almost 95 percent of the time since then. This ocean analogy is meant both in the sense of the incredibly vast amount of published writings of Luther (including those from eyewitnesses that quoted him speaking) and in the sense of the theological depth of this scriptural interpreter and Bible translator. With so much material available to an author over the years, it is to be expected that errors and oversight will occur—even for themes that constantly appear in many works of Luther—because Luther never pulled together his different explanations of the paradox he helped to create.

Of all the available types of writings of Luther, it is personal letters to friends and family, compared to funeral speeches and lectures recorded by devoted students, for example, that is probably the most reliable on this question of what he really believed. "It has been truly said that Luther's heart is seen in his letters, which he did not dream would see the light of day, while his talents may be seen from his other works."[1] However, there exist very few of them that are relevant to this book on the nature of death (and translated into English), even though about 2,600 personal letters written by Luther still remain available. It is very likely several more extant letters that have not been translated into English mention "death as sleep" in them (but are not identified here). Luther gave a plethora of sermons, though, and various objections

---

1. Currie, *Letters of Martin Luther*, xvii.

can be alleviated by finding several lectures and sermons that Luther directly composed. He would directly revise a published work from several years earlier for the purpose of issuing a new edition of it.

The amount of translated works of Luther available today is astounding when looking at just the two *Luther's Works* series (i.e., the completed one and the yet-to-be-completed one). The first series, running from 1955 to 1986, contains fifty-five volumes and is the most extensive collection of Luther's works in English. However, it does "not contain everything that has attracted the attention of historians and theologians in subsequent decades nor everything that Luther's contemporaries and successors esteemed and republished."[2] The second series of twenty-eight volumes in English as planned would amount to a total of over eighty volumes containing the writings of Luther.[3] This large number of books for an English reader or writer would seem to be the size of the Pacific ocean, with some authors summing it up with "Luther is an ocean."

Joseph Lortz (the Roman Catholic mentioned in the previous chapter) described Luther as an ocean, that is, an "inexhaustible ocean of religious strength" that referred more to the depth of the man as opposed to the expanse of his enormous literary output.[4] In Althaus's 1966 book on Luther, he wrote (translated) that "because our periods of time are no longer valid in God's eternity, the Last Day surrounds our life as an ocean surrounds an island."[5] Luther's literary output may certainly surround a scholar as far as the eye can see, but Althaus's point is that the details of the last day should be better understood. Due to the rarely discussed topic of *our* resurrection from the dead, these "last things" have been largely ignored by Christians. Consequently, what's happened for quite some time now—to use his same analogy—is that Christendom has been residing only in the middle of a very large island; for example, in the midst of the continent of Australia. Scripture recorded the eschatological details of the Return of Christ at the last day, and they can be clearly seen if only people would keep going to the beach to explore.

To put "Luther is an ocean" another way: a rough estimate of the number of pages to be eventually contained in these two *Luther's Works* series, and thereby accessible to the English reader, is in excess of 30,000 pages. The Erlangen edition contains over 50,000 pages of text in over a hundred

2. Brown, "General Introduction," vii.

3. The second series of *Luther's Works* has issued about twelve volumes to date, beginning in 2009, which was twenty-three years after the last volume in the first series was published.

4. Lortz, *Die Reformation in Deutschland*, 192.

5. Althaus, *Theology of Martin Luther*, 416.

volumes. Although Erlangen was the best collection as of the late-nineteenth century, regarding quality and quantity, it and other original-language editions in German and Latin, such as the St. Louis-Walch (Halle), have been replaced by the superior Weimar edition.

The Weimar, or Weimarer Ausgabe (WA), edition was initially released between 1883–1929, although the last part of the index was published in 2009. This complete edition of all works of Luther totals over 120 volumes and about 80,000 pages in either German or Latin. Luther authored 294 works in German and seventy-one in Latin, in addition to his German Bible, which was translated from the Hebrew and Greek instead of the Latin Vulgate (the only official Bible then).[6] So, the task of determining how often Luther raised this matter, or mentioned "death as sleep," requires the assistance of a computer for improved efficiency because Luther never published a comprehensive treatise on this topic. Unlike Aquinas, Calvin, or Melanchthon's *Loci*, which was an analysis of individual doctrines published in 1521 and revised in 1535, Luther did not publish a systematic treatise on any theological subject. This chapter next examines a still-referenced study that is most unique before beginning a journey, or a contest, showing why Luther should no longer be kept quiet on a strongly held belief of his that through its implications can affect other basic beliefs that many Christians assume to be scriptural.

Assessment of similar studies

Unfortunately, personal computers had not yet been invented at the time that a certain student attempted a broad survey of Luther on the nature of death, and the first volume of *Luther's Works* would not be published for another decade. In Toivo N. Ketola's thesis for a master's degree in 1946, it states that the "purpose of this study was to find out what Martin Luther taught about the state of the dead" between death and resurrection.[7] It included a couple other topics beyond those in my book, yet it is a short work (i.e., just thirty-nine pages, double spaced) and is unique for several reasons.

6. "In all Luther published over 350 works." Plass, *This is Luther*, 4.

7. Ketola, "Study of Martin Luther's Teaching," 1. Ketola was a faculty member of the Finland Mission School in Piikkio, Finland, as of 1956. That paper identifies the thesis advisor as Dr. Frank H. Yost, who was Professor of Church History. The source for the table in this thesis was the relevant contents of fifteen of the twenty-two volumes of the German-language Johann Georg Walch edition. Volume 23 contains an index of keywords that is more extensive than the similar index in the Erlangen edition. The Walch collection of Luther's works was first published in 1740–1753 with a revised edition in 1880–1910.

For at least two books that referenced the unpublished Ketola study, it was the bottom-line totals within a certain table in the thesis that became the headline. This tabulation table shows the repetition within Luther's writings of the "death as sleep" idea. The tabulation of the number of occurrences of this topic was performed in the Ketola study because "no detailed study concerned directly with his doctrine of the state of the dead is known by the writer."[8] It is probable that this 1946 study was the first time since 1546, the year of Luther's death, that anyone had conducted a broad tabulation that counts the individual number of times Luther mentioned death as sleep. There are several reasons for this claim by Ketola, but one would seem to be, as Williams was quoted above to say, that "little by little within Lutheranism the doctrine of the sleep of the soul was replaced by the idea of a natural immortality."[9] Whether or not Ketola's thesis was the first comprehensive search related to this subject at that time, it is likely the Ketola thesis remains as the only study of its kind available to us, with the exception of this present book. It is the last time anyone has done a study over the last seventy-five years that examines the pervasiveness of "death as sleep" by identifying the amount of emphasis or repetition seen throughout the writings of Luther.

The reason for this conjecture rests on the fact that a number of authors have referenced this particular study by Ketola (e.g., Froom, Secker, and Ball) while none of them have identified any other similar work that either supports or refutes Ketola. These include the following: "More than one hundred times, scattered over the years, Luther declared death to be a sleep."[10] "More than one hundred and twenty-five references to death as sleep and the unconscious state of the dead are said to be found in Luther's writings."[11] *Death until Resurrection* demonstrates these totals to be about half of what it could be while using very strict criteria for counting what's legitimate. I would be the first to say that my book has certainly not found them all either. It is theoretically possible that a search of the Weimar edition could show that I found only half of what it should be—given that it contains four times as many pages as the volumes issued to date as *Luther's Works*.

The thesis by Ketola should not be referenced anymore (as was done in 2008 by Ball, sixty-two years after Ketola wrote it) due to some serious deficiencies in it as explained next. The most glaring problem is its inconsistency with itself. This significant inconsistency can be seen between the conclusion and the summarized data found in a table. The final tally concludes at the end

---

8. Ketola, "Study of Martin Luther's Teaching," 2.
9. Williams, *Radical Reformation*, 197.
10. Froom, *Conditionalist Faith of Our Fathers*, 76.
11. Ball, *Soul Sleepers*, 32.

of this table, saying that "'death is a sleep' is mentioned in the above quoted places about 125 times."[12] The other part of this same table says the following: "'Death is a conscious state' is mentioned in the above quoted places about 32 times."[13] According to Ketola's own research, the quantity of 125 instances is four times the quantity of Luther saying death is not sleep. However, Ketola claims that Luther wrote about unconsciousness in death "sometimes" but "the main bulk of his teaching indicates that he believed in the conscious state of the dead."[14] Since 125 exceeds thirty-two, Ketola's data should not have been described as "sometimes" for "death as sleep." It is startling that Ketola does not discuss the reason for this major discrepancy between the tables and the end of the conclusion.

Another deficiency is that about 90 percent of the 125 instances of "death as sleep" discovered by Ketola are identified only by volume number, column number, and a year with no other identification, title of the work, or basic literary context around some keyword (which also is not typically provided). Predictably, the specific conclusions in Ketola have been noticed by writers as being useful either to support a position or to refute an opposing position. Consequently, it is a serious deficiency of the work because other authors who are defending opposing viewpoints between themselves can quote the same summary to obtain analytical support for their position. This result is unacceptable for both scholarly and popular-level books and articles, and it is being suggested that *Death until Resurrection* should replace it.

It is unfortunate that the methodology of that study was not expanded to include a theological assessment of those citations in the "death is not a sleep" category. There was no attempt in Ketola to offer a suggestion to explain Luther's apparently contradictory statements on the nature of death. For the few quotes that were provided in the thesis, none of them were the ones that explain how apparent contradictions on death made by the same person can be theologically explained. This is also a significant deficiency since Luther has repeatedly explained why it should not be confusing to people. This understanding would necessarily alter the classification of the "conscious state" citations in some instances, at least.

Philip Secker noticed the effect of this without realizing the internal inconsistency in Ketola's paper in his 1967 article published in *Concordia Theological Monthly*, writing the following: "The unpublished master of arts thesis [by Ketola] that Froom cites in support of his assertions draws a conclusion

---

12. Ketola, "Study of Martin Luther's Teaching," 28.
13. Ketola, "Study of Martin Luther's Teaching," 29.
14. Ketola, "Study of Martin Luther's Teaching," 35.

which is quite different from Froom's: 'although Luther sometimes expressed opinions in favor of the unconscious state of the dead . . . the main bulk of his teaching indicates that he believed in the conscious state of the dead.'"[15] So there we have one of the sources of the widespread confusion on what Luther believes about death. This book will clearly show that Ketola's claim is undoubtedly false regarding the "main bulk" of Luther's teaching. My search of fifty books on Luther has not turned up even one book that refers to any other study besides Ketola that includes this quantification of Luther's mention of "death as sleep" as being original research.[16]

The end result is that the voice of Luther on this topic has been silenced among many people. This silencing of Luther—effecting most readers of Luther—is ironic because he theoretically mentioned the idea (on average that is) in excess of every other month, every year for the last twenty-four years of his life, as this book will show the reader. So, I now present the start of a year-by-year analysis of the variety of fish and mammals in Luther's ocean so that a final determination can be reached on whether or not Luther was "vague" and actually held these views for "just a while."

My analysis begins in the winter of 1515–1516

Following his two-year lecture series on the Psalms, Luther decided that his second lecture series would be Paul's letter to the Romans. He "had prepared 123 pages of handwritten" commentary notes for his twice per week lectures that lasted from early summer 1515 until late summer 1516.[17] In addition to these notes, there are extant a number of student notebooks of these lectures which allow us to "get a very interesting and reliable account . . . [and] a very fair picture of what Luther actually said in the lectures" from a composite of this material.[18] These student notebooks have proven

---

15. Secker, "Martin Luther's Views on the Dead," 422.

16. The following list of authors of books that describe Luther at some length (usually with *Luther* in the book title) are provided for verification (see bibliography for titles): Althaus, Baker, H. Barth, Bayer, Blackburne, Boehmer, Bornkamm, Brecht (3), Canright, Childs, Ericksen, Froom, George, Gritsch, Hagen, Heinz, Hendrix, Holder, Hsia, Kolb et al., Kolb/Trueman, Kostlin, Lohse (2), Lull, Marius, Marty, Matheson, Maxfield, McGrath, McKim, Michelet, Noll, Oberman, O'Reggio, Paulson, Pelikan, Piper, Rosin, Selderhuis, Schwarz, Secker, Smith, Tavard, Thielicke, Thiselton, Whitford, and Williams.

17. Oswald, *LW*, 25:ix.

18. Oswald, *LW*, 25:x. Luther's own manuscript, including both the glosses and scholia, were published in WA 56, and the composite student notes of the lectures were published in WA 57. A copy of Luther's notes was published in the sixteenth century and it had found its way to the Vatican Library in the Thirty Years' War. After several

to be an "indispensable complement to the Reformer's own elaboration . . . [a] concrete echo . . . [and] the instruction of his students can be perceived in its immediate effect."[19]

At the very beginning of Luther's lecture notes we read that "the chief purpose of this letter [to the Romans] is to break down, to pluck up, and to destroy all wisdom and righteousness of the flesh."[20] This hyperbole of destroying all human wisdom led Marius to suggest that "already in his lectures on Romans, he prepares his way to stand alone or seemingly alone against centuries of Catholic tradition."[21] Johannes Ficker, the editor of this particular lecture series in the Weimar edition, concludes that Luther's lectures were distributed as follows: summer 1515 (Rom 1:1–3:4); winter 1515–16 (Rom 3:5–8:39); summer 1516 (Rom 9:1–16:27).[22]

The day that Luther had discussed Romans 6:3 (regarding the death of Jesus) which was around the middle of winter, 1515–16, is the point in time that my book starts the clock. The timeline of Luther's life on the matter of death starts when he was in his early thirties and continues through his early sixties when he finally died. Sometime in the dead of winter, when Luther reached this passage in Romans 6, he talked about the nature of death in the context of the Bible. The Reformer discussed death numerous times in the lecture hall with his students saying death is like natural sleep according to Scripture. He allowed for exceptions to this rule for those persons of the Bible, such as Enoch, whom God took without actual death occurring to them.[23]

The first time this lecture on Romans appeared in print, in either German, Latin, or English, was as late as 1908. It may be of little consequence whether Luther was actually born in 1483 or 1484, and whether this notable lecture on Romans 6:3 actually occurred at the end of 1515 or the beginning of 1516. It also is irrelevant that nothing he said throughout this lecture series on Romans can be categorized along with his many other statements made later that death is like a sleep. The value in starting here is to show the following:

---

centuries of its existence not being even suspected, but then found, a search for Luther's original manuscript was resumed around the beginning of the twentieth century, leading to a preliminary publication in 1908. The definitive edition prepared by Ficker did not appear until 1938 in the WA.

19. Oswald, *LW*, 25:xiii.
20. Oswald, *LW*, 25:xi.
21. Marius, *Martin Luther*, 109.
22. Oswald, *LW*, 25:x.
23. See Heb 11:5a (NRSV): "By faith Enoch was taken so that he did not experience death; and 'he was not found, because God had taken him.'"

1. That Luther, for the first time in his writings, chronologically, has briefly discussed "death as sleep."
2. In comparison with later writings (but not for very long), he had developed his interpretation of Scripture from uncertainty to certainty.
3. His description of the various senses of *sleep* in the Bible is useful in this book for evaluating my categorization of his later quotes.
4. Luther's preference for prioritizing the literal interpretative method for biblical exegesis can be highlighted related to his view of *sleep* in Scripture.
5. My methodology and evaluation criteria can be illustrated at the start of this analysis with actual Luther quotes.

Specified criteria are required for determining how *sleep* is to be understood during the process of identifying legitimate expressions of "death as sleep." It needs to be demonstrated that a particular use of *sleep* is not referring to a metaphorical use of death, but rather to literal death. Similarly, it is obvious that a use of *sleep* by Luther that refers to natural sleep at night, even within a discussion of actual human death, cannot count either.

Luther told his students that "in the Scripture it [death] is very often called a sleep, a rest, a slumber."[24] The immediate context shows that literal death is referred to by Luther when he says "natural [death], or better, temporal death."[25] However, this use of *sleep* likely meant for Luther at that time only a temporary situation where the person is waiting for the next life, rather than referring to the mind of the deceased person being unconscious or asleep. What is certain is that Luther did not say the deceased person is without consciousness. Therefore, it does not meet the strict criteria I have identified and is not included in the count total. The inclusion of this particular observation by Luther shows that he had recognized that it is not irrelevant or infrequent in the OT and NT that *sleep* is used to either describe death or to refer to it.

This choice to place a literal meaning onto *sleep* when death is compared to sleep in Scripture helps to show that Luther ascribed to the belief that a literal interpretation of Scripture should not be the last resort. However, he did not believe that way as a very young man, as seen below:

> Two centuries earlier Nicholas of Lyra had written extensively in favor of the literal and historical interpretation and had pointed out that by the use of the fourfold sense, dogma could be found

---

24. Oswald, *LW*, 25:310.
25. Oswald, *LW*, 25:310.

in any passage, all in the name of exegesis.²⁶ Luther at first opposed Lyra, calling him a literalist and a rabbi, but in later years, especially as he began studying Hebrew and Greek, he became much more appreciative of Lyra's insistence upon the *primacy of what the text actually said*. . . . In the years preceding the Reformation, it was still considered by many to be the least important of the four [regarding putting literalism ahead].²⁷

As Luther refined his method of biblical interpretation, "the hermeneutical principle which he laid down in his early period implicitly and inevitably implied the abandonment of the fourfold meaning of scripture . . . and was quite clearly replaced by a concern for the fundamental theme of the scripture in its literal sense."²⁸ The next quote shows that Luther took his reversal seriously regarding putting the formerly last of four methods of biblical interpretation to the top of the list.

In the treatment of individual passages Luther insisted that where points of doctrine were at stake only the literal meaning of the text, in its original context, could be used. By 'original' he meant 'original intent,' and not just one of many grammatical possibilities. And the 'original intent' was always to be derived from the message of the Gospel. There were only three possible reasons for departing from this rule: the statement of the text itself that it was to be taken figuratively; a strong indication to the same effect in another passage of Scripture; or the clash between a literal interpretation and a 'clear article of faith.' . . . But where specific points of doctrine are not involved, allegory may be used for 'illustrative purposes,' though it should otherwise be avoided.²⁹

Luther altered his opinion and criticism of Lyra who eventually became one of his favorite commentators. George described him by writing that Lyra "made use of the Hebrew text of the Old Testament and quoted liberally from works of Jewish scholars, especially the learned French rabbi Salomon Rashi (d. 1105). After Aquinas, Lyra was the strongest defender of the literal, historical meaning of Scripture as the primary basis of theological disputation. . . . More than any other commentator from the period of high scholasticism,

---

26. Allegorical, tropological, anagogical, and literal/historical are four ways to read Scripture. See de Lubac, *Medieval Exegesis*.

27. Doermann, "Luther's Principles of Biblical Interpretation," 16–17. The emphasis by italics is original.

28. Ebeling, *Luther*, 107.

29. Doermann, *Interpreting Luther's Legacy*, 22.

Lyra and his work were greatly valued by the early reformers."[30] George's reference to Thomas Aquinas above also included the following: "Thomas did not abandon the principle senses of Scripture but declared that all the senses were founded on one—the literal—and this sense eclipsed allegory as the basis of sacred doctrine."[31] At the start of his lecture series on Psalms (near the beginning of his career), Luther asserted that "our first concern will be for the grammatical meaning, for this is the truly theological meaning."[32] Ebeling writes that "it is now clear that he considers that there is only one genuine meaning of scripture, and that is the literal sense. . . . Admittedly it was still possible for Luther to use allegory as a homiletic device to obtain a more striking application of the text, particularly in his sermons, though he did this with decreasing frequency."[33]

When Luther was in his early fifties, he told his students that as "a young man, my own attempts at allegory met with fair success. . . . And so anyone who was somewhat more skilled in contriving allegories was also regarded as a rather learned theologian. Augustine, too, was led astray by this conviction . . . Ever since I began to adhere to the historical meaning, I myself have always had a strong dislike for allegories and did not make use of them unless the text itself indicated them."[34]

Near the end of his life (in his lecture series on Genesis where he quoted Lyra "more than one hundred times"[35])—Luther told his students that he "prefer[ed] him to almost all other interpreters of Scripture."[36] Although excessive reliance on allegorical interpretation and the other methods common in Luther's day could make fruitful use of some passage on occasion without risk to church dogma, this "concealed the dangers inherent in this procedure. There was no longer any serious respect for the biblical text itself. It was always possible to avoid strict attention to the actual text. And wherever there was any risk of conflict with prevailing Church teaching, the art of interpretation had to be used in such a way that it became in fact the act of concealed reinterpretation."[37]

Here is another quote of Luther from the Romans 6 lecture, and it highlights a critical distinction between one biblical meaning of *death* and

30. George, "General Introduction," xxix.
31. George, "General Introduction," xxix.
32. Ebeling, *Luther*, 107. See WA 5:27.
33. Ebeling, *Luther*, 107–8.
34. Pelikan, *LW*, 1:232.
35. George, "Introduction," xxii.
36. Pelikan and Poellot, *LW*, 2:164.
37. Ebeling, *Luther*, 102.

the common notion of *death* today (and in Luther's day): "This is death ['eternal death'] in the most proper sense of the word, for in all other forms of death something remains that is mixed with life, but not in this kind of death."[38] This understanding of death is an echo often seen in the OT, whenever a scriptural writer does not have in mind the promise of a Messiah who will turn eternal death into everlasting life through the once-absurd concept of a bodily resurrection.

In the summer of 1516, Luther gave a classroom lecture on Romans 13:11 in which he said "to wake from sleep."[39] However, this mention of "sleep" cannot count as a reference to the resurrection of the dead because the immediate context clearly shows that symbolic sleep is the sense of the word (i.e., "it is full time now for us to wake from sleep").[40] Another example of this illegitimate inclusion in my accounting is seen in the sentence by Luther that immediately follows this quote: "It says the same thing in 1 Cor. 15:34: 'Awake, you righteous, and sin not.'"[41] Luther's very next sentence says, "Eph. 5:14: Awake, O sleeper, and arise from the dead, and Christ shall give you light." Consider the following observations of this last quote, as it relates to characterizing Luther by counting up his mentions of the "death as sleep" idea:

1. *Sleeper* is obviously referring to a person who sleeps.

2. Its immediate context (i.e., "arise from the dead") does not obviously disqualify it from being included in this count (i.e., it is not clearly referring to symbolic sleep).

3. The wider context in the fifth chapter of Ephesians clearly shows that *dead* does not refer to literal death since the next verse (v. 15) says the following: "Therefore be careful how you walk, not as unwise men but as wise."

4. The still wider context of Ephesians 5:14 (which both the NRSV and NIV, for example, have reformatted the verse as poetry) and which shows a note in the NASB that refers to Isaiah 51:17 ("Rouse yourself! Arise O Jerusalem; you who have drunk from the Lord's hand the cup of His anger") in which its context (at Isa 51:23) shows that *arise* is probably referring to the inability of people to resurrect themselves from literal death. This would indicate the possibility that "awake O

---

38. Oswald, *Luther's Works*, 25:310.
39. Oswald, *Luther's Works*, 25:478.
40. Oswald, *Luther's Works*, 25:478.
41. Oswald, *Luther's Works*, 25:478.

sleeper" actually was originally referring to a literal, not metaphorical, death.

5. Luther is quoting from Scripture (Eph 5:14) and therefore the use of *awake* and *sleeper* cannot count under the criteria established in my book.

Luther told his students in 1516 that "the word 'sleep' is used in Scripture in various ways. In the first place, it is used in the literal sense with reference to physical death, as in John 11:11: 'Our friend Lazarus has fallen asleep' and in the second place, it is used with reference to spiritual sleep and in a twofold manner."[42] This use here of *asleep* referring to Lazarus cannot count either, even though he said it refers to literal sleep and literal death, because he is quoting the Bible.[43] To summarize: Luther briefly discussed "death as a sleep" for the first time ever, publicly, either at the end of 1515 or at the beginning of 1516.

Luther in 1517

Luther gave a university lecture on Hebrews 2:14 sometime between April and October of 1517, during his series on the book of Hebrews, which was first published (in any language) "finally in 1929."[44] This passage refers to the death of Jesus as well as to the death of other people. What is interesting about his comments that day is that Luther referenced John Chrysostom, the Archbishop of Constantinople, who was an important early church father of the late fourth century, and his opinion about death. Chrysostom was among the most prolific authors in the early Christian Church, exceeded only by Augustine of Hippo in the quantity of his surviving writings.[45] Luther told his students the following: "Therefore Chrysostom says on this passage . . . Why do you fear death? It is no longer terrible, but it has been trodden underfoot . . . and further on he [Chrysostom] says: 'For death is no longer bitter, because it does not differ from sleep.'"[46]

42. Oswald, *Luther's Works*, 25:478.

43. There's another Luther quote in this lecture on Rom 13 that discusses literal death, but it is not applicable either. And there's another one that uses *sleeping* in the "spiritual sleep" sense.

44. Hagen, *Theology of the Young Luther*, 5, 7. "It has only been in the twentieth century that these lectures [Titus, Philemon, and Hebrews] have been prepared for publication at all." Pelikan, "Introduction to Volume 29," ix.

45. There are six volumes of his writings in the Christian Classics Ethereal Library edition of the *Nicene and Post-Nicene Fathers*, compared to eight volumes for Augustine.

46. Chrysostom, source unknown, quoted in Pelikan and Hansen, *LW*, 29:136–37.

Not only is this another instance of Luther discussing the topic, about a year and a half later, but it also shows that Luther is telling his students something different now. At first, it likely was an observation that it is not infrequent throughout the scriptural materials that death is called a sleep. Recall that there are fifty-six passages in Scripture that refer to, or more likely describe, literal death as a sleep.[47] We see Luther here taking another step toward more specificity on the concept itself by telling the class that a highly-respected preacher of the fourth century taught his many followers that death does not differ from sleep. Instead of it being just a scriptural reference to saying "he fell asleep," when they actually meant "he died," Luther has demonstrated that it is possible that their repeated use of this term throughout the Bible had not just become a meaningless euphemism, but rather, it is possible, at least, that this usage actually was intended originally to describe the nature of death.

This usage of *sleep* by Luther does not count in my running total, however, even though it refers to literal death as sleep, and he's *not* quoting Scripture. Under my criteria, this use of *sleep* does not count because previous uses of *sleep* by Luther do not explicitly describe "death as sleep" in the sense of unconsciousness, instead of it just being a temporary situation before resurrection. Additionally, Luther is quoting another person (Chrysostom), so at this early stage in Luther's timeline discussing the subject, it cannot legitimately be an example.[48] Since about the time of Luther's death until the end of the nineteenth century, nobody knew about Luther's student, Sigismund Reichenbach, and his notebook on the Hebrews lectures, because "for well over 300 years these two sets of student notes lay dormant, unknown to the world of Luther scholarship. . . . It has been only recently that Luther's lectures on Hebrews have been edited and published. . . . In 1899 . . . Ficker discovered Aurifaber's copy of student notes in the Vatican Library [identified with the year 1517 in its Latin title]. . . . Finally in 1929, tired of waiting for Ficker's edition . . . Hirsch . . . and Ruckert came out with a critical edition of the Vatican manuscript."[49]

---

47. The NT has fifteen "death as sleep" verses (Matt 9:24; 27:52; John 11:11; Acts 7:60; 13:36; 1 Cor 11:30; 15:6, 18, 20, 51; Eph 5:14; 1 Thess 4:13–15, and 5:10). The OT has forty-one "death as sleep" verses (Jer 51:39, 57; Dan 12:2 Pss 13:3; 90:5; 1 Kgs 11:43; plus another thirty-five verses in the OT very similar to this one, which says, "Solomon slept with his fathers, and was buried").

48. It is possible that Luther had read the *Thessalonians Homilies* by Chrysostom (at 6, 8, and 9) based on the similarity of the phrase, "death does not differ from sleep" in those writings. Over eleven centuries prior to Luther's day, Chrysostom had written a very large number of commentaries on different books of the Bible.

49. Hagen, *Theology of the Young Luther*, 6.

We know that neither of the two students in class that day in 1517 bothered to record which specific commentary, or homily, Luther was referencing, of those still in existence (only two notebooks), and Luther's own lecture notes are not extant. Only the author and the fact that it was a commentary appear in the original composite manuscripts at this Luther quote. Because it is possible that Luther obtained his Chrysostom quote from the Thessalonians Homily, it may be appropriate to include three other quotes of Chrysostom here as follows:

1. "But if to grieve for the departed is the part of heathens, then tell me whose part it is to beat one's self, and tear the cheeks? On what account dost thou lament, if thou believest that he will rise again, that he has not perished, that it is but a slumber *and* a sleep?";[50]

2. "If anyone looked into their souls, no one is so cruel, no one so hardhearted, no one so firm, as not to have his soul dejected, and relaxed with fear and despair. And if when others are taken off by this death which differs *nothing* from sleep?";[51]

3. "Again, whether we wake or sleep; but by sleep there he means one thing, and here another. For here whether we sleep signifies the death of the body, that is, fear not dangers; though we should die, we shall live."[52]

To summarize 1517: Luther's students heard him quote Saint Chrysostom saying, "death is no longer bitter, because it does not differ from sleep."[53] However, it is not yet evident that Luther described *sleep* as an unconscious sleep.

Luther in 1519

When Luther's elector, Frederick of Saxony, became seriously ill in the summer of 1519, he was urged by Spalatin to prepare a spiritual consolation for him. The title of this tender, devotional treatise is *The Fourteen of Consolation*, which was composed in September 1519 and first published in both Latin and German in February 1520.[54] The *fourteen* refers to fourteen patron

---

50. Chrysostom, "Homily VI: 1 Thess. 4:9–10," 399.
51. Chrysostom, "Homily VIII: 1 Thess. 4:15–17," 418.
52. Chrysostom, "Homily IX: 1 Thess. 5:1–2," 434.
53. Pelikan and Hansen, *LW*, 29:137.
54. An alternative title is "The Consolatory Tesseradecad for the Weary and Heavy Laden" as seen in the table of contents of Cole, *Select Works of Martin Luther*, vol. 2.

saints (that were described by a Franconian shepherd in Germany in a 1446 vision), each of whom was a defender against some particular danger or disease. Luther's booklet soon became very popular, being published in the Netherlands in 1521, and by 1525, five Latin and seven German editions had been published. Johannes Mathesius (1504–65), Luther's biographer and compiler of the informal *Table Talk* of Luther, judged that there had never before been such words of comfort written in the German language.

In 1535, Luther issued this treatise in a new and final edition, adding a brief postscript and correcting many parts back to their original form that had become corrupted.[55] Over fifteen years after first writing it, Luther no longer held several of his former views seen in it. But he let that which he had outgrown all stand. Luther intended the set to be a historical record that shows the world how far he had developed. Another translation of this same brief note renders a part of it as follows: "For it is my purpose in this book to put forth a public record of my progress."[56]

Regarding death, Luther wrote the following after describing Moses and his serpent: "So, the just seem to die, in the eyes of the foolish, whereas, they [actually] rest in peace."[57] What did the young Luther really mean by "rest in peace"? Then, a few pages later we find the following: "Through death the whole tragedy of the world's ills is brought to a close; as it is written (Ps 4:8) . . . 'I will lay me down in peace and sleep.'"[58] Finally, Luther concludes by saying (under part 2): "Therefore it is, that the Scriptures call it a sleep, rather than death."[59]

These three examples of Luther describing death as being similar to sleep have been judged by me to be not legitimate instances under the criteria set within my book. Although "rest in peace" may have become, in just two or three years for Luther, a general funeral phrase that stood in contrast to the belief in a turbulent purgatory, it cannot count here without a literary context that shows it meant actual unconsciousness for him. Previous uses of *sleep* by Luther have not explicitly described "death as sleep" in the sense of unawareness. The second one is a quote of Scripture and is thereby excluded from my accounting of instances. The last one is a nominal observation of Bible verses that "call it a sleep, rather than death" and fails to suggest in and of itself (or its context) that unconsciousness is implied by *sleep*, instead of it just being a temporary situation before resurrection.

---

55. See Cole, "Consolatory Tesseradecad," in *Select Works of Martin Luther*, 2:174.
56. Luther, "Fourteen of Consolation (Tessaradecas Consolatoria)," para. 15.
57. Cole, *Select Works of Martin Luther*, 2:147.
58. Kerr, *Compend of Luther's Theology*, 240.
59. Cole, *Select Works of Martin Luther*, 2:156.

Although they are similar to the Chrysostom occurrence from 1517 above and are excluded from my tally, this treatise from two years later is quite noteworthy since it clearly shows that Luther was willing to tell everyone that "death, to them that believe"[60]—and not just to honored saints—is a "rest in peace." Although this point about commonality from the divine point of view between Saint Chrysostom and his many followers, for example, is remarkable, there are two other important points Luther made in this treatise. These include Luther's observations that death consists of "peace and sleep," and that the Bible repeatedly calls death a "sleep."

In Luther's "Sermon on Preparing to Die" (1519), there also were no valid expressions of "death as sleep" since he did not describe death until resurrection as consisting of unconsciousness here, nor did he imply it is just a temporary condition. This is also the case for the "Treatise on Baptism" (published in November 1519), although his interesting analogy of resurrection to baptism is worth quoting here. "So, then, the life of a Christian, from baptism to the grave, is nothing else than the beginning of a blessed death, for at the Last Day God will make him altogether new. In like manner the lifting up out of baptism is quickly done, but the thing it signifies, the spiritual birth, the increase of grace and righteousness, though it begins indeed in baptism, lasts until death, nay, even until the Last Day. Only then will that be finished which the lifting up out of baptism signifies. Then shall we arise from death . . . Then shall we be truly lifted up out of baptism and completely born, and we shall put on the true baptismal garment of immortal life in heaven."[61] The issues and key phrases above to be analyzed in chapters 8 and 9 (in the context of his later writings on death) include:

1. "at the Last Day God will make him altogether new": so what specifically happens to a deceased person's soul between death and resurrection such that it is raised altogether new?

2. "lasts until death, nay, even until the Last Day. Only then will that be finished": so the process of personal renewal doesn't end at death, but rather, it continues during the period of death even though the mind of the deceased person is unconscious?

3. "[and we will be] completely born, and we shall put on the true baptismal garment of immortal life in heaven": so it is only when we are born again at the Last Day that we actually fulfill the symbolism of baptism and only then that we put on the clothes of deathlessness for both body and soul?

60. Cole, *Select Works of Martin Luther*, 2:156.
61. Jacobs and Spaeth, *Works of Martin Luther*, 1:58.

Luther in 1521

Volume 75 of *Luther's Works*, published in 2013, provides a translated sermon titled, "Second Sunday in Advent: Luke 21," which Luther delivered on January 1, 1521, that discusses an advance topic under the category of "death as sleep." As a side note, the calendar was changed throughout the Holy Roman Empire to make January 1 the start of the new year (at the location of this sermon) about forty years afterwards (although its Catholic states changed it in 1544)—see footnote 11 in chapter 3 for additional detail. What is especially interesting about the contents of this sermon is that it shows that Luther had given some deep thought to the question of the location of the soul between death and resurrection, and that the condition of the soul during death had perhaps no spatiality. He certainly was not dogmatic on this point in this 1521 sermon, representing an early stage in his development, but it is clear from the questions Luther asked the congregants that day that his thinking was at a sophisticated level already.

Luther shows that he was contemplating God's method of preserving the soul/mind of a person while it was asleep in some sense. This part of the sermon began to wonder just *where specifically* a deceased person who is at rest would be according to Scripture. He asked the following questions: "Where do our souls remain when all of creation is on fire and there is nothing to stand on? Do you think that God cannot preserve souls in His hand? Or do you think that He must have a physical stall, as a shepherd does for his sheep? . . . Our bodies also [become new] and become alive again."[62] Chapter 8 of this book will examine these questions about the "where and how" of death and resurrection using Luther's more-developed quotes over the next twenty-four years of his life. The explanation within chapter 8 could work in the reverse as well for some readers, as an aid for believing Luther's claim about death as unconscious sleep, and thereby its specificity may resolve one's question related to *why* God would create souls that temporarily lose their consciousness.

Some social context may be helpful for interpreting Luther's next writing presented here by describing some events and persons in history. Luther's July 1519 debate opponent in the city of Leipzig, Germany was John Eck, who was a high-ranking member of the clergy and a published prelate

---

62. Mayes and Langebartels, *LW*, 75:109. Although most of the "sermons of the *Winter Postil* were written by Luther as 'explanations' and were not really sermons, so most were far too long to be preached, even by sixteenth-century standards" in contrast to the *Summer Postils*, which "were actually preached by Luther, recorded by a stenographer, and revised by an editor," this Luke 21 sermon was actually preached by Luther as shown in the Comparison Chart of Luther's Postil Publications at Mayes and Langebartels, *LW*, 75:xxxii. See also xxv.

at the time with a doctorate in theology. Following this debate, but before his April 1521 appearance in the city of Worms by order of the Emperor of the Holy Roman Empire, Charles, two papal bulls had been issued against Luther. The threat of immediate excommunication through admonition in June 1520 was followed by a January 1521 bull that made his excommunication effective. After Luther completed the first version of his reply in November 1520, as required by Pope Leo X, he burned a copy of the pope's official bull in December 1520 outside the gates of Wittenberg in the presence of the students of the university.

The 1520 bull from Rome "called dramatically upon Christ, the Apostle Peter, the Apostle Paul, and the entire communion of saints to take action against Luther and his teachings. . . . [and] anyone who held or defended these views . . . was condemned. . . . In the meantime he was ordered to keep silent and his books were to be burned [which Eck ceremoniously had done in 1520]."[63] Eck was a university professor whose birth and death were within about three years of Luther's. He "was largely responsible for securing Luther's excommunication by Rome in 1520."[64] The remainder of this 1521 section will examine an interesting portion of Luther's *Defense and Explanation of All the Articles* reply that was finally completed in March 1521, after four months' time, following some brief and relevant historical context.

About three years had elapsed since Luther called on Archbishop Albert of Brandenburg for supporting an academic debate using his ninety-five theses. At first Albert brushed off Luther's request, but he soon realized that this issue could affect him personally. Albert was the younger brother of Elector Joachim I of Brandenburg, a neighbor and rival of Elector Frederick of Saxony. Frederick "was offering indulgences of his own and was therefore competing with Albert."[65] In November 1518, one full year after Luther's ninety-five theses began to circulate widely, Pope Leo X "had issued a decree that upheld [John] Tetzel's claims about indulgences, claims which Luther had ridiculed in the ninety-five theses."[66] This pope designated this archbishop in 1516 who then selected this infamous-to-be Dominican friar, and licensed theology instructor (Tetzel), to continue promoting indulgences in the archdioceses of Mainz and Magdeburg.[67]

Consider Luther's reaction as seen in his *Explanations* at the twenty-seventh article. First, however, a bit more background for context: A papal

63. Mayes and Langebartels, *LW*, 75:x.
64. Lehmann and Bachmann, *Luther's Works*, 35:408n92.
65. Lehmann and Bachmann, *Luther's Works*, 35:408n92.
66. Lehmann and Bachmann, *Luther's Works*, 35:77.
67. See Hendrix, *Martin Luther: Visionary Reformer*, 56–57.

bull was promulgated from Rome in December 1513 (which was eight years prior to those sent to Luther) that intended to challenge the growing momentum in the universities on the subject of innate immortality of the soul as seen in the recent writings of the Catholic professor of philosophy, Pietro Pomponazzi, and other Aristotelian philosophers.[68] The issue for Rome was more of a philosophical character, not a wholly religious one, in that the focus was on what happens to the human soul when the body dies, rather than it relating to the eternal life of a saved person. This basic confusion is common even today when "soul immortality" is identified without any hint that the argument is about the natural properties of a person at birth, and the consequential effect on the mind/soul at death, rather than deathlessness in a heavenly life after our resurrection. To avoid this confusion, some have prefixed something to *immortality*—such as *natural, native, inherent,* or *innate* immortality of the soul—to separate it as being around birth instead of after death or at resurrection.

To demonstrate that Pomponazzi was discussing this ontological aspect (i.e., the nature of being) of the constituent makeup of a person as seen at death, rather than the soteriological aspect of receiving the gift of everlasting life, consider the following brief extract from his *On the Immortality of the Soul* (1516). Additionally, Aristotle was being interpreted at that time as being in support of the view, in direct opposition to Plato, that the soul does not remain in existence at death, because the mind/soul depends on the body to continue to function. At the risk of delving too deeply into an explanation of Pomponazzi's point within the document that largely contributed to the 1513 bull (and copies of Pomponazzi's writing were ceremoniously burned in Venice), may the following brief summarizing quote suffice, to mainly show which sense of immortality was being referred to by both Pomponazzi and the pope's advisors: "Because the human intellectual soul depends on the . . . perishable body, it cannot function after the body has been destroyed."[69]

Pope Leo X attended the eighth session of the Fifth Lateran Council (1512–17) which, by a vote of the Magisterium, produced this bull that "stands out as one of the few doctrinal decisions of that predominantly

---

68. Regarding the question of whether or not the proclamation from Rome was actually a bull containing a seal or ink impression: At the second paragraph of the introduction to the section titled "Lateran V, 1512–1517" appears the following: "The seven sessions after [Pope] Leo's election gave approval to a number of constitutions, among which are to be noted the condemnation of the teaching of the philosopher Pomponazzi (session eight) . . . All the decrees of this council, at which the pope presided in person, are in the form of bulls. . . . The fathers confirmed all the decrees by their votes." Roman Catholic Church, *Decrees of the Ecumenical Councils*, 593.

69. Martin, "Pietro Pomponazzi," para. 11.

political and reform-minded council."[70] At just thirty-seven years old, the new pope was persuaded to officially declare for the first time in the church's history that the soul is immortal, meaning that the soul does not perish immediately at death, as followers of Aristotle had separated themselves from the Neoplatonists, Augustinians, and the Thomists on this point. Part of the bull reads as follows: "We condemn and reject all those who insist that the intellectual soul is mortal. . . . it is also immortal."[71] See footnote 53 in chapter 3 for a longer quote from this official statement on the nature of the soul. This unusual bull furthermore commanded that all university professors of philosophy, when lecturing on doctrines that deviated from it, make every effort to teach the truth of the Christian religion and to refute any philosophical arguments that challenged it, subject to punishment as a heretic.

This threat of death at the stake is an important point to remember when evaluating the nuance seen within several of Luther's university lectures on immortality including the whereabouts and nature of the soul of the deceased. And it is directly relevant to our interpretation of the following *Explanations* reply of Luther to the pope's bulls regarding excommunication and further threats including death. If Luther's letter had clearly said "the Bible teaches that only God has the characteristic of immortality of the soul/mind, which is more authoritative than decrees that contradict this declaration to Timothy, as issued by the pope, therefore, because this passage excludes people, their soul is mortal (from 1 Tim 6:16)"; then Luther probably would have been signing his own death warrant (to be executed at age thirty-seven or so).

It seems many Catholics, Roman and Eastern; many Protestants, liberal and conservative; and most of everyone else in the West who believe in some kind of afterlife hold to the notion that people remain conscious after death. Our culture, with its television shows and movies depicting a ghost as a deceased person, constantly reinforces the notion that all human beings are immortal from birth. However, "God . . . alone is immortal" (1 Tim 6:13, 16, NIV), and this verse may actually mean what it seems to say.[72]

---

70. Constant, "Fifth Lateran Council Decree *Apostolici regiminis*," 353.

71. Roman Catholic Church, *Decrees of the Ecumenical Councils*, 605. See also Papal Encyclicals Online, "Fifth Lateran Council 1512-17 A.D," (which is not a Vatican site, although the Vatican Publishing House has granted permission for the site to reprint; see session eight).

72. "God . . . alone possesses immortality" (NASB) and "God . . . alone who has immortality" (NRSV) could possibly be ruling out the natural possession of immortality of the soul by any human being (except Jesus Christ, of course, who was fully God and fully man, in my view).

Under the twenty-seventh article in the *Explanations*, as seen in its final version from 1521, Luther wrote (in part):

> Hence the experts in Rome have recently pronounced a holy decree which establishes that the soul of man is immortal, acting as if we did not all say in our common creed, "I believe in the life everlasting." And, with the assistance of the mastermind Aristotle, they decreed further that the soul is "essentially the form of the human body," and many other splendid articles of a similar nature. These decrees are, indeed, most appropriate to the papal church, for they make it possible for them to hold fast to human dreams and the doctrines of devils while they trample upon and destroy faith and the teaching of Christ.[73]

Later, Luther would write that in this article "it was decreed that one must believe the soul to be immortal. From this one may gather that they make eternal life an object of sheer mockery and contempt. In this way they confess that it is a common belief among them that there is no eternal life, but that they now wish to proclaim this by means of a bull."[74] The current catechism of the Catholic Church presently teaches "that every spiritual soul is . . . immortal; it does not perish when it separates from the body at death."[75]

The first observation that could be made from the twenty-seventh article of Luther's reply is that he assumed that *soul immortality* (from the bull) obviously refers to *life everlasting* (as seen in his reply). It appears Luther had made either a mistake or a clever circumvention. However, the church leaders made it clear in Venice that they were then objecting to Pomponazzi's short philosophical treatise, *On the Immortality of the Soul*, written four years earlier. The bull itself "reaffirmed the doctrine of the immortality of the soul over against the teaching of some Averroists or neo-Aristotelians who taught that the human soul was mortal."[76] Furthermore, the Roman

---

73. Lehmann and Forell, *LW*, 32:77–78. This translation is based on the revised German version of March 1521 rather than his three previous versions in Latin and German. This translation also is a revision of the C. M. Jacobs translation from the Philadelphia edition of the works of Luther. For the original German, see WA 7:308–57.

74. Lehmann and Sherman, *LW*, 47:37–38. "Luther's Warning to his Dear German People," which contains this quote, was written in 1531.

75. *Catechism of the Catholic Church*, 83.

76. Lehmann and Sherman, *LW*, 47:38n41. Regarding the resurrection of the flesh, Luther preached the following in an Easter Wednesday sermon on Col 3:1–7: "The body . . . the tabernacle, or the corruptible flesh-and-blood garment, must also be raised." Lenker, *Luther's Epistle Sermons*, 2:220.

Catholic Church confirmed in a 1990 publication (that provided the full text of this bull) that Pomponazzi was, in fact, the target then.[77]

Therefore, the particular meaning of "soul immortality" in the bull of 1513 was clearly not related to the idea seen at the end of the Apostles' Creed (i.e., "and the life everlasting. Amen") as Luther suggested in the twenty-seventh article.[78] Rather, it was related to the philosophical controversy (i.e., the state of the person's soul/mind at death) that Pope Leo X was objecting to, given that the text of the bull also offers "to apply suitable remedies against the infection . . . [from] philosophy" and it allows "for cleansing and healing the infected sources of philosophy . . . [provided that] he actively devotes himself to theology or the sacred canons."[79]

Although it is possible that Luther was ill-informed of the controversy over the timing of obtaining immortality of the soul (e.g., around birth, around death, or around resurrection) or perhaps he was confused, this significant indicator on Luther's probable beliefs must be kept in mind when interpreting him on this question of immortality. The option exists which cannot be ruled out, given the deadly nature of the times in which he lived related to immortality debates, which is that Luther was not being sincere about his confusion or his objection to Rome's "common belief among them that there is no eternal life"[80]—which seems to be a suspicious charge in this context.

Luther's hesitancy in clarifying his specific meaning of *immortality*, or for *sleep* (as in "death as sleep"), undoubtedly relates to the quite hot topic in the sixteenth century of Christian mortalism (i.e., physicalism). As a derivative of the soul-sleep debates then (which could possibly be taken as literal sleep in a literal death), some of the radical reformers of the sixteenth century preferred instead to interpret this generic label as referring to the death of the soul when the body dies in this world. In later centuries, this mortalism of the soul became known as *conditional immortality* as opposed to *innate immortality of the soul* when interpreting some biblical uses of *sleep* in the context of death. To push back against this talk of mortalism or sleeping souls in death, John Calvin's first theological work, written in 1534, rebutted both the notion of soul-sleep and the claim that the soul/mind dies with the body. This can be seen from the titles of the following two separate English translations of Calvin's book. *Soul Sleep: Psychopannychia*

77. See Roman Catholic Church, *Decrees*, 593.

78. Althaus quotes Luther as saying the Apostles' Creed is "the finest of all, a brief and true summary of the articles of faith" in *Theology of Martin Luther*, 7 (no reference provided).

79. Roman Catholic Church, *Decrees of the Ecumenical Councils*, 606.

80. Lehmann and Sherman, *LW*, 47:37–38.

was published in 2011 by Amazon/CreateSpace Publishing; and *A Treatise of the Immortality of the Soule* was published in 1581 in London.[81]

Certain Catholic defenders of the faith made quite clear this challenge to purgatory and prayer to the saints would be met with burnings at the stake. It bears repeating that Calvin's book forcefully "refuted the strange opinion that the soul falls asleep at the death of its body and wakes up at the final resurrection."[82] At the very beginning of his preface, Calvin wrote the following: "Long ago, when certain pious persons invited, and even urged me, to publish something for the purpose of repressing the extravagance of those who, alike ignorantly and tumultuously, maintain that the soul dies or sleeps, I could not be induced by all their urgency, so averse did I feel to engage in that kind of dispute."[83] Eck remained a "persistent adversary since the Leipzig debate" and his "strategy was to put all non-Catholics into one heretical basket by arguing that the beliefs of Anabaptists [e.g., mortalism of the soul, adult baptism, etc.], whom both Lutherans and Catholics opposed, originated with Luther."[84] Eck assembled

> 404 theological statements . . . excerpted from writings by various reformers and stamped as heresy. . . . After Eck sent an elegant hand-written copy of the 404 statements to Emperor Charles V, Elector John and the Lutheran theologians feared that Charles might prejudice the Lutherans as no better than Anabaptists. In the [*Augsburg*] *Confession* [which "became the litmus test of Lutheranism"], therefore, Melanchthon made a sharp distinction between Lutheran beliefs and the unorthodox view held by Anabaptists.[85]

For an observer at the time of this controversy over the existence of purgatory, the question of a replacement teaching of what happens to souls at death was paramount. Peter Matheson's take on this historical period may be helpful, as follows:

> Belief in purgatory, despite its undoubted terrors, offered an effective guarantee that the great majority of Christians were saved and would live with Christ in heaven. Could the new Protestant churches do as much? The most pertinent question, then, was what would actually happen to the souls of the dead.

---

81. Calvin, "Psychopannychia," xvi. "The title page is as follows: 'A Treatise of the Immortality of the Soule' . . . Translated out of French by Tho. Stocke 1581."
82. Tavard, *Calvin's Theology*, 1.
83. Calvin, *Soul Sleep: Psychopannychia*, 5.
84. Hendrix, *Martin Luther: Visionary Reformer*, 163, 214.
85. Hendrix, *Martin Luther: Visionary Reformer*, 214.

There were, initially at least, no uniform answers about this from official Protestant teaching. Martin Luther proclaimed the "sleep of the soul," idea that the dead would remain insensible and unconscious until the last judgment and resurrection of the dead. But Calvin condemned the doctrine, and most mainstream reformers gradually fell into line, particularly as "psychopannichism" (soul-sleeping) came to be associated with radical Anabaptists.[86]

There are different ways to interpret Luther's twenty-seventh article in the *Explanations* regarding Luther's discussion of soul immortality and the bull. Some interpreters (e.g., Froom) seem to be unaware of the emphasis Luther may have put on the Magisterium's questionable priorities or methodological issues compared to the conclusion itself. To extend the context a bit within this twenty-seventh article, Luther wrote the following immediately before the quote above: "See here! Shouldn't the pope have power to establish doctrines and articles of faith, when this prophecy of him is so clear that even the spirits who inspire him are expressly mentioned? Moreover, in Col. 2(:8), St. Paul teaches us how we should deal with such doctrines when he says, 'See to it, that no one makes a prey of you by philosophy and empty deceit, according to human tradition, and temporal commandments which do not teach of Christ.'"[87]

Althaus wrote that "this does not mean that the teachers of the church and their theological work and teachings are to be despised and rejected. Their validity however depends on their conformity to Scripture. They must substantiate their statements from Scripture and may be judged and criticized on the basis of Scripture. . . . The authority of the theologians of the church is relative and conditional."[88] Luther's exegesis of Colossians 2:8 included the following: "Here we see that we should listen to Christ alone and flee from the commandments of man. Such commandments may appear to make us godly, but are only deceit and the destruction of faith. . . . Even St. Peter is not silent and says in 2 Pet. 2 (:1), "There will be false teachers among you who will teach according to their whim."[89] Luther "firmly believed that the Roman Church had obscured the gospel message over the course of many centuries. Luther once confessed that he would not object to the pope if the pope would only preach the gospel."[90]

86. Matheson, *Reformation Christianity*, 184.
87. Lehmann and Forell, *LW*, 32:77.
88. Althaus, *Theology of Martin Luther*, 6–7.
89. Lehmann and Forell, *LW*, 32:77.
90. Hughes, "Restoration, Historical Models of," 638. Note the contribution made

Two of the ways to interpret the whole statement by Luther at the twenty-seventh article can be described as follows: (1) Luther was mainly objecting to the method often used by the church for preferring mostly philosophical explanations over those that dwell on scriptural texts (i.e., he had *not* made a clear proposition that innate soul immortality is a false doctrine), or alternatively; (2) Luther was objecting to the conclusion itself (i.e., the error of "holding fast" to the neoplatonic view of immortality).

My opinion is that several other comments by Luther on immortality throughout his writings should be considered as being relevant context, and then brought to bear, before either of these two possibilities can be cited as stand-alone proof. That is the purpose of chapter 9 (the last chapter) of *Death until Resurrection*. Further study is needed to penetrate Luther's perceived ambiguity that occasionally appears with his "death as sleep" assertion to then focus on the problems associated with the now-still-common belief seen in traditional dualism, neoplatonism, or innate immortality of the soul.[91]

The author of the following assessment of Luther's quote above clearly has chosen the first of these two ways of reading this, since he has nothing to say about Luther's stance on the idea itself. "Luther objects to the substitution of philosophical ideas concerning the immortality of the soul for the Biblical teaching of the resurrection and the life everlasting."[92] As an example of an author who takes the other interpretation of Luther, Froom uses the following grounds:

> "Immortal soul" included among pope's "monstrous opinions". . . He lists five in the series including the "immortality of the soul" as the fifth, all and each of which Luther expressly rejects [e.g., "the bread and wine are transubstantiated"]. The significance of including "the soul is immortal". . . in what he denominates "monstrous opinions" and "Roman corruptions," is, of course, obvious. And he added immediately that these "all" came out of the "Roman dunghill of decretals" thus harking back to the pope's bull of December 19, 1513, wherein he declared the natural immortality of the soul to be a doctrine of the Catholic Church.[93]

---

by Scott Seay who is identified in the list of contributors within this encyclopedia (and who assisted me in the writing of my book manuscript by contributing suggestions).

91. See Gabor, "Doctrine of the Soul's Immortality."

92. Forell, "Introduction," 32:78n92. Forell is suggesting that Luther objects, and he references Stange, *Studien zur Theologie Luthers*, 287–344.

93. Froom, *Conditionalist Faith of Our Fathers*, 73. See WA 7:131–32 for Luther's reply that contains the "Roman dunghill" quote from 1520.

Chapters 8 and 9 delve into the ramifications of interpreting "death as unconscious sleep" as meaning symbolic sleep during death (i.e., the temporary death of the soul/mind). And, they address how this view of humanity's constitutional nature can affect one's reading of Scripture regarding its many descriptions of hell. It is easy to see how people went historically from Plato's type of "immortal soul for all from birth" to a hell that consists of these indestructible spirits; hence, there's non-stop torture there because it is logical. However, if Aristotle was closer to the truth on the soul, and if the Bible is seen as describing a reality closer to Aristotle's view, then many passages throughout Scripture can be legitimately interpreted as supporting a hell that eventually ends in a literal death for the entire person. Some of the benefits for the reader in following a sequential study of human creation, death, resurrection, and hell include the following:

1. Seeing God's vengeance more clearly as consisting of a literal "second death" (Rev 20:14).

2. Understanding the "everlasting" descriptions of hell in Scripture as referring to an irreversible divine judgment rather than eternal conscious torment and nonstop physical pain.

3. Realizing that "God is love" applies to everyone and everywhere, both the forgiven and the unforgiven, unrepentant lost. This new way of perceiving our Christian God who graciously ends a person's life after a period of mental torment in a real hell (with actual fire that consumes instead of only burning a person forever) can be appreciated as a good balance between justice and love. And it can be quite helpful to a person's well-being who has been a follower of Christ. And to the outside, skeptical observer of our religion, a belief in a more courteous hell would make our God less monstrous and sadistic, likely with tangible results that are positive. Evaluating parts of Scripture is beyond the scope of this book regarding those passages that may be supportive of any of the three main options for hell: conditional immortality, universal salvation, and the traditional "torment forever" view.

Alternatively, if the reader prefers to stick with a study on just "death as sleep," meaning a complete death of body and soul until our resurrection, then real comfort can be found in that as well, including reducing our common fear of death after understanding its details as given in the Bible. Developing more awareness of your trust and dependence on our loving Creator for both the challenges within our lives and on our very existence after death can result from rethinking the soul and reconsidering the meaning of "death as sleep" seen throughout the OT and the NT.

Natural immortality from birth, as opposed to one that is conditional on an act of God sometime after death, implies that the mind/soul of a deceased person naturally remains conscious. Alternatively, the view sometimes called mortalism, physicalism, monism, or conditional immortality (in contrast to "innate immortality of the soul" at one's birth) means the soul/mind of the dead no longer exists as a functioning person, except in God for use at resurrection. The presumption is that the mind or soul inside a person depends on the embodied nature (as evident in Pomponazzi and Luther) or on the neural processes in the brain as understood in neuroscience, rather than on an invisible brain.[94]

In recent decades the term *non-reductive physicalism* has been used especially in the area of philosophy as an alternative to various forms of dualism (i.e., body/soul relationships). Murphy, who is professor of Christian philosophy at Fuller Theological Seminary, suggested in a 2016 lecture at Villanova University titled "Does neuroscience teach that we have no souls?" that this label above could be replaced by *multi-aspect monism*. Perhaps another characterization that also pushes back against secular physicalism/materialism and different types of dualism would be *divinely monitored physicalism* or perhaps *unconscious dualism* (as explained in chapter 8). This is the view that Luther seems to have invented, although he didn't name it, and it:

1. emphasizes that God remembers in great detail each person born

2. for use at resurrecting everyone who remains unconscious in batches

3. even though God had required a complete death of our entire person

4. including that part of us that chooses to disobey and sin (which is the interior soul/mind)

---

94. In addition to the two books referenced in chapter 2 (at footnote 22) related to a quote from Nancey Murphy, see the following five books which are all also books of essays from writers of various backgrounds on the topic of mind/soul/personal identity: Crisp et al., *Neuroscience and the Soul: The Human Person in Philosophy, Science, and Theology* (2016); Murphy and Knight, *Human Identity at the Intersection of Science, Technology, and Religion* (2010); Green and Palmer, *In Search of the Soul: Four Views of the Mind-Body Problem* (2005); Green, *What about the Soul? Neuroscience and Christian Anthropology* (2004); and Peters et al., *Resurrection: Theological and Scientific Assessments* (2002). This group of seven books of essays involves seventy-nine contributors (after removing duplicates) representing philosophy, science, and the largest camp 57 percent, those holding positions as a Christian (based on their biographical descriptions in these books). The common theme in each of them is that a growing number of Christians are agreeing with the observations of neuroscience against the traditional view of the soul and have articulated positions that may be consistent with Scripture's promises.

5. and thus, God can create us again such that our personal identity and uniqueness is continued and autonomously recognized by others.

At the deliberative assembly in Worms, Germany in April 1521, at which Emperor Charles attended with Eck serving as the presiding officer, Luther was accompanied by a Wittenberg professor of law to act as his lawyer before the Diet. At the moment everyone had been waiting for, regarding Luther giving up the fight against Rome and just settling down, he said: "I am bound by the Scriptures I have quoted, and my conscience is captive to the Word of God. I cannot and will not retract anything."[95] Luther was "prepared to claim nothing for himself, personally. He was ready to say that he was 'the lowest scum and able to do nothing except err.' But as far as he was concerned, the controversy was not about his person or his opinions but rather whether the Word or the ecclesiastical dignitaries in Rome should be the final authority in the church."[96] As he saw these issues, it was the task of theologians to stand up for the word of God against its adversaries. Luther "was convinced that the 'sophists' were betraying it out of a mixture of ignorance, cowardice, and conceit."[97]

The 1521 treatise, *Against Latomus*, was a response to Jacob Latomus, the professor of theology at the University of Louvain (Belgium) who had published a comprehensive defense of the condemnation of Luther's writings.[98] In the treatise Luther asserted that "one ought to respect superiors, but not to the extent of offending against the Word of God—which is God himself.... Thrice cursed be the man who does the Lord's work fraudulently ... who winks at and plays along with hell's wolf."[99] Beginning in May 1521, Luther was clandestinely installed in the Wartburg Castle for ten months, which served as a rest and turning point for the Reformer, who was then in his late thirties. "The protracted journey—from Worms to the Wartburg—was quite different from the secretive mad dash portrayed in popular accounts. The friendly abduction in the forest was the climax of a long trip that, while no victory parade, was public and dignified nonetheless."[100]

---

95. Lehmann and Forell, *LW*, 32:112.

96. Forell, "Introduction," *LW*, 32:xv.

97. Forell, "Introduction," *LW*, 32:xvii. The term *sophists* would apply to the Scholastic theologians and perhaps to those theologians before them that dealt with purgatory, etc.

98. In Table Talk #DCLXVIII, Luther told some friends one day that "Latomus was the best among all my adversaries." Hazlitt, *Table Talk of Luther*, 282.

99. Lehmann and Forell, *LW*, 32:xvii.

100. Hendrix, *Martin Luther: Visionary Reformer*, 109.

During his peaceful stay hidden from public view, except for one foray in disguise,[101] Luther "now believed he was called to lead a movement that would bring to other children the same freedom that he now enjoyed.... To be free, however, Luther had to subject himself to a new authority, one which replaced both his father and the pope to whom his conscience had once been bound."[102] Beginning with his exit from Worms and his time put in at the fortress, "freedom for Luther meant living bound to Christ, and that freedom made him much more than a protester against indulgences or a critic of the pope. Now he was a man with a larger vision of what religion could be and a mission to realize that vision by making other people free."[103] The crucial turning point in Luther's life of over sixty years was not that associated with his ninety-five theses or at the Diet of Worms. It happened, instead, during his long seclusion at the Wartburg, "where he adopted a new identity and a new purpose that he believed to have come from God."[104]

To summarize 1521 for the purpose of this book: While preaching, Luther asked, where are the souls of the deceased located? "Do you think that God cannot preserve souls in His hand?"[105] Also, in the revised version of his *Explanations* reply to the pope, Luther mentioned the traditional belief in "soul immortality" negatively, in the context of the papal bull of 1513, although in a somewhat ambiguous manner. These two examples suggest that he had been thinking about Chrysostom's startling proposition on the nature of death sometime after he quoted the saint in his Hebrews lecture of 1517. The count for the number of mentions on the topic of "death as sleep" remains at zero.

The next chapter, however, which begins at 1522, was an earth-shattering year for him, and I have found twenty-one mentions of "death as unconscious sleep" in his surviving writings from the visionary Reformer in just that year alone. It will soon become more exciting for Luther with a refocused purpose for his life and more challenging to those who had read some of his many writings, attended some of his plentiful sermons, or enrolled at the university to hear his numerous lectures on the meaning of various books of the Bible.

---

101. In December 1521, Luther went to Wittenberg and while there, sat for the artist, Lucas Cranach, who painted nearly all of our authentic reproductions of Luther, and he also produced illustrations for many of Luther's printed works.

102. Hendrix, *Martin Luther: Visionary Reformer*, 114.

103. Hendrix, *Martin Luther: Visionary Reformer*, 115.

104. Hendrix, *Martin Luther: Visionary Reformer*, 115.

105. Mayes and Langebartels, *LW*, 75:109.

― CHAPTER 5 ―

An Investigation of Luther's Early Period

Luther in 1522

This chapter will show that during his ten months of seclusion in 1521–22, Luther's turning point was not just a reenergized commitment to the Gospel of Christ, but also was a strategic one related to helping his followers obtain a better understanding of human death. The year 1522 was Luther's first year of proclaiming death as being an unconscious sleep. This chapter alone will clearly demonstrate that Luther mentioned "death as unconscious sleep" over sixty times. Instead of using the name his parents gave him, Martin, the Reformer was known as George at the Wartburg Castle.[1] In the months immediately following Knight George's departure from the Wartburg in March 1522, to become known as Martin again, his zeal can be easily seen on the topic of death. In sermons delivered and published, Luther described death very differently compared to the instruction the church had been giving for centuries.

One benefit for Luther's readers and hearers from this new teaching, aside from better appreciating the good news of eternal life through bodily resurrection, was a healthier and less fearful view of one's own death. However, the primary impetus of Luther's constant reminders of the biblical references to "death as sleep" was the contrasting view of purgatory seen by many throughout Luther's life. The turmoil and pain of the traditional teaching on what happens at death for most people (including Christians) was, for Luther, inconsistent with the Bible's many references to something quite different from purgatory. Still, he talked repeatedly about other benefits of this issue. Luther believed that God has intentionally provided us help—through a better understanding of what death actually is—for the

---

1. The distance of this fortress, near Eisenach, from Wittenberg was about a forty-five-hour walk, or thirty hours by a walking horse.

purpose of allowing believers to overcome our natural fear of dying through more specific information on it.

The plan for this chapter, and the two following it, is to examine the relevant writings of Luther's entire life. It is absolutely necessary to include his last few years to determine whether he changed his mind shortly before his death. Additionally, it is critical to include the early years as he produced several helpful works that discussed the issue of death being similar to sleep. It is also obligatory to include the middle years, and the goal is to combine the early and middle periods to then compare this twenty-year segment against the last five or six years of his life. "There is the theory that the consolidator of the Reformation, old and conservative, departed from the idealism of his youth in both policy and doctrine. . . . In a very real sense, Luther's true inner unity can be seen best not from the early years, nor yet in the greatness of his finest hour, but in the full sweep of his whole life."[2] This 1522 section begins with two personal letters, then describes two major and two minor sermons, and then ends with a "sermon/explanation."[3]

On January 13, 1522, Luther wrote a private letter to his friend and fellow professor of both philosophy and theology at the University of Wittenberg, Nicholas von Amsdorf. He was his traveling companion to and from Worms and to the Leipzig Debate in 1519. Amsdorf became the first German Lutheran bishop twenty years after this particular letter, and held this position for twenty-three years until his death. "The major part of this letter deals with eschatological questions. Replying to Amsdorf, Luther discusses the question of the whereabouts of departed souls and the nature of Purgatory."[4] It marks a major milestone for Luther related to his "death as sleep" theme and was written in Latin while he was sequestered in the Wartburg. This letter made no mention of a desire by Luther or anyone else to publish these thoughts he made in reply to Amsdorf. It begins with the following: "Concerning your souls, I have not enough ['insight into the problem'] to answer you. I am inclined to agree with your opinion that the souls of the just are asleep and that they do not know where they are up to the Day of Judgment. I am drawn to this opinion by the word of Scripture. . . . It is most probable, however, that with few exceptions all ['departed souls'] sleep without possessing any capacity of feeling."[5]

2. Spitz, "Introduction," xi.

3. Major sermons are defined here as those that dwell on the subject of this book and therefore produce a large number of examples where Luther had emphasized his point through repetition.

4. Krodel, "Letter 111 Introduction," 360.

5. Lehmann and Krodel, *LW*, 48:360. See WA-Br 2:422 In both instances above, the brackets appear in the *LW* translation. Regarding just the purgatory and "death as sleep"

Prior to this letter, Luther had only quoted other authors rather than saying what he believed about "death as sleep." For the very first time, at least in this timeline five hundred years later, we see that Luther has expressed his own opinion for once on the topic—at about thirty-nine years old. Although he chose to bring up the subject before, he did not expound on the difference between *sleep* meant only as a temporary pause between death and resurrection, compared to the view that *sleep* means even more than this: it is a type of unconsciousness. Because this declaration to Amsdorf is quite significant in this book, a brief explanation of this letter follows, beginning with his main point, which is made in the second sentence of the letter:

1. Luther believed that literal death involves "souls . . . [being] . . . asleep."[6]

2. Luther based this view on his reading of the Bible. He assessed this opinion to be at the level of "most probable."[7]

3. He allowed for exceptions and identified Elijah and Moses by clarifying that they "certainly did not appear as phantoms on Mount Tabor."[8]

4. Luther asserted that departed souls "do not know where they are up to the Day of Judgment."[9] And this period during death is like natural sleep in that it is a temporary situation combined with the characteristic of not "possessing any capacity of feeling."[10]

5. His first response (seen in the letter's second sentence) is qualified to refer to only the righteous dead, or the "just"[11]—and without any expansion of this portion of humanity shortly after this sentence—whereas his final response to the same question refers to "all" the dead.[12] There is no explanation or even an acknowledgement within this letter for this contradiction or developing situation as he wrote it. This shows it is quite probable that Luther had not spoken of, or

---

part of the letter, Luther's elucidation takes up nearly 700 words (in English, excluding footnotes). Luther provided only a few brief biblical quotes and summaries in this letter to support his position.

6. Lehmann and Krodel, *LW*, 48:360.

7. Lehmann and Krodel, *LW*, 48:361.

8. Lehmann and Krodel, *LW*, 48:361. See Matt 17:3. "According to tradition this took place on Mount Tabor." Lehmann and Krodel, *LW*, 48:361n9. See WA-Br 8:662.

9. Lehmann and Krodel, *LW*, 48:360.

10. Lehmann and Krodel, *LW*, 48:361.

11. Lehmann and Krodel, *LW*, 48:360.

12. Lehmann and Krodel, *LW*, 48:361.

written on, this specific topic before penning this private letter to a close friend.

An accounting of the frequency of the "death as sleep" idea throughout Luther's works is a fundamental purpose of this book. Although Luther wrote *sleep* in his quote of Scripture in the sense of referring not to natural sleep before death, but rather to the situation after death, it does not count as an example because Luther was quoting a passage of Scripture. There are another two instances in this letter where natural sleep is the obvious sense of the word, and those cannot be counted either. Whenever a legitimate use of *sleep* appears in brackets, it also is not counted because Luther did not actually write it, but rather is a clarification by an editor. For example, "sleep on and off (or for as long as he wishes [them to sleep])."

The word *sleep* appears five times in a context allowing them all to be counted as legitimate examples of "death as unconscious sleep." This group of five instances is a measure of the density, or intensity, of Luther on this point. Another example uses the phrase "awakened from sleep,"[13] and this counts as only one instance instead of two since these indications of unconsciousness during death are contiguous. Finally, there are three other instances that show Luther is clarifying his use of *sleep*—as not just a temporary death but as unconsciousness—with the phrase, "they do not know where they are" and "they did not know where they had been."[14] These two instances count because in their context they do not mean that the person is confused or lost in space. Rather, the third instance confirms their meaning as follows: "all departed souls sleep without possessing any capacity of feeling."[15] Luther is saying that souls who are supposedly in purgatory are actually unable to feel either physical or emotional pain; they do not feel anything at all because they are completely unaware. In later works, Luther fills in the blanks to provide a better description of this characterization of the nature of death.

The running count in this book will total up each of these instances within a letter, sermon, or other writing of Luther. Consequently, the count begins here, and I have identified nine discrete instances of Luther referring to "death as sleep" (5 + 1 + 3). Under my criteria, the score is not just "one" for this letter because there is a significant difference between a letter that uses the word *sleep* just once in an answer to a friend's question, and this particular one where Luther emphasizes his degree of relative

---

13. Lehmann and Krodel, *LW*, 48:360.
14. Lehmann and Krodel, *LW*, 48:360.
15. Lehmann and Krodel, *LW*, 48:361.

certainty by repeating these concepts and keywords in the letter, usually with further clarification.

About five years had elapsed between Luther quoting Chrysostom to his students (that death does not differ from sleep) and his emergence from the Wartburg Castle in March 1522. The next letter indicates the likelihood that Luther's students carried this 1517 Chrysostom quote off campus and discussed among themselves some implications of death not differing from sleep. Naturally, it would be expected that such a proposition would lead to questions among Luther's Catholic theology students (being just prior to his famous ninety-five theses). For example: If the deceased are unconscious, do they hear our prayers to them, and do they feel any discomfort in purgatory? Undoubtedly, Luther was approached from time to time by those who desired his response on supplication for the saints and on purgatory. It seems likely that the friends and family of some of Luther's students had joined into the conversation over the years, thus multiplying the number of people who wished they knew what had happened to the professor during his long, ten-month absence, so they could approach him with a question on this.

On May 29, 1522, Luther wrote a letter to someone after about three months' time of re-engagement with friends following his confinement at the Wartburg. The relevant section reads as follows: "The whole world so pesters one with questions, a thing I wonder at, about the worship of saints, that I find myself compelled, once [and] for all, to publish my judgment on the matter."[16] Although there are no qualifying keywords in this letter, it shows the motivation for Luther to go public with his beliefs on this subject of the saints' ability to hear their prayers. Even though the implications of Luther's admission of agreeing with Amsdorf on this "death as sleep" idea raised a great difficulty, he not only felt compelled to publish it, but had quickly decided to express these views in a sermon at church.

Three weeks later, Luther gave a titanic sermon on June 22, 1522, which was probably his first-ever voyage in public on "death as unconscious sleep." It is titled "First Sunday after Trinity" on Luke 16:19–31 and discusses the parable, or historical account, of the "Rich Man and Lazarus." At least eight pamphlet editions of this sermon were printed during the period, 1522–24, but without Luther's authorization.[17] This unusual sermon was included in Stephan Roth's 1526 edition of the *Summer Postil* which included, in this specific case, Luther's revision and authorization. Later, it was included in Casper Cruciger's 1544 *Summer Postil* collection of

---

16. Michelet, *Life of Luther*, 133.
17. See Mayes and Langebartels, *LW*, 75:55.

Luther's sermons—twenty-two years later—probably because of its ice-breaking status. This publication history shows there likely was a need or a demand for this particular sermon and its unique contents. This interesting sermon appeared only recently in the *Luther's Works* edition as volume 78 in 2015. However, the first English translation of it appeared in a 1904 book by John Lenker (1858–1929).

The following excerpt from Luther's first public pronouncement on his personal view of the nature of death clearly says that the OT fathers remain in a state of sleep until the last day, in addition to describing the condition of their souls as being enfolded, preserved, and protected in God. Luther's understanding of the situation of a deceased person's soul during this initial sermon is remarkable. His conception of the human soul was such that it would be securely enclosed, in some sense, between death and resurrection. His statement does not appear as a tentative question or as a quotation of Scripture's use of *fell asleep* in death, as before. Rather, it appears Luther is somewhat sure of himself and his interpretation of Scripture. However, before the end of this year, 1522, a very important aspect of his explanation on death would be significantly altered by Luther. However, the new aspect of it would remain with him for the rest of his life. This June sermon was preached about four months after Luther completed his initial translation into German of the entire NT from Desiderius Erasmus's second version (1519) of the NT in Greek and Latin.[18] About halfway through the sermon, the preacher/professor said the following: "Thus, all the fathers before Christ's birth went into the bosom of Abraham; that is, they continued at death in firm faith in these words of God and fell *asleep* in the same words. They were enfolded and preserved as in a bosom, and still *sleep* there until the Last Day . . . falling *asleep* and being enfolded and preserved in Christ's bosom . . . Abraham's bosom is God's Word, in which the believers *rest, sleep*, and are preserved through faith until the Last Day."[19]

Throughout this book, each keyword (or each group of keywords) has been italicized as an aid to the reader. This statement above by Luther clearly implies that the BC/AD cutoff in our calendar is quite significant here, in a divine sense, because he referred only to the OT fathers falling asleep in death, and not those after Christ. This would be an inaccurate description of Luther over his lifetime if taken out of context since he evolved very quickly in his understanding of the Bible's teaching on this point. Luther "never wanted to be anything else than an obedient hearer and student of

---

18. See Metzger and Ehrman, *Text of the New Testament*, 145. Also, Tregelles, *Text of the Greek New Testament*, 25.

19. Mayes and Langebartels, *LW*, 75:62. See WA 22:5. An alternate translation of it appears in Lenker, *Church Postil Gospels*, 4:26–27.

the Scripture. In this Luther was a perfect example of his own teachings concerning the authority of Holy Scripture in the church."[20] This sermon contributes four distinct instances of the idea of "death as unconscious sleep" because they refer to literal death, and they all meet the other criteria identified in this book. The word *rest* in the context of literal death can possibly be a keyword; however, in this example, "rest, sleep" is considered one instance instead of two, since they appear consecutively. Chapter 8 will further explain Luther on the esoteric topic of "preserving souls in Christ's bosom" upon death, and then propose a claim related to this and a description of the divine method for ensuring the resurrection of the soul/mind. With this sermon probably being Luther's first-ever shot in public, or the first example of many chronologically to be seen in this chapter, these four instances raise the count to thirteen.

The next work of Luther is another monumental one like the previous sermon regarding Luther's own understanding of "death as sleep." It is titled "First Sunday in Advent, Matt 21" and was published in his *Advent Postil* of 1522.[21] This particular Advent sermon has been classified as a "sermon/explanation" previously because it is unknown whether Luther actually preached it from the sermon notes that Luther certainly wrote. There was at least one critical difference between these two writings of Luther (i.e., this "First Sunday in Advent" and the previous "First Sunday after Trinity" sermon): the separation of those "before Christ" from everyone else. Luther changed his mind on who is in the group of people that lose their consciousness at death. This second sermon was probably the first time ever that followers of Luther either heard or read him correlate his unusual view of death directly to Christians, and not just to the fathers of the OT. Within a period of less than six months at most, perhaps just a month after delivering the June 1522 sermon, Luther altered his opinion about who are unconscious after dying.

Luther's scriptural review of the matter resulted in the sudden realization that he was wrong, and that those living in AD 1522 were no different, in God's eyes, to those living in 1522 BC. It is clear Luther once believed strongly enough to tell a group of followers that only the BC era was subject to "death as unconscious sleep." However, he quickly wrote another sermon saying instead this should include those born in the *anno Domini nostril*

---

20. Althaus, *Theology of Martin Luther*, 5.

21. "More commonly, these two parts [the *Christmas Postil* and the *Advent Postil*] were published together and are now known as the *Wartburg Postil* (1522)." Mayes and Langebartels, *LW*, 75:xv. See the "Comparison Chart of Luther's Postil Publications" in Mayes and Langebartels, *LW* 75:xxxii. This work appeared in WA 10/1.2:21–62, and in the Lenker edition (*Luther's Church Postil Gospels*, 1:17–58).

Jesu Christi era as well. That which is common for nearly everyone is a state of unconsciousness between dying and resurrecting back to life. The exceptions to this rule of commonality in death were identified by Luther (e.g., Enoch, who was taken to heaven without dying first). This expansion of his timeline shows that Luther was more concerned with an honest reading of the Bible than personal embarrassment from these public pronouncements that contradicted themselves within a short period of time. Luther "intends to bring the old truth of Scripture and of dogma out of obscurity into the light, and to let its real meaning shine forth."[22]

Following the combination of the *Advent Postil* and the *Christmas Postil* into the *Wartburg Postil* (1522), Luther finished writing another collection of his sermons in 1525 called the *Lent Postil*. "Soon the *Lent Postil* was added to the *Wartburg Postil* and printed under the subtitle: 'corrected for the second time by Martin Luther,' indicating that the *Wartburg Postil* sermons were in their second revised edition."[23] This means that Luther had the opportunity to revise his "First Sunday in Advent, Matt 21" sermon/explanation during these three years. If further examination of Scripture by Luther were to show him that it was just the OT fathers who are asleep in death, instead of everyone since then including them, he probably would have reverted back and said this in his revised *Wartburg Postil*. However, that did not happen; consequently, more dependability can be placed on this writing and its unique claim about "death as unconscious sleep." This assertion is based on there being no other writing after 1522 in which Luther claims it is just the OT fathers who sleep during death. Therefore, the change in Luther's thinking in the second half of 1522 was permanent.

Although this sermon/explanation is based on Matthew 21:1–9, this biblical text does not mention death at all. Rather, it provides the account of the preparation for Jesus' entry into Jerusalem with verse 10 describing the entrance. Therefore, the question is raised: What led Luther to say something so shocking that was perhaps never said by him in public before? He asked the following three questions before discussing who specifically sleeps during death: "What does everyone desire more deeply than to be free from death and hell? Who would not gladly be without sin and have a good, joyful conscience before God? Do we not see how all people have striven for this with praying, fasting, pilgrimages, contributing money, monasticism, and priestcraft?"[24]

---

22. Althaus, *Theology of Martin Luther*, 8.
23. Mayes and Langebartels, *LW*, 75:xvi.
24. Mayes and Langebartels, *LW*, 75:46.

Then a half page later Luther wrote the following (as seen from John Lenker's 1905 translation of the 1522 version): "Hence the death of the believer in Christ is not death but a *sleep*, for he neither sees nor tastes death, as is said in Ps. 4:8: 'In peace will I both lay me down and sleep, for thou, Jehovah, alone makest me dwell in safety.' Therefore death is also called a *sleep* in the Scriptures."[25] By including the phrase "he neither sees nor tastes death" right after "not death but a sleep," it is clear that Luther is describing death as unconscious sleep, and the second appearance of *sleep* at the end of this quote of Luther by Lenker is included for this reason. This moment in Luther's life, at about age thirty-nine, represents a colossal mark on the timeline in *Death until Resurrection*.

The keyword *sleep* in this quote above meets the accounting criteria that I have established here, and it clearly refers to literal death rather than symbolic death or to either natural or symbolic sleep (e.g., slothfulness). Two points are earned with this sermon; therefore, the running total is now fifteen. Luther was not just using the analogy of natural sleep to say death is temporary, due to resurrection, but also that the mind of the person during death is unable to ascertain that death has come upon the person, because they are not conscious, and are unable to employ their senses of taste and sight.

Luther shows that he likely had decided to go in the direction of belief that the soul/mind of nearly everyone who has died is unconscious since he wrote that Christ calls death a sleep because, in Luther's words, "they neither see nor taste death." Unfortunately, we do not know with complete certainty, similar to his birth year, whether Luther preached this sermon to some followers, or alternatively, just kept his thoughts to himself and his pen, until his new book would, in fact, be published in several weeks to then reverse Luther's earlier claim.

---

25. Lenker, "First Sunday in Advent," 39. The preliminary title page indicates this volume is part of the series, "*The Precious and Sacred Writings of Martin Luther*, vol. 10. It also states that it is based on the Kaiser edition with reference to the Erlangen and Walch editions. The sermon preface on page 17 states that this sermon ("First Sunday in Advent") is found in E 10:1 and StL 11:1. The acknowledgement page by Lenker of this vol. 10/vol. 1 work says the following: "We gratefully record our hearty thanks . . . to Rev. E. H. Caselmann, Secretary of the German Iowa Synod, for translating the sermon of the first Sunday in Advent." See WA 10/1.2:42–43, WA 10/1.2:xli–xliv, and WA 7:459–537 (for the preliminary 1521 Latin sermons). The 1540 version of this part of the sermon/explanation in Mayes and Langebartels, *LW*, vol. 75 ends with "as Christ says here" without including the text of Psalm 4 as most of the earlier versions included it. The 1522, 1528, and 1532 publications of this sermon continue (after "as Christ says here" and the Psalm 4:8 quote, to then read "Therefore, death is also called a sleep in Scripture").

"Luther's sermons were among his most influential writings, especially the collection of sermons known as the *Church Postil*."[26] This collection includes the *Winter Postil* and the *Summer Postil* groups of sermons. "From 1525 to 1529, some twenty-five editions of Luther's postil were published, while in the next half-decade the number rose to more than fifty, and publication remained strong for the remainder of Luther's life."[27] Despite some difficulty between the mid-1520s until the late-1530s with a former student at Wittenberg (i.e., Roth) translating Luther's Latin manuscripts and publishing them usually without Luther's authorization, Luther's 1540 edition of the *Winter Postil* put an end to Roth's publication of his *Summer Postil* collection of sermons. The sermon just focused on here, "First Sunday in Advent: Matt 21," appeared in the *Winter Postil* collection, and thus, was specifically reviewed and approved individually by Luther for the 1540 edition. Some literary context around the keyword's immediate context in this sermon/explanation may be appropriate since this particular "death as sleep for Christians too" statement is significant historically.[28]

Luther preached two more sermons in 1522 that discussed death and resurrection in more detail by implication. The text for the first sermon is 1 Peter 1:4 in which Luther said: "So will it be with us when we are raised from the dead and have been a thousand years or more under the ground, we will think it is a short time that we *slept* in the grave."[29] The keyword *slept* meets all the criteria for being counted among the previous examples. The accounting criteria used in this book appears in the first section of the

26. Lenker, "First Sunday in Advent," 39.
27. Lenker, "First Sunday in Advent," 39.
28. Luther wrote the following: "If Christ himself were surrounded by death, sin, and hell, as we are, he would wish that someone would free him from it, take his sin away, and give him a good conscience. Since he would have others do this for him, he proceeds and does it for others, as the Law says. He steps into our sin, goes into death, and overcomes for us sin, death, and hell, so that henceforth all who believe in him and call upon his name shall be justified and saved, be without sin and death, and have a good, joyful, secure, fearless, and blessed conscience forever, as he says: 'If anyone keeps my Word, he will never taste death' (John 8:51); and 'I am the resurrection and the life. Whoever believes in me shall never die, and though he dies, yet shall he live' (John 11:25–26). See, this is the great joy, to which the prophet exhorts when he says: 'Rejoice greatly, O daughter of Zion! Shout aloud, O daughter of Jerusalem!' (Zech 9:9). This is the righteousness and the salvation for which this Savior and King comes. These are good works done for us by which he fulfills the Law. Therefore, the death of Christian believers is not death but a sleep, for they neither see nor taste death, as Christ says here." Mayes and Langebartels, *LW*, 75:46.
29. Lenker, *Peter and Jude*, 220. The preliminary title page identifies the work as part of the series *The Precious and Sacred Writings of Martin Luther*. There is no volume number on either title page.

next chapter. The reason the use of *slept* in this sermon does not refer just to a temporary situation, but rather a combination of this and unconsciousness, is because my criteria evaluates Luther's likely belief at the time he said or wrote it, instead of what people heard or read then. For the remainder of this book, a running total of occurrences will typically be shown in the following format: [16 total occurrences].

The emphasis here is on the questions of what Luther knew and when he knew it. If someone were to object by saying that Luther's comments on death in this 1 Peter sermon were not necessarily a combination of the two, meaning only a temporary situation is being related, then the timing of the sermon becomes critical. It would be an incredulous claim to assert that "slept in the grave" (seen at the end of the last quote) does not also refer to unconsciousness in the grave, given Luther's previous, January 13, 1522 letter to Amsdorf which included the following statement: "all departed souls sleep without possessing any capacity of feeling."[30] Consequently, for Luther at the time of this sermon, *slept* meant unconsciousness when seen in its context.

In this sermon on 1 Peter 1:4, which speaks of an inheritance reserved in heaven for followers of Christ, Luther uses the following two phrases in the same sentence: "slept in the grave" and "raised from the dead." It is the promise of being raised from the condition of being dead (i.e., in its ancient sense of a final end) and thus having eternal life upon resurrection, that prompts Paul to tell his followers that death (i.e., as an enemy) has been overcome. The death and bodily resurrection of Jesus into one who will not die again brought a victory over the sting of death as a "firstfruit" or first example. Therefore, others will also receive the gift of life and be literally raised from the dead.

For Luther, theology "was his calling, his trade, a subject of which he had a thorough understanding, and which it was his duty to understand thoroughly."[31] There is a testimonial in a letter Luther wrote in March 1509 (which was shortly before he received a bachelor's degree in Biblical studies) regarding his personal attitude to theology. "The statement unconsciously expresses a principle of fundamental significance for the entirety of his subsequent career . . . [especially] for the basic orientation of his thinking as a whole. . . . The type of theology Luther preferred was one] which explored "the kernel of the nut and the germ of the wheat and the marrow of the bones" . . . We see Luther making a decisive choice here . . . about the way of practicing theology . . . [and not in a way that is] superficial or satisfied

---

30. Lehmann and Krodel, *Luther's Works*, 48:360.
31. Ebeling, *Luther*, 93.

with mere outward appearance, but penetrating to what is really decisive, and touching the heart of the individual through a real understanding of the central point at issue."[32]

Throughout Luther's life, he "strove for a truly theological theology"[33] —and this passionate determination was applied to the subject of death and resurrection regarding the nature of the soul/mind. Exploring the inner "marrow of the bones" was how Luther described his objective to not be "satisfied by a theology in which philosophy still represented the dominant element, a theology overgrown with philosophy, such as was to be found in systematic scholastic theology."[34] In one of Luther's lectures in the Romans series a few years later, he told his students that he certainly believes that he owes it "as a matter of obedience to the Lord to bark against philosophy . . . [yet still] obtain knowledge of [its] errors in order to overcome them . . . to reject [erroneous parts of philosophy]. For it is time for us to devote ourselves to other studies, and to learn Jesus Christ, and him crucified. . . . Luther considered himself entitled to adopt such an attitude because he had made a thorough study of philosophy. . . . He was an acute and thorough thinker."[35]

For Luther, "theology consisted of the interpretation of the holy scripture. . . . For he never doubted that the will of God was revealed and comprehensible to men solely through the holy scripture."[36] Althaus has provided a useful description of what theology meant to Luther, what it should mean today, and why philosophers over the centuries usually fail at adequately explaining the nature of the soul/mind in an anthropological context, as follows:

> Luther very carefully considered the subject matter of theology. Theology is concerned with the knowledge of God and of man. It is therefore both theology in the narrower sense—the doctrine of God—and anthropology. These two are inseparably joined together. . . . Theology is thus concerned neither with an objective doctrine of God nor with an anthropology that asks questions about man other than those involving his relationship to God.[37]

Attempts at explaining the soul, or the essence of a human being (i.e., the literal nature of the invisible aspects of a person that provide uniqueness

32. Ebeling, *Luther*, 76–77.
33. Ebeling, *Luther*, 77.
34. Ebeling, *Luther*, 77.
35. Ebeling, *Luther*, 78–79.
36. Ebeling, *Luther*, 96.
37. Althaus, *Theology of Martin Luther*, 9.

and identity) has been done of course by philosophy (e.g., Plato, Aristotle, Descartes, etc.). However, Althaus asserted that secular philosophy cannot ever adequately describe a person's soul or mind, because this mystery is necessarily intertwined with theology. According to Althaus, this quest to understand the fundamental nature of humanity is not only a worthwhile pursuit, but it is possible to describe it completely using Scripture as a primary component. He explained how theology, compared to ontological anthropology, are related as follows: "This means that theological knowledge of God and of man is 'relative' knowledge in the sense that each is known only in relationship to the other, a relationship that is ontological as well as personal. . . . Philosophy however is not concerned with man as 'theological' man, with man in his relationship to God. . . . Only theology therefore is able fully and completely to describe the essence of man; and it can do this on the basis of Scripture."[38]

The next sermon was based on 2 Peter 3:8–11, and provides a good example for modern-day researchers for when computer word searches cannot be successful.[39] The best excerpt from the sermon, regarding the purpose of this book, would have been overlooked if one's methodology includes only word search (e.g., sleep, slept, wake, etc.). Since longer phrases using common words are used in this 2 Peter sermon, instead of any typical keywords, Luther's explanation on the nature of death takes up a bit more space, as follows:

> Since now in God's sight there is no reckoning of time, a thousand years must be with him, as it were, a day. Therefore the first man, Adam, is just as near to him as he who shall be born last before the day of judgment. For God sees not time lengthwise but obliquely . . . but before God it is all one. So when man dies the body is buried and wastes away, lies in the earth and *knows nothing*; but when the first man rises at the last day, he *will think he has lain there scarcely an hour* when he will look about and become assured that so many people were born of him and have come after him, of whom he had *no knowledge at all*.[40]

---

38. Althaus, *Theology of Martin Luther*, 9–10.

39. Nearly all of Luther's quotes in this book were discovered using the electronic word-search function (in English), rather than by Plass's examples (being too few of them) or by Ketola (being a German-language source but without a name or title of the work). The CD-ROM disc of *LW* was not available to me, and it was not my goal to locate all of his "death as sleep" examples anyway. The objective was to discover a sufficient number of them to defend my main claim, and to hope that more legitimate ones are found than the number identified in Ketola (i.e., 125 instances of "death as sleep").

40. Lenker, *Peter and Jude*, 363–64.

The absence of any typical keywords does not matter though. Luther raised the twin topics of the nature of death and of resurrection in a unique sense. The following phrases can be identified for the purpose of measuring the extent of repetition that Luther placed on these topics: "knows nothing," "will think he has lain there scarcely an hour," and "no knowledge at all." [3 instances, for a total of 19 occurrences]

A sermon/explanation titled "St. Stephen's Day" on Acts 6:8–15 and Acts 7:54–60 was prepared by Luther as a *Christmas Postil*. This work was first published in 1524 by Luther and it also appeared in the new edition that Luther had closely reviewed, edited, and published in 1540 as a *Winter Postil*. It did not appear in the *Luther's Works* series until 2013. Luther wrote the following: "This epistle provides not only a strong teaching and example of faith and love but also comfort and encouragement. It not only teaches but also excites and stimulates by calling death a '*sleep*,' at which all the world is horrified.... The Christian's death is a *sleep*."[41] This brings the number of total occurrences to twenty-one since *sleep* was repeated twice for emphasis.

Naturally, Catholics of Luther's day and age would be expected to be absolutely "horrified" since their calendar commonly and very frequently invoked a large number of honored saints, in addition to, of course, the very common practice of offering prayers to saints, which would be a constant reminder of the church's long-standing tradition of opposing "death as sleep." Luther's proposals were seen by his contemporaries as most shocking for these reasons.

However, for Protestants and other non-Catholics today, this question is raised: Why is it the case that mentioning "death as sleep" would similarly cause this horrified, although disguised, reaction? In my experience these last nine years (when I changed my mind as a result of extensive personal study), there have been many Christians who strongly objected to this break with tradition. Perhaps the answer for some people is that the common objection that Luther pointed to (i.e., "the church cannot err") continues to resonate among Christians nowadays as well. Under a Psalm 2 commentary, Luther wrote the following: "And therefore, being puffed up with this inflated and false confidence, they resisted the true prophets, just in the same way as, at this day, all those prating flatterers about the popes, resist every appearance of the truth, because they cannot once imagine, as they pretend, that the head of so high a personage can err, etc. The church cannot err they cry. The pope cannot err. The council cannot err, etc."[42]

---

41. Mayes and Langebartels, *LW*, 75:327. See WA 10/1.1:265–66.
42. Lenker, *Luther's Commentary on the First Twenty-Two Psalms*, 1:93.

In my opinion, the remedy includes the sharing of information to other followers of Christ. Whether someone is in academia or the church, a person should constantly show others, when appropriate, that which its leading theologians over the last two hundred years, as well as the last 2,000 years, have said about the subject. There are many leading voices from several different centuries who would agree with Luther on the issue of "death as unconscious sleep" (particularly in the metaphorical sense of sleep).

If you are thinking, so what? Does it really matter that Luther taught that death should be seen as unconscious sleep? I would respond by suggesting it does matter very much, and this issue can even be practical, significant, and helpful in one's relationship to God. This is possible after considering the implications of "death as sleep" including neoplatonic dualism, innate immortality of the soul, the nature of hell, and the type of God that would, or would not, assign a portion of God's creation to possibly enduring nonstop torture as punishment for rejecting God's offer of love to them. And on the other hand, it is possible to reduce our common fear of death by learning what exactly the Bible has said about the nature of death.

Luther in 1523 to 1525

The next four sermons are presented in a brief manner and include minimal description of death in that these messages are of an elementary nature. They were probably written in either 1523 or 1524, but certainly no later than 1525. In the one titled "Third Sunday after Easter" on 1 Peter 2:11–20, Luther referred to death as being similar to falling asleep, as follows: "Peter ... did not ascend into the heavens, but, having fulfilled the will of God, *fell asleep*."[43] [22 total occurrences so far] Luther wrote a sermon for Pentecost Wednesday on John 6:44–51 in which he said the following: "The saints, nevertheless, died, and Abraham and the prophets likewise died. We reply to this: The death of Christians is only a *sleep*, as the Scriptures everywhere call it. A Christian *neither tastes nor sees death*; that is, he is *never conscious of any death*."[44] [3 instances, for a running total of 25 occurrences]

43. Lenker, *Epistle Sermons*, 2:282.

44. Lenker, *Luther's Church Postil Gospels*, 3:402. See E 12:397 and StL 11:1137. The title page also identifies it as "Volume VII of *Luther's Complete Works*." The preliminary title page identifies it as part of the series *The Precious and Sacred Writings of Martin Luther*, vol. 12, edited by John Nicholas Lenker, 1907. "These sermons ... in 1581, were translated and printed in English ... also several obsolete words changed into modern [in this 1767 edition]." An alternate translation of the Luther quote is as follows: "The holy die notwithstanding, for Abraham and the holy prophets are dead ... I answer, The death of Christians is only a sleep, as the Scriptures also commonly calleth it: For

The sermon titled "Second Sunday in Lent" on 1 Thessalonians 4:1–7 says the following: "Paul tells us (1 Cor 11:30) that many were sickly and many had succumbed to the *sleep* of death."[45] [twenty-six occurrences] Luther wrote a sermon for the feast day of Epiphany on Isaiah 60:1–6 which says the following: "Plainly the injunction is addressed to one not risen, one who lies *sleeping* or is dead."[46] [27 total occurrences]

Luther wrote a hymn titled, "In Peace and Joy I Now Depart" (also known as "Asleep in Jesus"[47]) that was first published in *Walter's Wittenberg Hymnal* in 1524. Luther "pictured the peace which Christ's victory brings to the believer. This poem has been called the *Nunc Dimittis* of the ancient church."[48] "Luther called upon the services of Johann Walter . . . to assist him in preparing the hymns for singing."[49] Luther prepared a new preface for a second hymnbook in 1529, the *Klug Gesangbuch* (published by Joseph Klug) that contained all twenty-four of Luther's hymns in the 1524 edition plus four new ones (in addition to twenty-six numbers not by Luther). This "Peace and Joy" hymn also appeared in another booklet with just three other Luther hymns that was "probably the first hymnal ever prepared for this distinctive and specifically limited use: namely, in connection with the burial of the dead. It is the first evangelical collection of this character."[50] In the first of four stanzas of this hymn, the lyrics went something like this:

> In peace and joy I now depart
> [*Mit Fried und Freud ich fahr duhin*]
>
> As God wants me.
>
> Content and still is mind and heart,

---

a Christian tasteth and seeth no death, that is, he hath the feeling of no death." Luther, "Sermon XVII," 266.

45. Lenker, *Luther's Church Postil Gospels*, 3:147. See E 8 and StL 12.

46. Lenker, *Epistle Sermons*, 1:312. See E 7 and StL 12.

47. See "1108" in Plass, *What Luther Says*, s.v. "death," 376. This work contains over 5,000 quotes of Luther on various topics.

48. Plass, What Luther Says, 376. *Nunc Dimittis* is the Latin name for the song of Simeon (in Luke 2:29–32), which is used as a canticle in various liturgies and is defined as a farewell from life. The Lutheran Church–Missouri Synod today retains this Latin classification for this Luther hymn.

49. Strodach, "Hymn Book Prefaces," 278. See WA 35:438. Also, E 56:331 and StL 10:1455. This quote continues as follows: "This book contained twenty-four of Luther's hymns as follows: . . . *Mit Fried und Freud ich fahr duhin* [which is German for 'In Peace and Joy I Now Depart']."

50. Strodach, "Hymn Book Prefaces," 280. Its title is *Klug's Burial Hymnal,* or, *Christian Songs Latin and German for Use at Funerals,* from 1542. See Lehmann and Leupold, *LW*, 53:325.

He doth save me.

As my God hath promised me,

Death has become my *slumber*.[51]
[*Der Tod ist mein Schläf worden*].

This brings the running total of occurrences to 28. Notice at the last line that Luther did not write either the noun *Schläfrigkeit* or *Verschläfenheit*, which mean "drowsiness or sleepiness,"[52] but rather *Schläf* was his term, which means "sleep" or perhaps "slumber."[53] If there was a secondary meaning of *Schläf* as "in-and-out-of sleep" in the sixteenth century, then it cannot apply here. The reason is that Luther has clearly shown many times, as seen in this book, that the primary definition of *Schläf* (i.e., sleep) is to be instead taken. If an English-speaker uses "slumber" here (as seen above), then it should be primarily defined as *sleep*.[54] The secondary definition of *slumber*—"a state of inactivity or dormancy"—should be relegated as inapplicable due to its inconsistency with Luther's typical usage.[55] If one assumes that the secondary definition of *slumber* applies to this hymn instead, then this would be an example of taking it out of context inappropriately. Obviously, the point of this chapter is to show that the primary, rather than the secondary, definition of slumber applies here given the context of Luther's other writings.

The question by some authors, including recent ones, on whether Luther was certain or dogmatic on his beliefs about death at any point in his life can be partially answered by his hymn lyrics. Writing that a Protestant can now believe instead that "death has become my sleep" in the first stanza is an indication that Luther was certain in his mind. If he did not really believe it, then some of the thousands of Lutherans who sang it aloud over the decades, at times in his presence, would confront Luther for some explanation if needed. When anyone who had written the lyrics to this song, and then later heard his church sing "*mit Fried und Freud*" ("In Peace and Joy"), that individual would eventually need to answer people. The fact that eighteen years elapsed between the two publications with Luther's direct

---

51. Lehmann and Leupold, *LW*, 53:248. Also see Oswald, *LW*, 28:110n which shows the last line in German.

52. See "*Schläfrigkeit*" in the Beolingus online dictionary, https://dict.tu-chemnitz.de/dings.cgi?service=deen& opterrors=0&optpro=0&query=schlafrigkeit&iservice=.

53. "*Schläf*," https://dict.tu-chemnitz.de/dings.cgi?service=deen&opterrors= 0&opt pro=0&query=schlaf&iservice=.

54. *American Heritage College Dictionary*, s.v. "slumber," 1284.

55. *American Heritage College Dictionary*, s.v. "slumber," 1284.

authorization and the inclusion of this same hymn in them is significant, in addition to the fact that it was a very popular hymn that was among the last remaining four to be later published. The 1542 hymnal shows there was probably not some suspicious disagreement at that time over the supposedly dubious claim that Luther was unsure of his opinion.

The staying power and depth of the tradition for "In Peace and Joy I Now Depart" is also reflected in much more recent collections of hymns as reported by Plass, and as seen in the following hymnbooks: "This hymn is No. 137 in *The Lutheran Hymnal* of the Synodical Conference. . . . Also the Church Hymnal of the Lutheran Church–Missouri Synod has it among [its] hymns [as] No. 65."[56] There have been two hymnal editions published for this particular Lutheran denomination since this 1959 quote by Plass. The current hymnal used by the Lutheran Church–Missouri Synod was issued in 2006, and "In Peace and Joy I Now Depart" appears in it as #938. Its lyrics at the end of the first stanza are as follows: "For the Lord has promised me that death is but a slumber."[57] The "Topical Index of Hymns and Songs" in this 2006 hymnal shows this hymn under the "*Nunc Dimittis*" category with one other hymn, and is not under the group, "Death and Burial" which has sixteen hymns listed, nor is it under the "Presentation of Our Lord" grouping which is where it was formerly categorized as numbers 137 and 65 as referenced above.

There are at least two other hymns in the current hymnal used by the Lutheran Church–Missouri Synod (numbers 696 and 697) in which the lyrics of the first one, from the seventeenth century, uses the phrase, "*sleep in peace*" in the context of literal death. The other one, from the twentieth century, includes the following: "*Awake*, O *sleeper*, rise from death . . . *Awake*, arise, go forth in faith, and Christ shall *give you life*."[58]

It would not be surprising that other denominations would select hymns that refer to literal death being like sleep, and to resurrection being an awakening from death's sleep. For example, the current hymnal for the

---

56. Plass, What Luther Says, 377n14.

57. The Commission on Worship of the Lutheran Church–Missouri Synod, *Lutheran Service Book*, s.v. #938. Although this edition attributes the text of the hymn to Martin Luther on the same page that hymn #938 appears, the "Composers and Sources of Hymns and Songs" index of this book omits #938 from the list of hymn numbers appearing under "Luther" which shows six other hymns by him. Also, in the index, "Tunes—Alphabetical," this hymn is not listed with the other nineteen entries under "I," for "In Peace and Joy," nor is it under "P." However, this index contains the song under "M" for "*Mit Fried und Freud*," although the title of the hymn in this same book is shown at "938" as "In Peace and Joy I Now Depart."

58. See the Commission on Worship of the Lutheran Church–Missouri Synod, *Lutheran Service Book*, s.v. #697.

Free Methodist Church includes one titled, "We Shall Behold Him" (number 237), written in 1980 by the southern Gospel singer, prolific songwriter, and Grammy winner, Dottie Rambo. The main editor of this 1986 hymnal (published by Word Music), Thomas Fettke, who wrote its preface, was also credited as the arranger for this particular hymn. The second stanza of it reads as follows (prior to the refrain):

> The angel shall sound the shout of his coming;
>
> *The sleeping shall rise from their slumbering place.*
>
> And those who remain shall be changed in a moment;
>
> And we shall behold Him *then* face to face.[59]

However, the number of hymns within a Free Methodist hymnal with lyrics like "We Shall Behold Him" have been steadily declining over the last century (where literal death and resurrection is described in the lyrics as being either a sleep or being awakened from it). For example, a hymnal published in 1883 by Benjamin Roberts, the founder of the denomination in 1860, contains about six hymns with lyrics that roughly fit these criteria.[60] Another hymnal from 1915 published by the Free Methodists also had about the same number while replacing half of them with similar new hymns.[61] However, their hymnal from 1951 contained only half this total number of hymns that reflected this idea.[62] The last two Free Methodist hymnals, from 1976 and 1986, contained only about one hymn on "death as sleep." It may be relevant to quickly survey a hymnal from the denomination that Roberts and his fellow ministers broke away from

---

59. Free Methodist Church, *Free Methodist Hymnal*, 1986, #237.

60. The hymn that had the most longevity of these six, "Asleep in Jesus" is attributed to Margaret Mackay from 1832, and it was included in their next hymnal—as well as in the 1951 FMC hymnal. The lyrics of this group of six include the following (in the context of literal death): "Asleep in Jesus blessed sleep" (Mackay), "O for the deaths of those who slumber in the Lord" (Montgomery), "Unveil thy bosom, faithful tomb . . . to slumber in the silent dust . . . the peaceful sleeper here" (Watts), "Tender Shepherd . . . 'tis sleeping" (Meinhold), "Why do we mourn for dying friends . . . awake ye nations underground" (Watts), and "How sweet the hour . . . wake to perfect happiness" (Bathurst).

61. The lyrics of this new group includes the following: "Beloved sleep . . . sweet, dreamless sleep" (Clark) and "Sleep on beloved sleep . . . thy slumber . . . but thou shalt wake" (Doudney).

62. Although only one hymn was retained ("Asleep in Jesus") from prior hymnals, the lyrics from the two new hymns include the following: "Come ye faithful . . . three days sleep in death" (John of Damascus, 8th century) and "This is the day of light . . . wake dead souls" (Ellerton, 1867)—which was retained for the next FMC hymnal.

in New York. A Methodist Episcopal Church hymnal from 1849 contains about six hymns of this type, with three of them having been carried over to the 1883 Free Methodist hymnal.[63]

Naturally, there is often ambiguity in poetry and hymn lyrics regarding whether the author was referring to the body or to the mind that is asleep during death as well as whether death is meant literally or spiritually. Indicators of literal death involving the person, or the mind of the person, include literal markers near the words *sleep*, *wake*, etc. For example, an unbeliever who is slothfully asleep in literal death with no hope of being saved can be contrasted with a deceased believer who died in hope of being saved. Attaching the condition of being *asleep* in Jesus would probably nullify the symbolic sense of sleep (i.e., where it would not mean unfaithfulness or rejection of God). When a hymn only points in the *direction* of possible unconsciousness during a deceased Christian's sleep, then other markers can clarify its trajectory more precisely. For example, using the images of "silent dust" and "tomb" with "the peaceful sleep here" phrase suggests a literal sense. When a hymn says "underground," combined with "awake" from death, literal resurrection from a literal death can possibly point to literal unconsciousness since waking from natural sleep (with its unconsciousness) is so common.

Other hymns are even more clear when an adjective such as "dreamless" is attached to "sleep" to show that it is a very deep, yet "sweet" sleep where "sleep as slothfulness" misses the mark. "Three days sleep" and "wake dead souls" can be perhaps even more explicit in their meaning. Since the originally intended theology in a song lyric depends on this poetic context for clues, rather than on explanatory prose (with it being poetry), the meaning of "being awakened out of death" and "being resurrected from the grave" is *not* 100 percent certain. What's more relevant than reaching full certainty on "death as unconscious sleep" in a song is instead settling for, and being content with, a still-significant 50 percent either way when "awake and rise up" out of death uses this imagery of sleep. For example, "Christ Is Risen" was released in 2009 on the *Alive Again* album by Matt Maher in which the

---

63. These include the following: "Unveil thy bosom, faithful tomb . . . to slumber in the silent dust . . . the peaceful sleeper here" (Watts), "O for the death of those who slumber in the Lord" (Montgomery), "Why do we mourn for dying friends . . . awake ye nations underground (Watts). The three others not retained include: "Shall man, O God of light and life . . . the trump shall sound—the dead shall wake" (Dwight), "Through sorrow's night . . . in solitude shall sleep the years away" (White), and "When the last trumpet's . . . and dust to life awake" (Bickersteth).

following refrain appears eight times: "Come *awake*, come *awake*; Come and rise up from the grave."[64]

A Catholic hymnal today probably would not contain a hymn written by Luther, but there is an interesting Catholic hymn titled "The Clouds' Veil," categorized in the hymnal under death, in which the second stanza reads as follows: "where saints shall gather in deep peace. Deep in heaven's light where sorrows pass beyond *death's sleep*."[65] Accepting the sleep of death proposition as a Catholic believer who may pray to saints could be based on it being only a general rule and thus, not applicable to everyone that passes away.

Imagine a situation, as seen in sixteenth-century Europe, where praying to deceased and honored saints was omnipresent for many people, even saturated in the culture, and for those who stopped the practice, it was not just some old background from their younger days. "Burial services and funeral liturgies were rewritten to remove any suggestion that participants were interceding with God on behalf of the departed. . . . There was pressure to move the bodies of the dead away from the places of worship of the living, so that the latter would not feel tempted to offer intercessory prayer. . . . Taken together, this package of reforms represented a remarkably revolutionary assault on deeply ingrained cultural habits."[66]

It was common for people to date their letters "according to the nearest festival on the ecclesiastical calendar in use for centuries. The church calendar . . . was a universal timekeeper, which tapped out the rhythms that governed the lives of most sixteenth-century Europeans."[67] Awareness of saint so-and-so yesterday and saint what's-his-name tomorrow served as a continuous reminder of dead people who were not asleep or unaware. Of course, Luther was an exception and he "knew that calendar by heart . . . that identified the saints' days within each month. . . . A saint was assigned to almost every day, and that day reminded the faithful where they were in the year of sacred time."[68]

---

64. "Christ Is Risen" lyrics by Matt Maher and Mia Fieldes and copyright by Essential Music Publishing, Capitol Christian Music Group.

65. Dobbs-Mickus, Cuddy, Macalintal, and Trumfio, GIA Publications, s.v. "710," *Gather*. This Roman Catholic hymnal shows the author of the hymn's text is Liam Lawton (b. 1959). Apparently, the hymns in this particular hymnal are not unique within US Catholicism since it probably is the case that most Catholics across America presently have easy access to this particular hymnal.

66. Matheson, *Reformation Christianity*, 180–81.

67. Hendrix, *Martin Luther: Visionary Reformer*, 3.

68. Hendrix, *Martin Luther: Visionary Reformer*, 3–4.

This constant barrage by Luther in his appeal to people to see the nature of death differently than the common view then was something that went directly against the culture of invisible saints everywhere hearing prayers. Imagine the turmoil the Reformer caused with his "death as sleep" idea pushing against the next due date for payment to the church regarding release from purgatory and its pain. Recall the opinion of Lohse who wrote less than twenty-five years ago the following in one of his two books on Luther: "It [is] doubtful that words concerning soul sleep, which are certainly more numerous, can really be promoted to the rank of a 'doctrine of Luther.'... We should not attempt to regard the one or the other idea as his true opinion."[69] The main thesis of this book is that Thiselton, Althaus, and others are correct in their characterizations of Luther on the unconsciousness of the soul/mind after dying, which means that others, such as Lohse and Williams, esteemed experts they may have been (i.e., both are deceased), were incorrect about the Reformer on this matter. The score remains at twenty-eight occurrences (from one instance within "In Peace and Joy I Now Depart").

The sermon titled, "Sixteenth Sunday after Trinity" on Luke 7:11–17 was probably first published in 1524 at the latest as a *Summer Postil*. Luther asserts:

1. "From this it must follow that those lying in the church-yards and under the ground *sleep* much more lightly than we sleep in our beds";[70]
2. "But the dead hear and *awaken* upon a single word of Christ, as we see in the case of the young man and of Lazarus";[71]
3. "Before the Lord death is no death at all. For us it is called and is death when we die. But before God it is a *light sleep* which could not be any lighter";[72]
4. "Christians, though they die, are not dead, but *sleep* so lightly that Christ can *awaken* them with a finger";[73]
5. "Christ will *awaken* him from that *sleep* by a word";[74]

---

69. Lohse, *Martin Luther's Theology*, 327–28. This translated book was originally published in 1995 in Gottingen, Germany.
70. Luther, *Sermons on the Gospels for Sundays and Principal Festivals*, 277.
71. Luther, *Sermons on the Gospels for Sundays and Principal Festivals*, 277.
72. Luther, *Sermons on the Gospels for Sundays and Principal Festivals*, 277.
73. Luther, *Sermons on the Gospels for Sundays and Principal Festivals*, 277.
74. Luther, *Sermons on the Gospels for Sundays and Principal Festivals*, 278.

6. "I only *sleep*";[75]

7. "and *sleep* so sweetly and so lightly that the Lord Jesus scarcely needs to open His mouth before I hear Him and arise to eternal life."[76]

One new addition chronologically is the adjective in *light* sleep within the context of resurrection from the dead. The literalness of "light sleep" mixed with literal graveyards and natural sleep at night, combined with the context of what all has preceded it in time, causes this use of *sleep* by Luther to be more certain in its meaning compared to the examples above from some hymnals. Another new addition is seen with *sweet* sleep. Adding these nine legitimate instances seen in this Luke 7 sermon to the previous running total of 28 yields a sum of 37 occurrences so far.

The sermon titled "Easter Tuesday—Second Sermon" on Acts 13:26-33 says the following: "In whatever manner God may call you home—in it all, look only upon me, whose Word promises that you shall not die, what seems death being but a sweet *sleep*; the entrance into life eternal."[77] The year of composition for this sermon was in the period 1523-25. [38 occurrences]

The next sermon was first published in 1525 as a *Lent Postil* and again in 1540. Being in the *Winter Postil* group, it was closely reviewed by Luther for this 1540 edition less than six years before he died. However, it will not be double-counted in this study, although others may view the situation differently. If it was the case that Luther rarely mentioned "death as sleep' in the last ten years of his life, then an inclusion of those *Winter Postil* writings that were certainly reviewed by him may be appropriate.

The sermon is titled, "Fifth Sunday in Lent (Judica)" on John 8:46-59. Luther said the following: (1) "The Christian *sleeps* in death and in that way enters into life";[78] (2) "Hence, death is also called in the Scriptures a *sleep*. For just as he who falls asleep does not know how it happens, and he greets the morning when he awakes, *so shall we suddenly arise* on the last day, and

---

75. Luther, *Sermons on the Gospels for Sundays and Principal Festivals*, 278.

76. Luther, *Sermons on the Gospels for Sundays and Principal Festivals*, 278-79.

77. Lenker, *Luther's Epistle Sermons*, 2:207. The (single) title page shows the following in parenthesis: "*Volume VIII of Luther's Complete Works.*" See E 8 and StL 12.

78. Lenker, *Church Postil Gospels*, 2:179. See WA 17/2:234-35. The preliminary title page identifies the work as part of the series *The Precious and Sacred Writings of Martin Luther*, vol. 11, 1906. For an alternate English translation, see Mayes and Langebartels, *LW* 76:412-13.

never know how we entered and passed through death";⁷⁹ (3) "They however only lie down and *sleep* in death."⁸⁰ [5 instances; 43 occurrences]

The next sermon is another major example of Luther's beliefs and has been titled, "Twenty-fourth Sunday after Trinity: (The Daughter of the Ruler of the Synagogue Raised from the Dead), Matt 9:18–26 (Second Sermon)." Of all the published works of Luther, it ranks second on the list regarding the amount of emphasis he placed on "death as unconscious sleep." It is likely the sermon was delivered in the period, 1523 to 1525. It appeared in Cruziger's 1544 edition instead of the one below following this sermon that is identified with the same name and the same Bible citation. Although the titles of the two sermons are identical (with the exception of "second sermon" being added), their contents are quite different, with the "second sermon" having much to say about death and resurrection, as follows:

1. "Learn this spiritual wisdom that death is not death to Christ, but only a *sleep*";⁸¹

2. "This passage, as a general expression, teaches you that your death in Christ is nothing more than a mere *sleep* so that you may be able to look through and beyond the horrible sight and frightful larva of death and the grave, yea, apprehend the same truth of death, if only you hear these words in faith and accept them as true in Christ";⁸²

3. "How can a person be said to *sleep* when he no longer has either breath or life is buried under ground and is in process of decomposition?";⁸³

4. "In this passage you hear that Christ says that to him the dying of a person is not death, but a *sleep*; yea, from his point of view none of those who have lived and died before our time are dead but are all alive, as those we see standing before us; for he has concluded that all shall live (but only upon resurrection back to life)";⁸⁴

5. "It is not difficult for Christ, in the hour when body and soul are separated to hold in his hand the soul and spirit of man, even though we

---

79. Lenker, *Church Postil Gospels*, 2:179.
80. Lenker, *Church Postil Gospels*, 2:180.
81. Lenker, *Church Postil Gospels*, 5:357. The preliminary title page identifies the work as part of the series, *The Precious and Sacred Writings of Martin Luther*, vol. 14, 1905. See E 14:331 and StL 11:1834.
82. Lenker, *Church Postil Gospels*, 5:357.
83. Lenker, *Church Postil Gospels*, 5:357.
84. Lenker, *Church Postil Gospels*, 5:358.

ourselves *neither feel nor see anything*, yea, even though the body be entirely consumed";[85]

6. "Thus we should learn to view our death in the right light, so that we need not become alarmed on account of it, as unbelief does; because in Christ, it is indeed not death, but a fine, sweet and brief *sleep*";[86]

7. "Which brings us release from this vale of tears, from sin and from the fear and extremity of real death and from all the misfortunes of this life, and we shall be secure and without care *rest sweetly and gently for a brief moment*, as on a sofa until the time when he shall call and *awaken* us together with all his dear children to his eternal glory and joy";[87]

8. "For since we call it a *sleep*, we know that we shall not remain in it but be again *awakened* and live";[88]

9. "That the time during which we *sleep*, shall seem no longer than if we had just fallen asleep";[89]

10. "Hence, we shall censure ourselves that we were surprised or alarmed at such a *sleep* in the hour of death, and suddenly come *alive* out of the grave and from decomposition, and entirely well, fresh, with a pure, clear, glorified life, meet our Lord and Savior Jesus Christ";[90]

11. "The maiden suddenly *arose, as if* she had been awakened from sleep";[91]

12. "Turns death into *sleep*, your grave into a soft sofa, the time from the death of Abel until the last day into a *brief hour*, a work which no creature has nor can attempt except through faith in Christ";[92]

13. "Therefore the early Christians . . . followed the custom of bringing their dead to honorable burial and wherever possible interred them in separate places, which they called, not places of burial or graveyards, but *caemeterium*, sleeping chambers, *dormitorium*, houses of *sleep*."[93] [17 instances, for a total of 60 occurrences]

---

85. Lenker, *Church Postil Gospels*, 5:358.
86. Lenker, *Church Postil Gospels*, 5:359.
87. Lenker, *Church Postil Gospels*, 5:359.
88. Lenker, *Church Postil Gospels*, 5:359.
89. Lenker, *Church Postil Gospels*, 5:359.
90. Lenker, *Church Postil Gospels*, 5:359.
91. Lenker, *Church Postil Gospels*, 5:359–60.
92. Lenker, *Church Postil Gospels*, 5:360.
93. Lenker, *Church Postil Gospels*, 5:360.

The sermon titled, "Twenty-fourth Sunday after Trinity: The Daughter of the Ruler of the Synagogue Raised from the Dead, Matt 9:18–26 [first sermon]" contains the following: "for he does not know what it is to *sleep* or enter the grave."[94] This early period of Luther's writings on "death as unconscious sleep" has now ended with 61 occurrences from 1522 to 1525.

---

94. Lenker, *Church Postil Gospels*, 5:341.

CHAPTER 6

An Investigation of Luther's Middle Period

Luther in 1526 to 1531

In his lecture series on Ecclesiastes, from July to November 1526, Luther had told his students how he interprets Ecclesiastes 9:5-6 and 9:10.[1] This work by Luther is grouped under 1526, rather than 1532 (its first year of publication), because my categorization scheme gives less priority to publication dates compared to the composition date, or when it was first preached. Luther said the following:

1. "Solomon seems to feel that the dead are *asleep* in such a way that they *know nothing* whatever. I do not believe that there is a more powerful passage in Scripture to show that the dead are *asleep* and *do not know anything* about our affairs—this in opposition to the invocation of the saints and the fiction of Purgatory. 'They have no reward' is a Hebraism for what we would say in German this way: 'It is all over for those who are dead'";[2]

2. "When Jerome raises the quibble that although the dead do not know anything of what goes on in the world, they do know other things, namely, those that go on in heaven, *this is an error*, and a foolish one at that";[3]

3. "This is another passage which proves that the dead *do not feel anything*. There is, he says, *no thought or art or knowledge or wisdom* there. Therefore Solomon thought that the dead are *completely asleep* and *do not feel anything at all*. The dead lie there without counting days

---

1. See Pelikan and Oswald, *LW*, 15:ix-x. The Ecclesiastes lectures were first published in 1532.
2. Pelikan and Oswald, *LW*, 15:147. See WA 20:160-63.
3. Pelikan and Oswald, *LW*, 15:148.

or years; but when they are raised, it will seem to them that they have only *slept* for a moment."[4] [10 instances; 71 occurrences]

One of the aims of this book is to evaluate that which Luther had said about the question, "Where do the souls of the deceased go? and, How does God preserve them, according to Scripture?" The assertion I make in chapter 8 that further explains the Luther paradox on death is based directly on several comments that Luther had made such as the following: "The nether region (*infernus*) [footnote: *sheol*] designates the pit, or the grave (*sepulchrum*). According to my judgment, it really designates that hidden recess in which the dead *sleep* beyond this life and whence the soul goes to its place, whatever its nature may be, for geographical (*corporalis*) it cannot be. You must therefore understand that here the nether region means that which contains the souls, a sort of grave for the soul, outside this geographic world, just as the earth is the grave of the body. But precisely what it is we do not know."[5] [72 occurrences]

An alternate translation of this advanced topic seen in the quote above is provided as a footnote.[6] Luther is suggesting that his understanding of the Hebrew term from the OT, *Sheol*, does not mean just the grave. It actually can be defined as gravedom, which refers to a "hidden resting-place" according to Luther,[7] and "which contains the souls . . . [that are] outside this geographic [or physical] world."[8] In seminary, I was taught recently by the OT professor, who also teaches Hebrew, that *Sheol* means the grave. However, Luther imagines this term refers to a holding place for unconscious souls in heaven rather than underground. It probably is a unique claim of his, but I find it quite interesting that *Sheol*—as explained by the prophets of God—could actually be where God resides rather than where some suspect the devil resides. Chapter 8 picks up on this.

At the very beginning of a lecture series on Titus, Luther said the following on November 11, 1527, according to the notebook once owned by

---

4. Pelikan and Oswald, *LW*, 15:150.

5. Plass, What Luther Says, 385. See WA 20:162–63. See Luther's comments on Eccl 9:10.

6. Luther wrote the following (significant translational differences are italicized): "Pit means the grave or the sepulcher. In my opinion it refers to the hidden *resting-place* in which the dead sleep outside of the present life, where the soul *departs* to its place. Whatever *it* may be, it cannot be *physical*. Thus you should understand the *pit* to mean *the place* where the souls are kept, a sort of *sepulcher* of the soul outside this *physical* world, just as the earth is the *sepulcher* of the body. What this is, however, is unknown to us." Pelikan and Oswald, *LW*, 15:150.

7. Pelikan and Oswald, *LW*, 15:150.

8. Plass, What Luther Says, 385.

the most faithful of his students, George Rorer: "We do not yet see the life which we attain through godliness. First we must fall *asleep*. Our life is prepared, but in hope." [73 occurrences]

One of the goals of this book is to determine whether Luther changed his mind, or became less certain, in his late fifties/early sixties by placing them in context with his earlier writings. Therefore, it is necessary to also characterize his descriptions of death within the middle period of his life as was done for the first year (i.e., 1522, around age forty) because a more legitimate comparison can be made between age sixty and earlier by also examining his work around age fifty. There is a large volume of writing in this middle period (1526 to 1535) that qualify for inclusion in the "death as sleep" count. Consequently, this part of the chapter now moves to a mostly brief presentation of the middle period, compared to its first five years (i.e., 1522 to 1526). The last five or six years of Luther's life (i.e., mid-1540 to early-1546) is critical to determining to what extent, when mentioning "death as sleep," did he become less dogmatic, or even show a reversal of his views on it.

On February 15, 1530, Luther wrote his father, who was approaching death, a fascinating letter in excess of one thousand words (as translated). This is a critically important piece of evidence, compared to other individual sermons and lectures—on their own as single works—since it is a personal letter to his father. It is excerpted as follows:

> Dear father! My brother James has written me that you are seriously ill . . . If it is His divine will you should still await that better life and suffer with us in this troubled and unhappy vale of tears, to see and hear sorrow and help other Christians to suffer and conquer, He will give you grace to receive all willingly and obediently. This execrable life is nothing but a vale of tears, the longer a man lives the more sin and wickedness and plague and sorrow he sees and feels, nor is there respite nor cessation this side of the grave; there is repose, and we can then *sleep* in the rest Christ gives us until He comes again to *wake* us with joy. . . . For our faith is certain, and we doubt not that we shall shortly see one another in the sight of Christ and God; our departure from this life is a smaller thing than the journey from here to Mansfeld. It is only an hour's *sleep*, after which all will be different.[9] [3 instances; 76 occurrences]

Luther sought protection, peace, and quiet at the time of the Diet Assembly of Augsburg within the Coburg Castle between April and October

---

9. Smith and Jacobs, *Luther's Correspondence*, 515–16.

1530, and was forced to wait for mostly disturbing updates on the Diet's progress as an outlaw of the Holy Roman Empire. During the first week of June 1530, upon hearing the terribly sad news for Luther that his father had just died, he wrote a letter to Melanchthon in which it conveys the following: "Even though it comforts me that my father, strong in faith in Christ, fell gently *asleep* . . . so that seldom if ever have I despised death as much as I do now."[10] [77 occurrences] His father died on May 29, 1530.

At the Coburg Castle, Luther wrote a commentary on Psalm 118 in June 1530, in addition to his Bible translation work there. Luther said the following regarding verse 17 ("I shall not die, but I shall live"): "It is impossible that they [the 'saints'] can die, or not enjoy eternal life . . . because, God cannot be the God of those who are dead or who are nothing, but must be the God of the living . . . hence death is not death to the saints, but a *sleep*."[11] [78 occurrences] This particular psalm "was Luther's favorite among all the psalms."[12] During Luther's earlier period of protection at the Wartburg Castle, he also wrote commentary on some of the Psalms (e.g., Psalm 68) in 1521.

In a letter written in 1530 from the Coburg fortress to his friend who was Germany's brightest composer at the time, Ludwig Senfl, Luther referred to Psalm 4:8, and wrote the following: "This melody has comforted me from boyhood, and even more now that I understand the words. . . . I hope that the end of my life is at hand. The world hates and scorns me and I in turn am disgusted with the world and despise it. May the Good Shepherd take my soul. That is why I am beginning to sing this song more frequently."[13] Psalm 4:8 reads, "I will both lay me down and sleep: for thou, Lord only makest me dwell in safety."[14] Senfl complied with Luther's request to arrange for him a particular type of song, however, the composer did not use the psalm Luther described in the letter. Instead, Senfl chose another of Luther's favorite verses, and his most favorite psalm, which goes like this: "I shall not die, but live, and declare the works of the Lord" from Psalm 118:17.

"This was the verse that Luther had written . . . on the wall of his study" at the Coburg fortress while in seclusion, as verified as late as 1550 by the eyewitness, Matthaeus Ratzeberger.[15] The circumstances of Luther's life in 1530 as he followed the negotiations in Augsburg from a distance, led him

10. Lehmann and Krodel, *Luther's Works*, 49:319. See WA-Br 5:351.
11. Cole, *Select Works of Martin Luther*, 1:349.
12. Pelikan, "Introduction to Volume 14," x.
13. Lehmann and Leupold, *LW*, 53:337. See WA-Br 5, no. 1727, p. 639.
14. Lehmann and Leupold, *LW*, 53:337n1.
15. Lehmann and Leupold, *LW*, 53:337, 337n1.

to write that he was ready to die with disgust for the world. But his friend had another idea (similar to Paul's outlook in prison): "you may prefer to be with the Lord in heaven, but the Lord may prefer you to continue teaching your students and the church." As it turned out, with Luther's death occurring in 1546, that would be another sixteen long years of putting up with the world after leaving the Coburg.

Whether for a classroom lecture as professor, church sermon as the preacher, or a biblical commentary as an author, Luther would talk about the Psalms throughout his life. In the preface to the revised edition of the *German Psalter* (1531), Luther wrote the following, which shows he wished the Psalms were held in higher regard: "There was handed about almost nothing but a multitude of legends of . . . [the] lives of saints; and the world was so filled with them, that the Psalter lay under the seat, and in such great darkness, that not one psalm was rightly understood . . . I think that a finer book . . . has never appeared [on] the earth, nor ever can appear, than the Psalter."[16] In the preface to the 1545 edition of the *Psalter*, Luther advised that "every Christian . . . ought . . . to make the Psalter [their] manual."[17] In his exposition on Psalm 3, Luther observed the following: "Now death is not death but a *sleep*; and the tomb not a tomb, but a bed and *resting place*."[18] [80 occurrences]

If you're wondering why *resting place* counts as an example here, then it is because the "tomb [is] . . . but a bed and resting place" refers to the soul/mind within us and not just to the body; also, Luther uses tomb in the broader sense. Recall the social/historical context of the sixteenth century where Luther was pushing back against the view that when some commoner goes to their grave, that meant going to a painful purgatory. In contrast to this view, Luther was saying that even for those not honored as a saint in the Catholic Church, death was a "rest in peace" for both body and soul. Now may be a good time to review a summary of the strict criteria I've set up for this book in determining when keywords count as examples for "death as sleep.": The accounting criterion include the following:

1. *Sleep, slept*, etc. must mean not having consciousness from the immediate literary context unless a prior use (chronologically sometime) of the word by Luther carried this meaning;

---

16. Lenker, *First Twenty-Two Psalms*, 9.

17. Lenker, *First Twenty-Two Psalms*, 14.

18. Lenker, *First Twenty-Two Psalms*, 132. The date of composition is unknown, but it was likely first written prior to 1532.

2. These words within the own phrase cannot refer to natural sleep, but rather to unconsciousness (in some sense, including nonexistence) following death;

3. Nor can they refer to symbolic sleep such as slothfulness or laziness;

4. *Death, dead*, etc. must be used in a literal sense of end-of-life in this world for a human being, rather than in a symbolic sense (e.g., "let the dead bury the dead" or "dead to sin");

5. *Wake, awakened*, etc. must mean a resurrection from literal death and unconscious sleep;

6. *Rest, peace*, etc. must mean during literal death and have a prior use of *sleep*, etc. as meaning unconsciousness during literal death;

7. Other words that are not associated with the above examples (e.g., before being aware, knows nothing, etc.) must, in its immediate literary context, refer to literal death or a bodily resurrection;

8. Contiguous and near-contiguous words, such as "peaceful sleep and rest" and "rest in peace," count as only one instance each, instead of two each, although *rest* could qualify, depending on context, as pointing to unconsciousness when a qualifying *sleep* appears nearby, but not too close;

9. Phrases that are quoted from either Scripture or from another commentator cannot count as a legitimate example for the purposes of this book.

Luther in 1532 to 1535

This book will now be shifting gears due to the amount of repetition seen. There is a value to repetition in that it increases the chances that the message is eventually understood. "As an educator no less than a theologian [Luther] knew that the 'hammering process' of constant repetition was necessary to achieve the desired end. . . . His repetitiousness at such times seems to have been largely the result of an intensity of conviction."[19] Repetition is a fairly common literary device used by specific scriptural writers, not to mention the Bible as a whole. Althaus describes Luther's view of how a divine message can break through into someone's thoughts, as follows: "He knew very well that God's speaking is always a spiritual and inner moving of the heart, always a matter of God reaching in and

---

19. Lenker, *First Twenty-Two Psalms*, xii.

touching the heart at just that moment. It is by God's will, however, that this inner spirituality is completely bound to the external word preached and heard by human beings. God speaks directly to the heart only through the external word; and in this direct communication he says nothing else than what the external word says."[20]

One day Luther said the following to some friends as they were perhaps sitting at a table talking: "'Whosoever keepeth my saying shall never see death.' Luther expounded this passage of St. John thus: we must die and suffer death, but whosoever holds on God's Word *shall not feel death*, but depart as in a *sleep*."[21] [82 occurrences]

Luther also told his friends the following: "If there were no hope of the resurrection, or of another and better world, after this short and miserable life . . . to what purpose should we hear his Word, and believe in him? . . . Therefore it is most certain, that we do not die away like the beasts that have no understanding; but so many of us . . . *sleep* in Christ, shall through him be raised again to life everlasting at the last day."[22] [83 occurrences]

The year 1532 encompassed many instances where Luther mentioned "death as sleep" due to the death of a very important person, and because he lectured on Paul's resurrection chapter in 1 Corinthians. Luther gave two speeches in 1532 for the funeral of Duke John, the Steadfast, who had organized the Lutheran Church in the Electorate of Saxony as a model that was later implemented beyond Saxony. The first one was delivered on August 18, 1532 (on 1 Thess 4:13–14), published the same year, and included fifteen instances. However, the second speech on 1 Thessalonians 4:13–18 included only one mention of "death as sleep." Due to several modern writers (e.g., Lohse) pointing to Luther's apparently contradictory comments made regarding the death of Urbanus Rhegius in 1542 (e.g., "he is still living and functioning in death"), it is necessary to see the repetition of "death as sleep" in the 1532 funeral speech. However, a quick rundown of only brief phrases around each keyword will be provided as follows (in chronological order):

1. "they have no hope after this life, but you know that you do not die but only fall *sleep*,"[23]

2. "but of us he says that we do not die, but only fall *asleep*,"[24]

---

20. Althaus, *Theology of Martin Luther*, 40–41.

21. Luther, *Table Talk*, trans. Hazlitt, s.v. "DCCXLII [#742]," 428. The year that Luther spoke this is unknown.

22. Luther, *Table Talk*, s.v. "XCVIII [#98]," 1848, 44–45. The year that Luther spoke this is unknown.

23. Lehmann and Doberstein, *LW*, 51:233. See WA 36:237–70.

24. Lehmann and Doberstein, *LW*, 51:233.

3. "he calls our death not a death, but a *sleep*,"[25]
4. "we should consider our death a *sleep*,"[26]
5. "now they are called, not dead, but *sleepers*,"[27]
6. "those who have fallen *asleep*,"[28]
7. "and have fallen *asleep* in Christ,"[29]
8. "our beloved prince is caught up and fallen *asleep* in Christ's death,"[30]
9. "for this reason we shall reckon our beloved sovereign among those who *sleep* in Jesus Christ,"[31]
10. "they are *sleeping* in Christ (they should not be called dead people but sleeping people),"[32]
11. "death should not be called death but a *sleep*,"[33]
12. "such a *deep sleep* that one will not even dream,"[34]
13. "without doubt our beloved lord and prince [Duke John] lies in a *sweet sleep*,"[35]
14. "and has become one of the *holy sleepers*."[36] [15 instances, for a total of 98 occurrences]

The single instance within the second funeral speech for Duke John was as follows: "If you have believed and understood that Christ died and rose again, then there can be no doubt that he will also raise up with him those who have fallen *asleep*."[37] [99 occurrences]

---

25. Lehmann and Doberstein, *LW*, 51:233.
26. Lehmann and Doberstein, *LW*, 51:234.
27. Lehmann and Doberstein, *LW*, 51:234.
28. Lehmann and Doberstein, *LW*, 51:235.
29. Lehmann and Doberstein, *LW*, 51:235.
30. Lehmann and Doberstein, *LW*, 51:237.
31. Lehmann and Doberstein, *LW*, 51:239.
32. Lehmann and Doberstein, *LW*, 51:240, 242.
33. Lehmann and Doberstein, *LW*, 51:242.
34. Lehmann and Doberstein, *LW*, 51:242.
35. Lehmann and Doberstein, *LW*, 51:242.
36. Lehmann and Doberstein, *LW*, 51:242.
37. Lehmann and Doberstein, *LW*, 51:249.

Luther's series of seventeen sermons on 1 Corinthians 15 began on August 11, 1532 and ended in April 1533. The sermons were usually delivered on Sunday afternoons, and were published in 1534.[38]

1. "He will also *awaken* him and transport him from death and every misfortune to joy eternal,"[39]

2. "For with the word 'Firstfruits' he implies that Christ is not the only one to *arise* but that *others will follow* later,"[40]

3. "Christ is the Firstfruits of those who have fallen *asleep*,"[41]

4. "Christ arose, not from *sleep* but 'from the dead.' For what was a true and eternal death prior to this and without Christ is now, since Christ has passed from death to life and has arisen, no longer death; now it has become merely a *sleep*,"[42]

5. "So the Christians who lie in the ground are no longer called dead, but *sleepers*, people who will surely also rise again,"[43]

6. "Therefore, by that very word '*asleep*' Scripture indicates the future resurrection,"[44]

7. "This remnant of death is to be regarded *as no more* than a deep [natural] sleep,"[45]

8. "The future resurrection of our body will not differ from suddenly *awaking* from such a sleep,"[46]

9. "Though we depart and rot in the ground. For now, this is no more than a *sleep*,"[47]

---

38. The full sermon schedule is not described in *LW*; however, it says that "George Rorer preserved both the dates and the sermons themselves." Oswald, *LW*, 28:x. Since Luther covered the entire chapter of fifty-eight verses, and because vv. 1–21 contain ten of the eighteen instances, it is very likely that the sermon on v. 21 was delivered within the nearly five months of 1532 [(21 / 58) x (8 months) = 2.9 months after August 11, which is the first week of November 1532.]

39. P107. See WA 36:542-44.
40. Oswald, *LW*, 28:109. See WA 36:546-47.
41. Oswald, *LW*, 28:109.
42. Oswald, *LW*, 28:109-10.
43. Oswald, *LW*, 28:110. See WA 36:547-48.
44. Oswald, *LW*, 28:110.
45. Oswald, *LW*, 28:110.
46. Oswald, *LW*, 28:110.
47. Oswald, *LW*, 28:110.

10. "It is but a night before He rouses us from the *sleep*,"[48]

11. "We will *wake* up again and come forth on that Day, when the trumpet will sound,"[49]

12. "Christ is our Firstfruits, that He has initiated the resurrection, that He has burst through the devil's kingdom, through hell and death, that He no longer dies or *sleeps* but rules and reigns up above eternally, in order to rescue us, too, from this prison and death,"[50]

13. "Nor will He *awaken* the Christians who die after Him individually, and one after the other,"[51]

14. "He will not *awaken* us before all who are His own have been gathered together,"[52]

15. "We shall not all *sleep*,"[53]

16. "This will cause everything to fall into ruin and all the dead to be *awakened*."[54] [18 instances, for a total of 117 occurrences]

These eighteen instances of keywords from the series fully meet my legitimacy criteria (keeping in mind the value of context within sequential sermons). It is likely that by the end of 1532, there were ten instances of "death as sleep" mentioned by Luther with the remaining ones given the next year.[55] Adding the sixteen instances from the August funeral with these ten produces a record twenty-six instances for 1532, which exceeds 1525 and its twenty-three examples. It would be worthwhile for interested readers to see how the Reformer explained Paul's fifteenth chapter on the resurrection of the dead. Luther's commentary on 1 Corinthians 15 encompasses 154 pages for just this single biblical chapter, as seen in *Luther's Works* (*LW*) 28. Luther also had much to say about the resurrection of the dead in four sermons preached in 1544 and 1545 (all on 1 Corinthians 15) as seen in *LW* 58.

---

48. Oswald, *LW*, 28:110.
49. Oswald, *LW*, 28:111. See WA 36:548–50.
50. Oswald, *LW*, 28:111.
51. Oswald, *LW*, 28:122. See WA 36:565–66.
52. Oswald, *LW*, 28:123. See WA 36:566–68.
53. Oswald, *LW*, 28:200. See WA 36:675–76.
54. Oswald, *LW*, 28:201. See WA 36:676–77.
55. This is done because a calendar-year basis is used here for year-to-year comparison purposes (rather than any consecutive twelve-month period, which would have produced thirty-four instances instead of twenty-six). See footnote 38 in this chapter regarding the full sermon schedule.

On September 29, 1533, Luther gave a Michaelmas sermon in commemoration of Michael the Archangel, in which he said, "there is a difference between going to sleep and dying; but for Christians there is, in truth, *no difference.*"[56] [118 occurrences]

At this point in the book, Luther will now be presented in a very brief manner for the purpose of showing the reader how limited the provided data was in the Ketola paper which was referenced in the first two chapters. Only the following information was given in that study for 90 percent of the 125 occurrences that Luther mentioned "death as sleep": volume, column, and year. Not even the name of the work, the type of work, nor the scriptural passage used by Luther, was typically shown in that thesis for identification (even for the ten percent that were quoted). Additionally, keywords such as *sleep, slept,* etc. were absent as well for 90 percent of the examples.

It was perhaps in 1534 or 1535 that Luther mentioned "death as sleep" seven times on pages 77, 78, and 304 in *LW,* volume 67.[57] [125 occurrences] This is indicative of how sparse the typical information was in Ketola's 1946 thesis, with very little means to assess the judgment of the writer. Yet the work has been repeatedly referenced by scholars (e.g., Ball in 2008, Froom in 1965, and Secker in 1967) and without any other studies referenced that may provide a total of Luther's reiteration of "death as sleep." This is because it was the only work that provided a numerical characterization of Luther's repetition on the nature of death. Also, it is because it seemingly supported these three authors' position since it appealed to those who had taken positions diametrically opposed to each other on whether or not Luther believed in "death as sleep." No attempt was made by Ketola to explain the internal inconsistency as seen within the conclusion itself.

In *The Theology of Martin Luther* (1966) by Althaus, there are some quotes of Luther in a footnote that should be included in the accounting of "death as sleep" mentions, as follows: "Then it must cease and let us *sleep* in the peace of Christ until he comes and *awakens* us with joy."[58] [127 occurrences] "There can be no doubt: he must be sweetly and softly *sleeping* in eternal peace of Christ."[59] [128 occurrences] "Adam, Eve, patriarchs, prophets, pious kings are *asleep* in this Dwelling Place. If, as I believe, they have not as yet risen with Christ, their bodies are indeed at rest in the grave, but their life is hidden with Christ in God [Col 3:3] and will be revealed in

---

56. See "1111" in Plass, What Luther Says, 378. See WA 34/2:276.

57. See Brown, *LW,* 67:77–78, 304. See WA 38:489–90 for chapter 9 (77–78) and WA 38:648–651 for chapter 16 (304).

58. Althaus, *Theology of Martin Luther,* 415n. See WA-Br 5:240.

59. Althaus, *Theology of Martin Luther,* 415n. See WA-Br 5:213.

glory on the Last Day.[60] [129 occurrences] These quotes don't have a year, title, or type of work; however, they are unique expressions by Luther in the context of my book.

Luther preached a sermon on July 4, 1535, based on Romans 6:3–11, that described death repeatedly and was titled, "Sixth Sunday after Trinity."[61] Luther said the following:

1. "they are physically dead—the body dies. But this is not really death; rather a gentle, soothing *sleep*";[62]
2. "in the Scriptures it is called a *sleep*";[63]
3. "it is truly only a *sleep*";[64]
4. "to be only a falling into a sweet and gentle *slumber*";[65]
5. God lays us—like a little child is laid in a cradle or . . . [a recliner]—where we shall sweetly *sleep* till the judgment day";[66]
6. "the spirit indeed is willing and desires bodily death as a gentle *sleep*. It does not consider it to be death."[67]

Additionally, Luther said the following regarding the natural fear of one's own death: "Flesh and blood cause you to fear and dread when there is nothing to fear or dread . . . God is laying me in my bed for sweet *sleep*, and I wish that my flesh would understand this, but I cannot get it to understand."[68] If one were to translate a part of this last example as, "God will be setting me down in a very comfortable recliner for a sweet nap," then an assessment on whether *nap* or *sleep* (from above) qualifies is necessary. Obviously, in the context of this sermon, Luther's last statement here is not referring to heavy sleepiness preventing him from writing another

---

60. Pelikan, *LW*, 13:85.

61. There are two sermons called "Sixth Sunday after Trinity" in Cruciger's *Summer Postil* (1544) preached about a year apart with one on Matt 5 and the other on Rom 6. See the "Comparison Chart of Luther's Postil Publications" in Mayes and Langebartels, *LW*, 75:xvi.

62. Lenker, *Luther's Epistle Sermons*, 3:149. The title page shows in parenthesis: "*Volume IX of Luther's Complete Works*." See WA 22:99–100.

63. Lenker, *Luther's Epistle Sermons*, 3:150.

64. Lenker, *Luther's Epistle Sermons*, 3:150.

65. Lenker, *Luther's Epistle Sermons*, 3:151.

66. Lenker, *Luther's Epistle Sermons*, 3:152.

67. Lenker, *Luther's Epistle Sermons*, 3:152.

68. Mayes and Langebartels, *LW*, 75:230.

sermon before turning in for the night; so, this use of *sleep* counts as a legitimate instance of "death as sleep."[69]

Regarding the convention by translators to use *slumber* at the very end of the first stanza in Luther's still-published hymn among Lutherans, "In Peace and Joy I Now Depart," notice that *sleep* appears in this sermon on Romans six times, in addition to *slumber* appearing once. Therefore, this "Independence Day" sermon can serve as a great example for why some Lutherans today could rethink their allegiance to a vague notion and instead use the same definition of *slumber* that Luther used (as seen at hymn 938 in the 2006 edition of their hymnal).[70] [7 instances, 136 occurrences]

Luther wrote a sermon on Luke 21 that was completely different from the Luke 21 sermon he delivered on January 1, 1521, which was the year immediately prior to Luther first describing "death as unconscious sleep" in his letter to Amsdorf.[71] Just as the previous sermon from July 4, 1535, was obviously not part of a "Fourth of July," Independence Day celebration, nor was this earlier, January 1, 1521 sermon delivered to people who thought it was New Year's Day. Decades before various countries and states switched from the Julian to the Gregorian calendar, the Protestant states of the Holy Roman Empire in 1559 made January 1 the start of the new year (the Catholic states in the Holy Roman Empire made the change in 1544). Near the end of this revised sermon on Luke 21, Luther said the following: "Both those who are alive, and are so afflicted and oppressed, and also those who are dead and *asleep* in their graves and waiting to come forth into their glory."[72] This translated sermon was published in 1826, and a year was not provided (for either the delivery of the sermon or any previous publication of it) although its contents indicate the sermon was not given in an early period of Luther's life.[73] This middle period of Luther's writings on "death

---

69. Lenker, *Luther's Epistle Sermons*, 3:153.

70. See chapter 5 (*Luther in 1523 to 1525*). The lyrics read (in part) as follows: "For the Lord has promised me that death is but a slumber." The Lutheran Church, s.v. "938," *Lutheran Service Book*.

71. Cf. Mayes and Langebartels, *LW*, vol. 75 and Lenker, *Luther's Epistle Sermons*, vol. 1. There were no legitimate expressions of "death as sleep" in the 1521 sermon on Luke 21, or in any other relevant extant writing during this year.

72. Cole, *Select Works of Martin Luther*, 1:568. The title, "Sermon IX: A Sermon of Consolation on the Coming of Christ and the Signs That Shall Precede the Last Day," is similar to others on Luke 21 (e.g., the "Second Sunday in Advent" sermon). It is possible this mystery sermon was written during the last five years of his life, however, it is being excluded from that critical time period since no date for it is known.

73. Luther wrote the following in this undated sermon: "With what shouting, with what expectations, did they wait for the arrival of the Emperor in Germany to annihilate the Lutherans, and to establish again their own power and tyranny." Cole, *Select Works of*

as unconscious sleep" has now ended with 76 examples from 1526 to 1535, for a total accumulation of 137 occurrences.

Martin Luther, 1:552. The phrase "annihilate the Lutherans" suggests it was likely written during the last fifteen years of his life. It may have been written shortly before the Schmalkaldic War of 1546–47 when Emperor Charles V defeated the Lutheran forces, and captured Elector John Frederick. For reference, the first sentence of the sermon (on p. 547) is as follows: "In the Gospel for to-day, Christ our Lord gives us a particular declaration of the state of things that there shall be in the world, when the end thereof shall be at hand." The last sentence (on p. 569) is as follows: "For our life and conversation are not here, but we look for another life, wherein our body shall be delivered; which life is now hidden by faith with Christ in heaven, (as Paul saith,)[*sic*] but which shall soon be revealed before the whole world in eternal life and everlasting glory."

—— CHAPTER 7 ——

An Investigation of Luther's Later Period

Luther in 1536 to mid-1540

This chapter provides the grounds for reaching a clear determination on which view of the nature of death—awake or asleep—Luther took with him to his grave. Will the research show that Luther had recanted on this topic sometime before he died? Or, is there an end-of-life writing by Luther that undoubtedly demonstrates his unwavering belief that death is like unconscious sleep? Imagine that Luther begged Saint Martin for some forgiveness to avoid the pains of purgatory for his error. How utterly stunned Luther's followers would have been if he had told them, "never mind," or "I am not so sure as I once was on this mystery of death."

While executing the research on Luther's writings in a way independent of the fatally flawed Ketola thesis (which is the only other count available), one of the secondary questions was whether my grand total would exceed Ketola's count of 125 examples of "death as sleep." The end of the previous chapter provided the answer (with its 137 examples). The usefulness of significantly exceeding that amount is seen when an even greater ratio of "is a sleep/is not a sleep" in Luther's writings is combined with a theological explanation of the Luther paradox that supposedly holds these two options in tension.

These questions can certainly be answered by examining the writings in this chapter since Luther continued to discuss death and our resurrection, and he even dwelled on them at times. This repetition at the end of his life on the "death as sleep" idea was likely done by him to hammer away on his new students, to be sure his point is taken by new church attendees, and perhaps to hopefully overwhelm any future doubt about "what Luther says." This last point should be seen in the context of the Lutheran Augsburg Confession of 1530 which was "composed and edited mainly by Melanchthon . . . [and it]

sought to obtain recognition from the [Catholic] emperor . . . by watering down Luther's religious convictions . . . not to antagonize him [the emperor]."[1] At the start of his thirty-year journey of holding firm on many differences with Christian tradition, such as that discussed at the beginning of his 1515 Romans lectures, Luther had presaged a lifetime of devotion to Scripture through unconventional biblical interpretation that maintained an independence from the Roman Catholic Church and its presiding popes.

On January 14, 1536, Luther wrote an academic disputation for use at his university titled "The Disputation Concerning Man" and it represents "a little known area of Luther literature."[2] It was first published in 1556 and was based on Romans 3:28. In it he said that deceased infants are also "*asleep*."[3] Luther was pointing out that the Catholic Church preferred the teaching that deceased infants are in a "middle [state] . . . [in which] they feel neither joy nor sorrow." [138 occurrences]

Ten years before that disputation (during the 1526 lectures on Ecclesiastes), Luther told his students about Jerome's flawed opinion (that although the deceased may not know about the affairs of our world, they are aware of those occurring in heaven). Luther made it clear then that he believed Jerome was wrong. In the context of this 1536 assertion, imagine that Luther was right, instead of the translator of the Vulgate Bible. The practical implication of Jerome's view is that many infants, toddlers, and other deceased children are being raised in heaven by people other than their parents. In the next life, being among our family and friends as a continuation and renewal of fellowship and community, these youngsters and their earthly parents will supposedly be nothing more than distant cousins. However, suppose that the young are not raised by someone else up there, but instead are to be raised by their designated or natural parent, or parents, following the mass resurrection of the unconscious dead. Which outcome would God likely want for his followers, knowing the grief of a father or mother who has lost a child, as was experienced by both the heavenly Father in Jesus' painful death, and by Jesus himself when he raised children back to life and presented them to their grieving parents?

In the final decade of the life of Luther, the preacher decided to explain to his congregants the meaning of nearly every part of the first book of the NT. In Luther's series of fifty-six sermons on Matthew, delivered sporadically (due to bouts of illness) from July 1537 to September 1540, Luther said

1. Hendrix, *Martin Luther: Visionary Reformer*, 214–15.
2. Lehmann and Spitz, *LW*, 34:xiii.
3. Academic disputations were brought back into use in 1533 for doctorate examinations at the University of Wittenberg after falling out of favor among the faculty for a few years; "Luther favored the disputations heartily." Lehmann and Spitz, *LW*, 34:xiii.

the following: "for faith is in the heart of one who *sleeps*, even when he dies."⁴ [139 occurrences]

In his comments on Matthew 22:32 ("I am the God of Abraham"), Luther discussed the waiting period between death and resurrection as being perceived as only a moment, from the deceased point of view, in the context of this passage on Abraham. Since his explanation (seen next) directly relates to the Luther paradox (death as sleep versus its opposite), an extended length is presented here:

> As you and I see it, Abraham is dead, but Christ says: "He is not dead to Me, for I have grasped him in such a way that I am his God. He shall remain whole, rise from the dead, and to Me he is already living, for I will awaken him" ... As to how this all happens, reason can neither see nor comprehend: a man dies—the body does not see, its work and deeds become dust and ashes, the soul also does not know its condition—and yet is not dead. ... Thus Abraham is also dead, and yet he lives through the resurrection ... The state of death shall abide with him only for a moment. We should regard this as he sees it and as it is before God. He regards it not even as a moment. Therefore, Abraham lives, as God sees it, though he is dead, as men see it. ... Let us hold fast to this article, for if it is lost, every townsman and peasant will come to despise the resurrection of the dead. Yes, they will become totally blind and like Caiaphas ... Therefore, let us pray to God that He preserve us in the light of the Gospel, that we recognize this article, and that our descendants also have the teaching.⁵

When he reached the sermon on Matthew 23:3, sometime between October 1539 and March 1540 (which was not published in any language until 1817), Luther said the following: "The churchyard (cemetery) is called a 'bedroom' and 'bed,' and the burial places themselves are held in special honor and called 'places for *sleeping*.' It is a very fine testimony, with which we confess that the dead we bury will surely rise again on the Last Day. ... And the Holy Spirit calls dying and being buried 'going to *sleep*.'"⁶ [141 occurrences]

---

4. Brown and Mayes, *LW*, 68:26. See WA 47:331–32. This sermon was given during the first half of 1538, and was "first printed 1796." Brown and Mayes, *LW*, 68:xviii. This quote on 1796 refers only to the sermons on Matthew 18–22.

5. Brown and Mayes, *LW*, 68:140. See WA 47:435–36.

6. Brown and Mayes, *LW*, 68:202. See WA 47:496–97. Regarding the 1817 publication date, see Brown and Mayes, *LW*, 68:xviii. This date includes only Matt 23:1–36, with the remainder of Matt 23 and Matt 24:1–34 being first published in any language

Luther continued this point when he arrived at Matthew 23:29-30 ("Woe to you, scribes and Pharisees, hypocrites"), which quotes the religious leaders of Jesus' day as saying they would not have made the disgraceful mistake of murdering the great prophets of the OT. Although Matthew was only referring to their shedding of blood, Luther took this reference to death as another opportunity, once again, to tell his fellow Lutherans the following: "We know that they *sleep* in the cemetery, and that we will follow them, and will rise again from the dead on the Last Day."[7] [142 occurrences]

For Professor Luther, the very beginning of Scripture, Genesis, was placed on his university syllabus at the end of his life. He began his last lecture series at the University of Wittenberg in early June 1535, starting with the first chapter and proceeding chapter by chapter as usual. Due to several interruptions from illnesses, plagues, travels, and other duties, it took him ten years to work his way through Genesis. Just a few short months before he died, Luther was able to complete his lecture series on the last chapter of the book near the end of 1545. The man who translated these lectures from Latin to English for the first time (over a century-and-a-half ago), said that "it is most remarkable that this ... commentary was the last public work of Luther's ministry and life."[8] Luther had much to say in this lecture series about "death as sleep" and the question is, on what did he change his mind, if at all? This study presents quotes of Luther's exposition on ten chapters of Genesis which are widely spread out as follows: 2, 5, 15, 25-26, 42, and 47-50. The quotes in this study come from several translators (e.g., Schick, Pahl, Schaller, Cole, etc.), and therefore, they come from three time periods, based on the series (1858, 1909-10, and 1958-2015) for this critical set of Genesis chapters.

Similar to some of the other works of Luther, these lectures have been edited by others from the sixteenth century. The *Lectures on Genesis* "is not a product of Luther's pen or even a transcript of his lectures; it is a transcript that has been reworked and edited. From the instance of other commentaries, where we have both the lecture notes and the printed version, it is evident that the editors of Luther's Biblical commentaries allowed themselves greater liberties in preparing his lectures for publication than the modern conventions of editing and publishing would justify."[9]

---

in 1847.

7. Brown and Mayes, *LW*, 68:209. See WA 47:502-3.

8. See Cole's "Translator's Preface" in Luther, *Commentary on Genesis*, vi. Cole referred to his previous experience in translating the four volumes of Luther's "Select Works" beginning thirty years prior to his Genesis translation.

9. Pelikan, *LW*, 1:x.

Small portions throughout Luther's *Lectures on Genesis* have been substantially supplemented to some extent, and "the problem of authenticity and integrity becomes most acute, however, not in the question of Luther's erudition but in the question of his actual theological position. And the researches of Peter Meinhold have led him to the conclusion that the theology of the *Lectures on Genesis* has also been adulterated by the editors to conform it to the growing orthodoxy of the second generation of Lutherans."[10]

Meinhold "bases this conclusion on a study of the theology of Veit Dietrich in relation to both Luther and Melanchthon; in several cases he has proved that Dietrich's brand of Melanchthonian theology has been superimposed upon Luther's thought and language, and in other cases he has shown that this is very likely."[11] The general editor of volumes 1–30 of *Luther's Works*, Jaroslav Pelikan, asked whether this skepticism is justified or not, in the introduction to volume 1. It is remarkable that in the following short list of just three examples of this illegitimate alteration of Luther, innate soul immortality is specified, and according to Pelikan's judgment, the studies of Professor Meinhold must certainly cast doubt on those sections of the commentary in which Luther sounds more like Melanchthon than like any Luther we know. One must have some misgivings about passages which present such novel ideas as these: the arguments for the existence of God, rationalistic arguments for the natural immortality of the human soul, defenses of astrology, and the like. . . . It must be asserted that Meinhold's skepticism is warranted.[12] After stating that "much material in the lectures . . . comes directly from Luther,"[13] Pelikan concludes by saying, on this question of authenticity, that "the hands are sometimes the hands of the editors, but the voice is nevertheless the voice of Luther."[14]

Sometime prior to July 18, 1535, when Luther's lectures were interrupted by an outbreak of the plague after about one month into the series, he gave a lecture on Genesis 2:21 saying the following: (1) "in such a departing *sleep* would he have been changed and translated into the glorified spiritual life, feeling no more in death";[15] and (2) "this nature of ours must experience the pangs of death. That dissolution of the body, however, is followed in the saints, by the sweetest of all *sleep*, until the day when we

---

10. Pelikan, *LW*, 1:xi.
11. Pelikan, *LW*, 1:xi.
12. Pelikan, *LW*, 1:xi–xii.
13. Pelikan, *LW*, 1:xii.
14. Pelikan, *LW*, 1:xii.
15. Cole, *Creation*, 174.

shall *awake* unto a newness of life, and a life eternal."[16] [145 occurrences] Luther often said that Scripture tells us that although a person loses their consciousness at death due to their being a sinner, the Good News is that a resurrection from the dead will occur at the Last Day at the command of God's trumpet. Althaus has written that Luther saw eschatological topics as not just last things to be placed at the end of a book on theology, but rather Luther brought them forward to permeate his own theology on other subjects, as follows: "Luther's theology is thoroughly eschatological in the strict sense of expecting the end of the world. His thoughts about the eschaton are not a conventional appendix but a section of his theology which is rooted in, indispensable to, and a decisive part of the substance of his theology. Luther did not merely repeat the old traditional answers to the central questions of eschatology. In this doctrine too, he is the Reformer."[17]

In the late winter of 1536, following the six-month shutdown of the Genesis lectures due to the plague, Luther reached Genesis 5:21–24 and may have said the following to his students: "Therefore they despised death in all holy assurance, as not being death indeed, but a certain *sleep*, out of which they should surely *awake* unto a life eternal. For to them that believe, death is not really death, but a certain sweet *sleep*."[18] [148 occurrences] The use of *awaking* by Luther near this previous quote, as referring to a resurrection from literal death, does not count here as a legitimate example of "death as sleep" because the context shows that a hypothetical situation had been constructed by him (i.e., if Adam had not sinned and not died). Did Luther really mean to say this to his students that day, regarding applying it to only Christians (i.e., "to them that believe")? At this point, ten years before he passed away, Luther had made a distinction, on six previous occurrences, on who specifically loses their consciousness at death.

Earlier in the same year, 1536, Luther showed in a disputation at the university that he concurred with the Roman Church that infants feel neither joy nor sorrow, and hence are asleep. A little over a year prior to this, Luther gave a lecture at the university that referred to the righteous in the context of the OT as being asleep. In a 1533 sermon he used the word *Christian* to indicate who sleeps in death. One year prior to this, Luther gave a funeral speech where he referred to the deceased as being a faithful Christian, and he was sleeping in death. Two years before that, in 1530, he wrote a commentary saying that the righteous, being in an OT context, sleep in death. Any or all of these examples could lead a student hearing this particular Genesis lecture

---

16. Cole, *Creation*, 175.
17. Althaus, *Theology of Martin Luther*, 404–5.
18. Althaus, *Theology of Martin Luther*, 460.

in 1536 to conclude that the wicked are the exception and go straight to hell without even a nap. However, Luther very rarely, prior to this point in time, if ever, referred to this exception to the rule.

In every instance I could find, he was not explicitly comparing Christians against non-Christians, or the wicked compared to the just. Recall the social context of 500 years ago when only the honored saints could avoid a lengthy stay-over in a painful purgatory. The distinction for Luther was between regular Christians and sainted Christians. Luther's message was that all the church loses their consciousness and all Christians can avoid paying indulgences for forgiveness of sins and its resultant escape from purgatory to heaven. The sixth example occurred in 1522 in a personal letter to Amsdorf and thereby set the precedent for each of these later instances. Luther questioned the common belief that the unrighteous go to hell right after dying (in his lecture on Genesis 25 in 1540) by pointing to Paul's statement that they will need to appear in heaven on Judgment Day. "But we do not know whether their damnation [i.e., the 'ungodly'] begins immediately after death; for it is written (Rom 14:10) that all will have to stand before the judgment seat."[19]

Although Luther first wrote in this letter the following, "the souls of *the just are asleep* and that they do not know where they are,"[20] he corrected himself in the same letter, written with pen and ink, to then say, "*all departed souls sleep* without possessing any capacity of feeling."[21] My opinion is that Luther held to the same belief from the beginning to the end (from 1522 to 1546, with the exception of one sermon in 1522) that everyone—before or after Christ, in or out of Christ—sleeps during the interval of death. Luther said the following to his students at the Genesis 25:7–10 lecture (sometime in late-1540): "But whether the souls of the ungodly are tortured immediately after death I am unable to affirm . . . In 2 Cor 5:10 Paul says: 'For we must all appear before the judgment seat of Christ, so that each one may receive good or evil, according to what he has done in the body.' It seems that they, too [the 'ungodly'], are *sleeping and resting* ['after death']."[22] [1 instance, and 149 total occurrences]

This does not seem to be an illegitimate overlay of an editor's opinion, and Pelikan did not include it in his list of suspicious assertions, probably because he knew that it parallels the claim Luther had made about nineteen years earlier. However, there is one example from a Genesis 42:38 lecture,

---

19. Althaus, *Theology of Martin Luther*, 460.
20. Luther, "Letter 111," 360. See WA-Br 2:422
21. Luther, "Letter 111," 361.
22. Pelikan and Hansen, *LW*, 4:314–15.

likely given in 1544, where the edited text says the following: "Nor do we know whether they ['the ungodly'] sleep after death."[23] Perhaps the most relevant point regarding this potential inconsistency here is that Luther saw a distinction between saying "nor do we *know*" versus "it *seems that* the ungodly are sleeping in death."

When Luther reached Genesis 15:13–16 in 1538, he said the following: "God declares that Abraham will die; yet He promises that He will be Abraham's reward. How are we going to harmonize these statements unless we conclude that after this life there remains another life, one that is better and eternal, to which we shall be *awakened* out of the very dust of death by the Son of God?"[24] [150 occurrences] "Throughout his Commentary on Genesis Luther contends against those who ignore the doctrine of the resurrection in the Old Testament; there, as here, his chief support is the pericope, Matt 22:29–32."[25]

Luther gave a sermon on Luke 1:68–79 on June 30, 1538 in which he told the assembled church the following: "The Fathers called churchyards *coemeteria* (cemeteries), that is, places in which one *sleeps*, sleeping quarters, where Christians are buried. . . . To them the grave is not a tomb but, as it were, a bed in which they *sleep* until the time comes when they are to be *awakened*."[26] [153 occurrences] Luther said the reason some burial plots were called cemeteries (as translated from German), which he told them comes from *coemeterium*, was because this Latin word comes from the Greek word, *koimeterion*, which Dictionary.com defines as "a sleeping place, equivalent to *koime* (a variant stem of *koiman*: to put to sleep)."[27] The Germans of the sixteenth century were using different names than before, Luther said, because more and more people were understanding their graveyards as being restful "houses of sleep . . . a *dormitorium*, sleeping chambers."[28]

When Luther arrived at Genesis 22:11 in late 1539, he told the class that "without fear death is not death but a *sleep*."[29] [154 occurrences] This concludes this part of his life (now in his late-fifties), and we have finally arrived at the last five-and-a-half years of Luther's life. If Luther had changed his mind about death in his later years, as some scholars have suggested,

23. Pelikan and Hansen, *LW*, 7:303. See WA 44:518.
24. Pelikan, *LW*, 3:39.
25. Pelikan, *LW*, 13:126–27, 127n82.
26. See "1112" in Plass, What Luther Says, 379. See WA 46:470.
27. See the origins for the word "cemetery" at https://www.dictionary.com/browse/cemetery?s=ts.
28. Lenker, *Church Postil Gospels*, 5:360.
29. See "1079" in Plass, What Luther Says, 367. See WA 43:218. For year, see Pelikan and Hansen, *LW*, 4:ix.

then the total count wouldn't go much beyond 154 times. As it turns out, it does go much higher. Luther still kept talking about there not being any consciousness between death and our resurrection.

Luther in mid-1540 to 1546

Sometime in 1540, between May and September, Luther gave a sermon on Matthew 24:29 (and first published in 1847) in which he said the following: "those will be *sleeping*, that is, lying dead in the grave."[30] [155 occurrences]

Luther was halfway through the book of Genesis when he gave an extraordinary lecture sometime in the second half of 1540. Prior to that particular day, Luther had mentioned "death as sleep" at least 155 times during the previous eighteen years. As an average, this quantity computes to over eight times per year over the entire period (155 / 18 = 8.6). There is not a single work of Luther—perhaps anywhere, anytime—that contains as much discussion, and repetition of "death as sleep," as does the next lecture on Genesis 25. He specifically mentioned this topic a greater number of times that single day than he did during his lectures on 1 Corinthians 15 (eighteen times) that were spread over six months or so. He repeated himself that day in 1540 more than he did the entire year of 1522, which was twenty-one times. In the following lecture to his divinity students, Luther discussed this subject extensively; amounting to a total of twenty-three instances in one day. This was almost three times the annual average compressed into a single lecture.

Why did Luther decide to do this heavy repetition at that time? "Before 1541 Luther had a long history of headaches, weakness, dizziness, depression, [gout, insomnia, ringing in his ears] and kidney stones . . . Luther's deteriorating health during the late 1530s" likely led him to complain in writing "more than once that he was tired of living in general."[31] Perhaps the answer to this question would be that Luther wanted to not only change minds at that time, but also to make sure before it was too late that future Christians would know about his emphasis on "death as sleep."

Luther was well aware that his associates, and particularly his closest associate, Melanchthon, disagreed with him on the wisdom of continuing to make bold stands on theology, especially those that gave support to the most radical reformers. He was very unlike Luther with his tendency to "tread so softly and quietly" on theological matters (as Luther described

---

30. Brown and Mayes, *LW*, 68:328. See WA 47:611–12.
31. Hendrix, *Martin Luther: Visionary Reformer*, 263, 282.

Melanchthon—who was fourteen years younger—after reading the draft of the 1530 *Confession* from the Coburg fortress).[32]

Within about a year or so of this Genesis 25 lecture, Luther became seriously ill again and perhaps realized death was fast approaching his worn-out body. On January 6, 1542, he finally wrote his will and testament to cover his modest net worth, even though "he was the highest-paid professor in the university" in Wittenberg.[33] Luther said the following to his students regarding Genesis 25:7–10:

1. "The saints do not taste death but most pleasantly fall *asleep*."[34]
2. "But they are sleeping a most pleasant *sleep*."[35]
3. "Our souls . . . are *sleeping* in peace, and that they are not being racked by any tortures."[36]
4. "He enters into peace; they *rest* in their beds. These are most extraordinary words. They [the Isaiah 57:1–2 passages] clearly indicate the state and condition of the dead after this life. 'They enter,' he says, 'not into death, purgatory, or hell; they enter into peace.'"[37]
5. "After they had been called away from the troubles and hardships of this life, they entered their chamber, *slept* there, and *rested in peace*."[38]
6. "Thus it is enough for us to know that souls do not go out of their bodies into the danger of tortures and punishments of hell, but that there is ready for them a chamber in which they may *sleep* in peace."[39]

---

32. Hendrix, *Martin Luther: Visionary Reformer*, 214.

33. Hillerbrand, "Luther's Will: 1542" in *Christian Life*. Hillerbrand was the editor-in-chief of *The Oxford Encyclopedia of the Reformation* referenced in chapter 3 of this book. Luther's will begins as follows: "I, Martin Luther, Doctor of Sacred Scripture, etc., acknowledge with this my own handwriting that I have given to my beloved and faithful wife Katherine as an endowment . . . which she will be at liberty to manage according to her desire and best interest." Hillerbrand, "Luther's Will: 1542" in *Christian Life*. See WA-Br 9:571–74 and Spitz, *LW*, 34:295–307. Luther's great respect and love for Katie (1499–1552) is reflected in it, given the legal situation of that century when it was uncommon for wives to inherit such responsibility in real estate properties. Elector Frederick eventually declared Luther's will to be valid.

34. Pelikan and Hansen, *LW*, 4:309. See WA 43:357–58.

35. Pelikan and Hansen, *LW*, 4:309.

36. Pelikan and Hansen, *LW*, 4:312. See WA 43:359–60.

37. Pelikan and Hansen, *LW*, 4:312. Another reason *rest* is counted here is because *rest* is taken by Luther to mean "sleep during death" given the context of this lecture on Gen 25:7–10 (e.g., on pp. 313–14).

38. Pelikan and Hansen, *LW*, 4:312.

39. Pelikan and Hansen, *LW*, 4:313. See WA 43:360–61.

7. "There is a difference between the sleep or rest of this life and that of the future life . . . the soul does not *sleep* in the same manner."[40]

8. "The *sleep* in the future life is deeper than it is in this life."[41]

9. "Thus after death the soul enters its chamber and is at peace; and while it *sleeps*, it is *not aware* of its sleep."[42]

10. "God preserves the *waking* soul. Thus God is able to awaken Elijah, Moses, etc., and so to control them that they live. But how? We do not know."[43]

11. "The resemblance to physical sleep—namely, that God declares that there is *sleep, rest, and peace*—is enough."[44]

12. "He who sleeps a natural sleep . . . feels nothing in his sleep. The *same thing will happen* in that life, but in a different and better way."[45]

13. "Just as a mother brings an infant into the bedchamber and puts it into a cradle—not that it may die, but that it may have a pleasant sleep and rest—so before the coming of Christ and much more after the coming of Christ all the souls of believers have entered and *are entering the bosom of Christ*."[46]

14. "Therefore the whereabouts of the souls is the Word of God or the promises in which we fall *asleep*. To be sure, it appears to be of no consequence and feeble when it is uttered through the mouth of man; but when we take hold of it in faith and fall *asleep* in the Word, the soul comes into infinite space."[47]

15. "As yet there is *rest* and peace among the saints."[48]

---

40. Pelikan and Hansen, *LW*, 4:313.
41. Pelikan and Hansen, *LW*, 4:313.
42. Pelikan and Hansen, *LW*, 4:313.
43. Pelikan and Hansen, *LW*, 4:313.
44. Pelikan and Hansen, *LW*, 4:313.
45. Pelikan and Hansen, *LW*, 4:313.
46. Pelikan and Hansen, *LW*, 4:313.
47. Pelikan and Hansen, *LW*, 4:314. See WA 43:361. Luther described Augustine on this point as follows: "There have also been discussions about where the souls are. In his *Enchiridion to Laurence* [footnote: chapter 29, par. 109] Augustine states that their whereabouts is concealed. He [Augustine] says: 'But the time that elapses between man's death and the final resurrection keeps the souls in hidden places, inasmuch as each one deserves either rest or distress, depending on what its lot was in the flesh while it was living.'" Pelikan and Hansen, *LW*, 4:314.
48. Pelikan and Hansen, *LW*, 4:316. See WA 43:362-63.

16. "For He [Christ] is always working and does not rest as do the saints who *sleep*, about whom it is stated in Is. 63:16: 'Abraham does not know us, and Israel does not acknowledge us.'"[49]

17. "There is a great difference between the *sleeping* saints and the ruling Christ. The former *sleep* and *do not know what is going on*. Nevertheless, they are *resting*."[50]

The entire set of these 23 instances appear on just eight pages of text in *Luther's Works*, volume 4, and each is under the heading of Genesis 25:7–10.[51] Therefore, it is very likely all of them came during a single lecture in one day in 1540. This is a great example of repetition of the "death as sleep" idea, and most significantly, it occurred near the end of Luther's life, being published in 1544. With this total now being 178 instances, could there be a few more perhaps as we head down the homestretch toward the finish line? Yes, more than just a few remain since Luther has another five years of life or more, and he was not to be kept quiet about this important teaching, ever.

In 1540 a revised edition of Luther's *Winter Postil* collection of sermons was published in which Luther himself chose to make "many significant changes to his sermons."[52] However, this close supervision of the editing process could not be said of the 1544 edition of the *Summer Postil* produced by his trusted aid, Cruciger (which was Luther's plan "as early as 1535"[53]). "It appears that Luther began with a thorough edit of the Advent sermons, then worked hastily, with the exception of those places where he excised lengthy sections and the complete replacement of the Gospel sermon for the First Sunday after Epiphany."[54] There is a good example of a particular *Winter Postil* sermon, published in 1522, 1525, and again in 1540 (as revisions), where it is certain that Luther reconsidered its contents for the 1540 edition, due to the detection of entire sentences appropriately added.[55] Consequently, we can have greater assurance that the

---

49. Pelikan and Hansen, *LW*, 4:316.

50. Pelikan and Hansen, *LW*, 4:316.

51. All of these quotes appear on seven consecutive pages (at most) in the Weimar edition (WA 43:357–63).

52. Mayes and Langebartels, *LW*, 75:xxii. The full title of the postils is *Explanation of the Epistles and Gospels from Advent to Easter, by Dr. Martin Luther, Corrected Anew*. "He removed sections in which he had previously tolerated Roman Catholic fasts and the cult of saints. . . . Some of Luther's changes demonstrate greater kindness toward Aristotle." Mayes and Langebartels, *LW*, 75:xxii.

53. Mayes and Langebartels, *LW*, 75:xxiii.

54. Mayes and Langebartels, *LW*, 75:xxii.

55. "These last two sentences were first added in the 1540 edition." See "First Sunday in Advent, Matt 21:1–9" in Mayes and Langebartels, *LW*, 75:32. Regarding the footnote

1540 edition of the sermon/explanation titled, "First Sunday in Advent, Matt 21:1–9" was closely reviewed by Luther personally, rather than being handled by Cruziger or Roth.[56]

This sermon from the young Luther (i.e., in 1522) was probably the first time ever that his followers either heard or read him correlate his unusual view of death and resurrection directly to Christians, and not just to the fathers of the OT. The fact that Luther originally wrote this *Winter Postil* eighteen years before he edited it in detail, less than six years before he died, is quite significant regarding Luther's true opinion on this subject. However, this work and others similar to it will not be double-counted in my running total since this will not be necessary to defend my claim. In the 1540 revised edition of his *Winter Postil*, Luther said the following: "Therefore, the death of Christian believers is not death but a *sleep*, for they neither see nor taste death, as Christ says here."[57] The main difference between the two versions is the inclusion of text for a cited Psalm; the latter version omits the text.

On January 9, 1541, Martinus wrote a personal letter in reply to Frederic Myconius in which he said the following: "It is a singular joy to me that you are so unterrified by death, that *sleep* into which all good men fall, nay, that you are rather desirous of being freed and living with Christ."[58] [179 occurrences] See chapters 3, 8, and 9 for discussions on how Luther had dealt with the perceived paradox of a deceased person being both asleep and not asleep at the same time.

"Several hymnals published in Wittenberg during Luther's lifetime were devoted exclusively to burial hymns. The first of these, published by Joseph Klug in Wittenberg in 1542, contained six German chorales and eight Latin chants. Luther supplied the preface, in which he outlined the guiding principles for the reform of the burial service."[59] Luther titled the

---

at the end of the statement, "they neither see nor taste death, as Christ says here" we read the following: "1522, 1528, 1532 add: 'of which the psalm speaks: "In peace I will both lie down and sleep; for You have put me in good safety" (Psalm 4[:8]).'" See "First Sunday in Advent, Matt 21:1–9" in Mayes and Langebartels, *LW*, 75:46n.

56. "Whereas Roth's edition presented the contents of his stenographic notes from Luther's preached sermons with little emendation, Cruziger's edition shaped his sources into a uniform whole, which Luther was able to claim as his own intellectual property. Luther's desire and intention was not at all to present to the reading public a literal transcript of his pulpit utterances. Therefore, while Luther disapproved of Roth's slavishly exact publication of his sermons, he was fully satisfied with Cruziger's revisions and acknowledged the latter's work as his own." Mayes and Langebartels, *LW*, 75:xxiv.

57. Mayes and Langebartels, *LW*, 75:46. See WA 10/1.2:42–43. See chapter 5 at the "Luther in 1522" section and its footnotes for detail.

58. Smith, *Life and Letters*, 391.

59. Lehmann and Leupold, *LW*, 53:325.

preface of the work called *Christian Songs, Latin and German, for Use at Funerals* as "To the Christian Reader." His preface for this particular hymnal by Klug was his longest one of all the hymnals in which he was directly associated, and he began it as follows: "St. Paul exhorts the Thessalonians (1 Thess 4:13–18) not to sorrow over the dead as others who have no hope, but to comfort each other with God's Word as having a certain hope of life and of the resurrection of the dead."[60] Luther continues by writing the following: "It is little wonder if those are sad who have no hope. Nor can they be blamed for it. Since they are beyond the pale of faith in Christ, they must either cherish this temporal life as the only thing worthwhile and hate to lose it, or they must expect that after this life they will receive eternal death and the wrath of God in hell and must fear to go there."[61] Following this, Luther wrote the following: "But we Christians, who have been redeemed from all this by the dear blood of the Son of God, should by faith train and accustom ourselves to despise death and to regard it as a deep, strong, and sweet *sleep*, to regard the coffin as nothing but paradise and the bosom of our Lord Christ, and the grave as nothing but a soft couch or sofa, which it really is in the sight of God; for he says, John 11:11, 'Our friend Lazarus has fallen asleep,' and Matthew 9:24, 'The girl is not dead but sleeping.'"[62] [180 occurrences]

Within the same preface, Luther wrote four sayings or proverbs. One of them is based on Luke 2:29–32, and has ten lines to it, that begins as follows:

> With peace and joy in sweet repose,
>
> Gladly will [my] eyelids close,
>
> And go to *sleep* the grave within.[63] [181 occurrences]

Luther also suggested the hymn "In Peace and Joy I Now Depart" be sung "on returning home from the internment" along with three other hymns he identified.[64] Looking back over the previous decades, Luther recounted the following: "We have removed from our churches and completely abolished the popish abominations, such as vigils, masses for the dead,

---

60. Lehmann and Leupold, *LW*, 53:325.
61. Lehmann and Leupold, *LW*, 53:325–26.
62. Lehmann and Leupold, *LW*, 53:326. See WA 35:478–83.
63. Lehmann and Leupold, *LW*, 53:330.
64. Lehmann and Leupold, *LW*, 53:331. See chapter 5 regarding this still-published hymn by the Lutheran Church–Missouri Synod.

processions, purgatory, and all other hocus-pocus on behalf of the dead."[65] He also said the following in this same preface: "If the graves should be honored in other ways, it would be fine to paint or write good epitaphs or verses from Scripture on the walls above (where there are such) so that they may be seen by those who go to a funeral or to the cemetery . . . [rather] than other secular emblems, such as shields and helmets."[66] He provided a list of twenty-two suggestions for this use on or near the tombstone of a Christian.[67] Only two keywords are italicized in the following list since the others are too similar to the scriptural passages cited by Luther or later editors to meet my criteria for inclusion in the count.

1. "He has fallen *asleep* with his fathers and has been gathered to his people. (Gen 25:8)";[68]
2. "I know that my Redeemer lives, and that he will *awaken* me out of the earth . . . I shall see God. Job 19:25–26";[69]
3. "I laid down and slept and awaked, for the Lord kept me. Ps 3:5";[70]
4. "I lie down and sleep in complete peace. Ps 4:8";[71]
5. "I shall behold thy face in righteousness: I shall be satisfied, when I awake, with thy likeness. Ps 17:15";[72]
6. "Awake and sing ye who lie under the earth. Isa 26:19";[73]
7. "Shall enter into peace and rest in their chambers. Isa 57:1–2";[74]
8. "Many who lie sleeping under the earth will awake, some to everlasting life, some to everlasting dishonor and shame. Dan 12:2";[75]
9. "I will redeem them from hell and rescue them from death. O death, I will be poison to you. O hell, I will be a plague to you. Hos 13:14";[76]

65. Lehmann and Leupold, *LW*, 53:326.
66. Lehmann and Leupold, *LW*, 53:328, 330.
67. Most of these twenty-two propositions originally included a biblical citation by Luther (book and chapter only, without a verse number which was added later).
68. Lehmann and Leupold, *LW*, 53:328.
69. Lehmann and Leupold, *LW*, 53:328.
70. See "Christian Songs for Funerals" in Luther, *Works of Martin Luther*, 6:290.
71. Lehmann and Leupold, *LW*, 53:328.
72. Lehmann and Leupold, *LW*, 53:328.
73. Jacobs and Spaeth, *Works of Martin Luther*, 6:291.
74. Jacobs and Spaeth, *Works of Martin Luther*, 6:291.
75. Jacobs and Spaeth, *Works of Martin Luther*, 6:291.
76. Lehmann and Leupold, *LW*, 53:329.

10. "For as in Adam all die, so also in Christ shall all be made alive. 1 Cor 15:22";[77]

11. "If we believe that Jesus died and rose again, so shall God also lead with him those who have fallen asleep through Jesus. 1 Thess 4:14."[78] [2 instances, 183 total occurrences]

Luther wrote a letter to Amsdorf on October 29, 1542, which was five weeks after his daughter had died.[79] "After fourteen years, after Magdalena had completely captured the big heart of her father by her winsome personality, God took her too [following his very young daughter Elizabeth]."[80] Luther wrote the following: "I rejoice that she is living with her Father in sweet *sleep* until that Day. . . . This is really *sleeping* in the Lord, not seeing or tasting death."[81] [185 occurrences] However, Luther had earlier stated the following immediately before she died according to an account given by someone in the household: "I am angry with myself that I cannot rejoice in heart . . . as I ought. . . . I love her very much."[82] Three days after her death, Luther wrote to Justus Jonas of Halle saying the following: "I ought only to give thanks and rejoice . . . yet so strong is natural affection that we must sob and groan in heart under the oppression of killing grief."[83]

Sometime in 1542, when the professor resumed his Genesis lectures at the university, Luther told his class the following at Genesis 26:2-5:

1. "The reason why death is bitter is that the hindrances of the flesh prevent us from believing [the words seen in Scripture]. Otherwise affliction would be a joy, and death would be a *sleep*";[84]

2. "What then, shall we suppose is the way in which the soul *rests* or lives? It undoubtedly has some way of its own in which it *sleeps*";[85]

---

77. Lehmann and Leupold, *LW*, 53:329.
78. Jacobs and Spaeth, *Works of Martin Luther*, 6:292.
79. Magdalena Luther died on September 20, 1542.
80. Plass, *Luther: A Character Study*, 268–69.
81. See "1120" in Plass, What Luther Says, 382. See WA-Br 10:169.
82. Smith, *Life and Letters*, 354.
83. Smith, *Life and Letters*, 354. Jonas was the man who had taken the last piece of paper that Luther had written on before dying (and then he lost it)—the famous, "We are beggars, this is true," according to Johannes Aurifaber who first found it and had written that he "'took the slip of paper with him' only to have long since disappeared." Kellerman, "Last Written Words of Luther."
84. Pelikan and Hansen, *LW*, 5:22. See WA 43:443–44.
85. Pelikan and Hansen, *LW*, 5:74. See WA 43:479–80.

3. "The souls of the saints are *resting*, as is stated in Isa. 26:20 and 57:2, and far more peacefully at that than people who are sleeping";[86]
4. "In the same way the souls, too, are *sleeping*";[87]
5. "Eventually he will live while he *sleeps* even though he is dead."[88] [191 occurrences]

Sometime during the winter of 1543–44, Luther said the following two years before he died: "Souls hear, think, see after death, but how they do it we do not understand. . . . If we think of it in terms of this life, we are fools. Christ has nicely solved it."[89] What Luther says, according to Plass, is that if someone claims that Luther said the deceased can think like people do in this life, and can employ their senses in the interim state as people do in this life, then they are acting like "a fool." The next chapter will attempt to further explain the paradox of how the soul/mind of a deceased person could be completely unconscious and yet functional in some way simultaneously, while not being a contradiction.

In 1544, when Luther reached Genesis 42:38 at the university, he said the following:

1. "But after leaving this life the godly enter their chamber or bed, in which they *sleep and rest* until body and soul are again united in the future and eternal life";[90]
2. "For hell did not keep His soul in a state of *sleep and rest*";[91]
3. "Those, however, who were raised from the dead by Christ were able to testify to nothing else than that they *slept* and lay in a bed";[92]
4. "This is the extent of the knowledge we have about the refuges for the bodies and the souls: [The grave] is the place for the body, but [Sheol] is the place for the *sleeping* soul. . . . What the nature of this rest is we do not know";[93]

---

86. Pelikan and Hansen, *LW*, 5:75. See WA 43:480–81.
87. Pelikan and Hansen, *LW*, 5:75.
88. Pelikan and Hansen, *LW*, 5:75.
89. See "1129" in Plass, *What Luther Says*, 384. See WA-Tr 5 (5534).
90. Pelikan and Hansen, *LW*, 5:293. See WA 44:516–17. Regarding the reasonable speculation by the *LW* editors that it is most likely that this particular lecture was given sometime in 1544, see Pelikan and Hansen, *LW*, 7:vii–viii.
91. Pelikan and Hansen, *LW*, 5:294. See WA 44:517–18.
92. Pelikan and Hansen, *LW*, 5:294.
93. Pelikan and Hansen, *LW*, 5:294.

5. "But that rest of the dead which Holy Scripture calls a *sleep* is much more wonderful";[94]

6. "But they are *asleep and resting*, as is true of all the godly, so that Christ is able to *awaken* them whenever it is His good pleasure to do so. Accordingly, it is not necessary to pray for them. Much less is it necessary to spend so much money to redeem their souls from purgatory";[95]

7. "But the doctrine of the Gospel, which bears witness that the godly are *asleep and at rest* in Christ, refutes and cancels this whole piece of godlessness concerning the offering of the body and blood of Christ to be made for the dead";[96]

8. "Nor do we know whether they ['the ungodly'] *sleep* after death or how they sleep. This is what I wanted to say in this place about the difference between the grave and Gehenna."[97] [With these 9 instances the total number of occurrences is now 200]

Luther preached a sermon on May 31, 1545 and spoke the following: "There he ['Isaiah' in Isa 26:19] says: 'Your dead shall live and rise with their bodies. You who lie beneath the earth, awake and shout!'... He speaks to the dead *as if* they were *already alive*. By this he wants to show that the resurrection from the dead is certain."[98] [1 instance; 201 occurrences] The reason this Luther quote serves as an example to be counted among the others is because his interpretation of this passage in Isaiah involves seeing that the writer understood death to not consist of consciousness or even some type of life. Saying that the mind of the deceased (which would cause the body to shout) was being spoken to by the writer *as if* resurrection had already happened shows us that Luther sees death as like some kind of sleep. When Luther's students heard the professor give a lecture on Genesis 47:29–30, sometime in mid-1545, he said the following: "He falls *asleep* most pleasantly with a calm and collected mind as he passes from

---

94. Pelikan and Hansen, *LW*, 5:295. See WA 44:518.

95. Pelikan and Hansen, *LW*, 5:296. See WA 44:518–19. At this point in time, twenty-seven years had elapsed since Luther's October 31, 1517 letter objecting to costly indulgences regarding purgatory was distributed and likely posted on the bulletin board at the local church (his ninety-five theses).

96. Pelikan and Hansen, *LW*, 5:297. See WA 44:519–20.

97. Pelikan and Hansen, *LW*, 7:303. See WA 44:523–24.

98. Brown, *LW*, 58:154. It was preached on Trinity Sunday in Wittenberg titled "The Fourth Sermon" and used 1 Cor 15:54–57.

this world in which he has spent a life that has been very bitter and full of very serious troubles."[99] [202 occurrences]

Luther said the following in mid-1545 on Genesis 48:21: "This is the theology we teach. It is altogether different from the theology which the blind and foolish scholastics and papists retain. These men are completely ignorant of it and despise faith. Therefore, let us listen to the patriarch Jacob as he speaks of death as if he were speaking of sleep.... In this confidence I shall die and fall *asleep* in peace."[100] [203 occurrences]

The following quotes from a lecture on Genesis 49:33 that occurred sometime in late-1545 (just a few months before he died) represent another flurry of repetition on the "death as sleep" theme:

1. "The words 'was gathered to his people' are truly splendid and full of meaning.... This way of speaking should be pleasing to us for it testifies that ever since the beginning of the world the saints fell *asleep* in faith and in the hope of the resurrection";[101] [204 occurrences]

2. "Where, then, did he go? God has a receptacle in which the saints and the elect rest without death, without pain and hell.... But it is certain that it is called, and is, a people.... But how these saints are kept in definite places, we do not know";[102] [205 occurrences]

3. "Or shall we not think that He will preserve the soul in such a way that even though I do not know where I am, I nevertheless am in a definite place... It is certain that it is not an evil place and that the saints are not tormented by any tortures but are *resting* in the grace of God";[103] [206 occurrences]

4. "Thus the place of the dead has no torments; but, as we say, they *rest in peace* [RIP]... We depart, and we return on the Last Day, *before we are aware* of it";[104] [208 occurrences]

5. "Sleeps in most peaceful *sleep and rest*."[105] The total is now 209 occurrences.

At this point in Luther's life, six months before he died (or less), I would like to ask the reader to respond to that which Robert A. Morey (1946–2019)

---

99. Pelikan and Hansen, *LW*, 8:138. See WA 44:680–81.
100. Pelikan and Hansen, *LW*, 8:191–92. See WA 44:718–20.
101. Pelikan and Hansen, *LW*, 8:315. See WA 44:811.
102. Pelikan and Hansen, *LW*, 8:315–16. See WA 44:811–12.
103. Pelikan and Hansen, *LW*, 8:317. See WA 44:812–13.
104. Pelikan and Hansen, *LW*, 8:318. See WA 44:813–14.
105. Pelikan and Hansen, *LW*, 8:319. See WA 44:814.

wrote in his 1984 book concerning Luther's view of death. After seeing this presentation of quotes from Luther over a long period of time, is it true that "Luther himself toyed with the idea of soul sleep as a quick and clean answer to the Catholic teaching of purgatory"?[106] It certainly was an answer to his church's teaching, and a clean and good one at that, but can over 200 mentions of "death as unconscious sleep" over the last twenty-four years of his life, be labeled as "quick"? Morey also wrote there that "later writings reveal that he changed his mind." Does it appear to the reader of *Death until Resurrection* that Luther changed his mind as he became older? Since this book has clearly demonstrated he had not, then it is a mistaken conclusion on Morey's part to characterize it as Luther toying with this particular idea of death and subsequently discarding his belief.

Although the original meaning of *Requiescat in pace* (Latin) by Luther refers to an immediate rest or sleep upon death, when the use of RIP on the tombs of Christians became ubiquitous by the eighteenth century, its meaning changed. To wish that the soul of the departed would eventually find peace in the afterlife, following an indefinite period of torment in purgatory allowed Roman Catholics and others to assume the referent still involved the soul, while other people assumed that it was the physical body that was enjoined to lie peacefully in the grave. Luther did not coin the phrase as an epitaph since it has been found on tombstones centuries before him, including Jewish burial inscriptions.

Luther finally arrived—after ten years—to the last verse of the last chapter of Genesis (i.e., Genesis 50:26) in November 1545. "Volume VI of the Latin section of the Wittenberg edition of Luther's works elaborates on this comment: 'Dr. Luther, the man of God, concluded his lectures on Genesis on November 17, 1545. He had begun them in the year 1535, when he said in his preface: "I shall linger over the exposition of this book and shall die in the process of doing so."'"[107]

Luther was out of town and away from his cherished wife when the end was near. He began a letter to his wife dated February 1, 1546 as follows: "To my dearly beloved housewife, Katherine Luther, owner of Zulsdorf and the Saumarket, and whatever else she may be. . . . Kathie, I became extremely weak when I was close to Eisleben." Luther had left Halle on January 28, 1546, and preached on Sunday, January 31, 1546 in Eisleben. Luther's last letter to his wife (dated February 14, 1546) begins and ends as follows: "To my dear, kind wife, Katherine Luther, at Wittenberg . . . we are provided with

---

106. Morey, *Death and the Afterlife*, 201.
107. Pelikan and Hansen, *LW*, 8:ix–x.

meat and drink like lords, and have every attention paid us, indeed too much . . . I am very well. . . . I commend you to God. Martin Luther."

Although Luther's thirty-two-year career teaching the Bible as a professor was about to end, his preaching career would not end until February 14, 1546, when he preached for the last time at Eisleben on Matthew 11:25. Previously in Wittenberg, Luther told his students the following to end his great lecture series on Genesis: "He wants that tomb to be before the eyes of all his descendants, in order that his children and grandchildren . . . may persevere in the same faith and promise in which he had fallen *asleep* with his fathers. This is now the dear Genesis. . . . I can do no more."[108]

This quote above shows that the very last point Luther made to his students at the final end of his professorship was that the nature of death was a topic he would again mention one last time in public. Obviously, Luther could have said several other things immediately before closing the book on his Genesis lecture series, but he chose to refer to the not-uncommon phrase from the OT—someone had fallen *asleep* in death with his fathers who preceded them. The grand total of this book is now 210 occurrences where Luther repeated his firmly held belief that the best interpretation of Scripture, as a whole, on death is to acknowledge that "fallen asleep" in death means falling into a type of unconsciousness whenever the person falls into death.

However, the good news is that this period of lifelessness ends on the day of the resurrection of nearly everyone who was ever born, based on both the OT and the NT. It can be imagined this last day will then permit us to ascertain what just happened to us, and to those around us, who also may not recall anything transpiring after their last day in this world. Our experience and our interaction with others on their recollection of the nature of death—asleep or awake—will confirm it, at a level of certainty, on what lies between death and resurrection. However, it is still worthwhile to investigate Luther's interpretation of the Bible and also, to determine what all Scripture says, as a whole, about this ongoing issue. This is because Luther mentioned "death as unconscious sleep" at least 210 times over the last twenty-four years of his life and because several other prominent scholars after Luther have also seen some importance in it.

Luther passed away exactly three months after his final lecture on Genesis shortly after midnight on February 18, 1546.

---

108. Pelikan and Hansen, *LW*, 8:333. See WA 44:824–25. At supper on February 17, 1546, the evening before Luther died (in Eisleben, rather than in Wittenberg), he had discussed death and everlasting life. Jonas, Colius, Goldschmid (Aurifaber), and his two sons (who had recently arrived from Mansfeld) were present when he passed away.

CHAPTER 8

The Where and How of Death and Resurrection

Luther's descriptions of where the deceased go

In Luther's study of the Bible, he noticed that the repetition of a certain phrase related to death in the OT was important. Luther said the following to his university students about five years before he died: "But where did Abraham go? Moses says: 'He was gathered to his people.'"[1] To Luther, "the words 'was gathered to his people' are truly splendid and full of meaning."[2] Luther interpreted Genesis 25:8 as saying that "this Word testifies that after this life there is a people."[3] Then, Luther told them that day "this is truly an outstanding and notable evidence of the resurrection and the future life."[4] A few months before Luther died, he told his class that he "is certain that it [the gathering place] is called, and is, a people.... But how these ... are kept in definite places, we do not know."[5]

This common phrase referring to death in the OT led to names being assigned to this place. Luther referred to theologians, popes, and "rabbis [that] make up anything you please out of anything you please. Christ alone says that Lazarus 'died and was carried by the angels to Abraham's bosom' (Luke 16:22). This Interpreter and Teacher must be believed, because He is God and man."[6] This action need not imply an actual *carrying* as Luther may have conceived it more generally; for example, when

---

1. Pelikan and Hansen, *LW*, 4:309.
2. Pelikan and Hansen, *LW*, 8:315.
3. Pelikan and Hansen, *LW*, 8:315.
4. Pelikan and Hansen, *LW*, 4:309.
5. Pelikan and Hansen, *LW*, 8:315.
6. Pelikan and Hansen, *LW*, 8:315.

someone dies their soul is "*transferred* by the angels into the bosom of Abraham, or to our people."[7]

Why was it originally called this, and is it still to be considered "Abraham's bosom"? In this context, *bosom* is defined as "a state of enclosing intimacy; warm closeness: the bosom of the family."[8] Luther answers this as follows: "Abraham is adduced because he was the father of the promise"[9] and "before the time of Christ this was called the bosom of Abraham."[10] However, the souls of the deceased "are now kept in the bosom of Christ"[11] since "Abraham's bosom has become Christ's bosom."[12] "For when we depart this life, we are carried into the bosom of Christ."[13] Luther used the analogy of a baby's bed—in addition to his own bed and his own couch—to describe the sleep of death. "Just as a mother brings an infant into the bedchamber and puts it into a cradle—not that it may die, but that it may have a pleasant sleep and rest—so before the coming of Christ and much more after the coming of Christ all the souls of believers have entered and are entering the bosom of Christ."[14]

The writers of the OT had given another name, a proper noun that can be capitalized, to the *bosom of Abraham*, that replaced it. Luther asserted that there is certainly a critical distinction between two Hebrew words regarding where people are put after dying: one is *Sheol* and the other one is translated as *grave* (or burial vault for the body). He quoted Psalm 16:10 ("because you *will not abandon me* to the realm of the dead, nor will you let your faithful one see decay").[15] Since *Sheol* is the name of "the realm of the dead," the NASB reads instead: "For You *will not abandon my soul* to Sheol; Nor will You allow Your Holy One to undergo decay."[16] Notice their preference for using "abandon my soul" instead of just saying "abandon me" which may lead to the following question. What specifically is given up

---

7. Pelikan and Hansen, *LW*, 8:315–16.
8. The definition of "bosom" seen at dictionary.com is particularly helpful.
9. Pelikan and Hansen, *LW*, 8:315.
10. Pelikan and Hansen, *LW*, 7:294.
11. Pelikan and Hansen, *LW*, 7:294.
12. Mayes and Langebartels, *LW*, 75:62.
13. Pelikan and Hansen, *LW*, 4:311–12. See WA 43:358–59.
14. Pelikan and Hansen, *LW*, 4:311–12.
15. The version here is from the NIV. The NRSV reads as follows: "For you do not give me up to Sheol, or let your faithful one see the Pit."
16. The NASB follows this verse with a footnote defining Sheol as "the nether world." Some have claimed Sheol refers to the grave, as opposed to hell. However, others (e.g., Luther) disagree that Sheol refers to either of them. Many understand Sheol to be the world of the dead.

to *Sheol* when the text says *me*: the body or the mind? The context of this passage (Ps 16:7–11) constantly refers to the mind of the person using the following phrases (as seen in these five verses in the NRSV): *I* bless, gives *me* counsel, *my heart* instructs me, *I* keep, before *me*, *I* shall not be moved, *my heart* is glad, *my soul* rejoices, and show *me* the path of life.

The Hebrew word Luther referenced in this passage, *Sheol*, is next to another Hebrew word, *nefesh*, in this same passage, which is usually translated as soul, life, person, mind, and heart (in order of decreasing frequency in the KJV throughout the OT with its 753 occurrences of *nefesh*). "As the suffering soul especially [as used in Job 19:2], and as the tortured mind, the *nefesh* is the precise subject of the psalms of lamentation; it is frightened (Ps 6:3), it despairs and is disquieted (Ps 42:5, 43:5) . . . suffers misery (Isa. 53:11). . . . The context . . . in many similar ones shows clearly that here it is a state of mind that is being thought of."[17] Therefore, the writer of Psalm 16 was likely referring to the mind, and not to the body, when writing that God would not "abandon me to *Sheol*." In this case it appears the better translation of *nefesh* in Psalm 16:10 is *soul* instead of *me* (from the NIV and NRSV) because the NASB better preserves the distinction implied by the context between the mind (heart and soul) versus the body which "decays." The use of *soul* is more specific than *me* and is appropriate since the *nefesh* stands in opposition to the body in death in this passage. Luther also quoted from the Apostles' Creed with this psalm to provide further grounds for his claim.[18] Both of these, for Luther, show that its writers had made a distinction between the body, which "died, suffered, was buried" on one hand and the soul on the other (which is not abandoned to *Sheol*). Luther said that *Sheol* is the place where the souls of all the dead are housed and quotes Augustine on this point. "In his *Enchiridion to Laurentius* Augustine mentions 'secret shelters for souls.'"[19] It is clear from Luther's writings (as seen below) that he pictured the grave (which contains only the body) as being a different place from that which contains the soul (i.e., *Sheol*).

Regarding the distinction between the righteous and the wicked and where their souls go immediately at death, without any regard to afterward

---

17. Wolff, *Anthropology of the Old Testament*, 17.

18. The Apostles' Creed says in part as follows: "Jesus Christ . . . suffered . . . was crucified, died and was buried. He descended into hell [or Hades]; the third day He rose again from the dead . . . from thence He shall come to judge the living and the dead. . . . I believe in the . . . resurrection of the body, and life everlasting. Amen." See "Apostles' Creed." "In its oldest form, the Apostles' Creed goes back to at least 140 A.D. . . . Though not written by the apostles, [it] is the oldest creed of the Christian church and is the basis for others that followed." See "What is the Apostles' Creed?," paras. 3, 1.

19. Pelikan and Hansen, *LW*, 7:292. Augustine, *Enchir.* 29.109. An alternative title is *Handbook to Laurentius*.

(i.e., heaven or hell), Luther wrote the following: "Nor is mention made [in the Bible] of one [type of] *Sheol* for the godly and another for the ungodly."[20] Luther implies that he is fairly certain of this claim since he states that "various arguments . . . [from the opposing view] do not particularly impress me."[21] It would appear that Luther is focusing on the time period prior to the last day, or the return of Christ, since he had elsewhere referred to the day of judgment before the throne of God determining the ultimate fate of a person (rather than immediately at death). Therefore, this particular exclusion would also apply to expectations within the mind of the deceased regarding their faith of being saved, or not (i.e., "the happy side of Hades" versus "the lowest part" of it).

When the Hebrew Bible was translated into Greek to become the Septuagint (or LXX), *Sheol* became *Hades*. Hades means this nether world of souls of the departed, as used in the original sense, rather than meaning hell. Another term for this common receptacle of all souls (i.e., *Sheol*) is the *grave*. However, with this term the distinction Luther made is lost; therefore, another English word could align better with this different place for the soul. Some prefer the term *gravedom* for *Sheol* and *Hades* to contrast the place containing bones with, on the other hand, the place containing the mind of the deceased. What Luther says is that "the nether region or pit means that which contains the souls, a sort of grave for the soul, outside this geographic world, just as the earth is the grave of the body. But precisely what it is we do not know."[22] Luther wrote this "nether region (*infernus*), or *Sheol*, actually designates that hidden recess in which the dead sleep beyond this life . . . Whatever its nature may be, for geographical (*corporalis*) it cannot be."[23]

Beyond these descriptions of this divine place, how does Luther describe this collection of the souls of people? "They were enfolded and are being preserved as they sleep there in secure protection."[24] Luther's emphasis on the protection of souls that are being guarded during death may have been based on 1 Peter 2:25 which reads as follows (NRSV): "For you were going astray like sheep, but now you have returned to the shepherd and guardian of your souls." The selection of the word *enfolded* (as seen in the Luther quote above) by the translator and assistant editor of volume 78 of *Luther's Works* (2015), James Langebartels, is unique. In Lenker's 1904 translation of this quote (which the title page says was the first time this collection of

20. Pelikan and Hansen, *LW*, 7:292–93.
21. Pelikan and Hansen, *LW*, 7:293.
22. Plass, *What Luther Says*, 385.
23. Plass, *What Luther Says*, 385.
24. Mayes and Langebartels, *LW*, 75:62.

sermons had been translated into English), we read the following: "die . . . be embraced and guarded." Instead of using *embraced*, Langebartels used *enfolded*. Although dictionary.com defines *enfold* to mean "to hug or clasp; embrace: She enfolded him in her arms" it shows this as the third definition. The first one listed there says, "to wrap up; envelop: to enfold someone in a cloak" or coat. The *American Heritage College Dictionary* (3rd ed.) shows *enfold* as meaning "to hold within limits; enclose."

What was Luther's specific meaning with this phrase from the sermon that Luther closely reviewed for Cruciger's *Summer Postil* (1544)? Did he imagine our first meeting with Jesus at the moment of our death as being an unconscious hug, or alternatively, is the mind of the deceased to be put into an enclosure of some sort? We know from further description of Luther's view of Sheol that when he said a person's soul is "embraced or enfolded" at death, he meant it in the sense of secure enclosure, and not as a long or a quick hug. "God has a receptacle,"[25] that is, a "place for the sleeping soul,"[26] which is "a definite place,"[27] just as the grave "is the place for the body."[28] It "is a kind of common receptacle"[29] in which its contents are very secure and are being "carefully preserved."[30] Upon our resurrection at the Last Day when we will consciously be in the presence of Jesus in Paradise, it is then that we will no longer be enfolded in some type of enclosure, but rather be enfolded in an embrace.

Luther wrote on occasion that "death as sleep" excludes even dreaming. "They are sleeping in Christ . . . such a deep sleep that one will not even dream."[31] What did Luther mean exactly by *in Christ* since Luther had, in a letter in 1522, placed all souls there and not just Christians? When he was explaining the nature of sleep for the deceased using Abraham as an example, Luther observed: "Christ says . . . for I have grasped him in such a way that I am his God."[32] So, *in Christ* may be perhaps interpreted not as, "with belief in Christ," but rather as, in the control of Christ, that is, a God who takes the role as recreator of the individual. When people die, they become wholly subject to the will of God. "The soul also does not know

---

25. Pelikan and Hansen, *LW*, 8:315.
26. Pelikan and Hansen, *LW*, 7:294.
27. Pelikan and Hansen, *LW*, 8:316.
28. Pelikan and Hansen, *LW*, 7:294.
29. Pelikan and Hansen, *LW*, 7:292.
30. Lenker, *Luther's Church Postil Gospels*, 5:359.
31. Lehmann and Doberstein, *Luther's Works*, 51:242.
32. Brown and Mayes, *LW*, 68:140.

its condition"[33] and "it is impossible that they [the 'saints'] can die, or not enjoy eternal life . . . because, God cannot be the God of those who are dead or who are nothing, but must be the God of the living . . . hence death is not death to the saints, but a sleep."[34] The "death as sleep" idea conveys a temporary situation of a complete absence of consciousness and willpower to be then interrupted as an alarm wakes a person from natural sleep to return to normal living. "Shall we not think that He will preserve the soul in such a way that even though I do not know where I am, I nevertheless am in a definite place . . . It is certain that it is not an evil place . . . so after this life the souls of the righteous are in God's hand."[35]

Luther described the unconscious individuals in *Sheol* who are under the full control of God, as specifically consisting of the *lives* of these individuals. "We should entrust and commend to our true Savior and Redeemer ourselves, body, soul and life."[36] The Greek *psuche* is translated (in order of frequency in the KJV) as: soul, life, mind, and heart. Of course, Luther was very knowledgeable of biblical Greek, having translated from Greek to German, rather than from the Latin Vulgate (the official Bible), for the Luther Bible. What did Luther mean by "ourselves: body, soul, and life" being delivered over at death to the care of the Lord and Savior of the world? What distinction was he making by repeating *soul* and *life*? Luther grounds his assertion once again on the following scriptural claim: "Paul employs almost the same language ['place of refuge'] when he writes: 'Your life is hid with Christ in God' (Col 3:3)."[37] Why would Paul tell the church in Colossae that the life of a person is hid in God? It is probably because Paul knew what Luther knew about *Sheol, Hades,* and the nether region of souls, who Paul had called *sleepers* in death, and who had been gathered to their people. They were securely hidden from forces of evil and it is not, for Luther, just a deceased person's soul, but more specifically it is their unique life, in the sense of the effect of living life, that is there with Christ in God. The distinction Luther had made between *soul* and *life* is emphasized by saying that "their life is hidden with Christ in God and will be revealed in glory on the Last Day."[38] "Hence we must conclude that he holds in his hand the life [i.e., that was lived] of those who have died for if this power did not belong to

---

33. Brown and Mayes, *LW*, 68:26.
34. Cole, *Select Works of Martin Luther*, 1:349.
35. Pelikan and Hansen, *LW*, 8:317.
36. Lenker, *Luther's Church Postil Gospels*, 5:359.
37. Pelikan, *LW*, 13:84.
38. Pelikan, *LW*, 13:85.

him, he could not restore life."[39] It is very relevant to my claim later in this chapter for the reader to see the difference between a person's soul/mind (as a living entity) and a person's life (as a nonliving collection of memories, knowledge, attitudes, and wisdom).

Since Luther believed the soul is not in a conscious state there, this event on "the last day" involving a bodily resurrection, amounts to a glorious revealing of newly conscious people. But what is life like right before this awakening happens? Luther asked, "What, then, shall we suppose is the way in which the soul rests or lives? It undoubtedly has some way of its own in which it sleeps."[40] Regarding Genesis 26:2–5, Luther told his class in 1542 the following: "I hear in this passage that there is life in death and after death, and that there is a resurrection of the dead."[41] "There is a difference between the sleep or rest of this life and that of the future life . . . the soul does not *sleep* in the same manner."[42]

While he was using natural sleep as an example of a different kind of living, compared to our waking hours (in addition to living in the womb), Luther asked, "Would God not have more ways of living than these two, so that there is a life without life? Thus the soul can have some way of its own of living."[43] What Luther probably means by "a life without life" is that although the individual is completely without consciousness in gravedom, that does not mean there is not divine action applied to the mind of the deceased. A fetus, or even an infant, to use Luther's examples here, do not have much of a life, even though life is associated with them at that time. So, Luther is simply suggesting that another type of life may be what is planned for the dead.

Luther even told people, in the context of a funeral or the death of a famous person, that the deceased was even now communicating presently, in some sense, with God. Luther knew he could easily explain this apparent paradox of "being asleep while being not asleep" to the confused. One of the ways Luther explained this conundrum related different perspectives on time itself, on one hand, from the viewpoint of both God and of the unconscious person, and on the other hand, to those who are alive in this temporal world. Another way to explain "a life without a life" is to describe the divine activity on the contents of the person's mind during death (i.e., their *life* of memories and attitudes). Luther realized this mystery of death involves

---

39. Pelikan, *LW*, 13:85.
40. Pelikan and Hansen, *LW*, 5:74.
41. Pelikan and Hansen, *LW*, 5:75.
42. Pelikan and Hansen, *LW*, 5:75.
43. Pelikan and Hansen, *LW*, 5:76.

some divine process of communication with the mind of the deceased (as in our regular lives) even though the individual was in a most deep sleep. Consider how this mental interaction is described at Ezekiel 36:26 (GNT): "I will give you a new heart and a new mind. I will take away your stubborn heart of stone and give you an obedient heart."

Psalm 121 provides another good example where Luther's comments on verses 7 and 8 show that he conceptualized death as referring especially to the role God has in it for the purpose of preserving, or keeping one's soul (or the unique life of the person) for use on "the last day." Psalm 121:7–8 (NRSV) reads as follows: "The Lord will keep you from all evil; he will keep your life. The Lord will keep your going out and your coming in from this time on and forevermore." Instead of "your life" the NASB translates this part as "He will keep your soul." In the following quote, Luther shows these two verses to mean that God preserves the life or soul of a deceased person, now and forever, in the sense of all we do: "God keepeth thy life. . . . thou seemest to die, but indeed it is not so, because thy life . . . liveth. . . . He will preserve thee . . . To go out, is to go to the works of thy vocation. To come in again signifieth to return from labour and travail, to rest and quietness."[44]

It may be helpful to show how Jewish tradition, as seen in their targumim, had interpreted these passages in Psalm 121. The interesting move they had made was to explain *the Lord* as meaning in this particular context, *the word of the Lord*, as follows: "The Targum makes a significant comment at the beginning of the verse: 'The word of the Lord shall preserve thee from all evil: he shall preserve thy soul.' . . . The Targum paraphrases it ['the Lord'] that the Word of the Lord did so and so. . . . See a most striking indication that the authors of the Targum conceived of a personality attaching to the Word of the Lord."[45]

The Targum on Psalm 124:6–8 further explains this alternate exegesis; and it would be helpful to first quote the passage as follows: "Blessed be the Lord, Who has not given us to be torn by their teeth. Our soul has escaped as a bird out of the snare of the trapper; The snare is broken and we have escaped. Our help is in the name of the Lord" (NASB). Notice below how the Targum attempted to differentiate, in the context of Psalms 121 and 124, between "a statement from the Lord" and "a possession of the Lord consisting of words" which can be distinguished by giving this personal monograph an identifying name, as follows:

---

44. Vautroullier, *Commentary on the Psalms*, 156–57. The original English translation of Luther's Latin commentary from his lecture series on "Psalms 120–34 [was published in] London in 1577." Smith, "Complete List of Works of Luther in English," 495. A total of one hundred works in English were identified from 1526 to 1915.

45. Armfield, *Gradual Psalms*, 160–61.

The Targum again enlarges "Lord" (see above on Ps 121:7): "Our support is in the Name of the Word of the Lord, who made Heaven and earth." This is a most important instance of the introduction of the phrase "Word of the Lord;" because it tends to show that the authors of the Targum conceived of the "Word of the Lord" as a person, and not merely as an attribute, an emanation, or an abstraction. If in their phrase "the Word of the Lord" meant no more than "the declaration of the Lord," [or] "the saying of the Lord," they could hardly have spoken of its "Name."[46]

What is the nature of this divine activity in *Sheol* that consists of something similar to brain activity but without a brain (since it perished)? Exactly where are the souls of the deceased? Luther grounds his claim that addresses these questions eventually. First, on Paul's assertion in Colossians 3:3 that the contents of a deceased person's mind, which amounts to their personal life and its events, etc., is hidden with Christ in God. Also, Luther quoted Psalm 4:8 by writing, "In peace I will both lie down and sleep, for You have put me in good safety."[47] That the deceased dwell in a high level of security in the afterlife, immediately after death, is Luther's emphasis here.

There is a notable lecture on Psalm 90 Luther gave in 1534 and published in 1541, which is purportedly written by Moses himself. If that attribution is truthful, then it is very likely that Moses's claim in Psalm 90:1 is also as truthful as his more well-known claim that both sets of the stone tablets containing the ten commandments were actually divinely engraved at the mountaintop. (Recall that Moses intentionally broke the first set in anger.) Luther first quoted Psalm 90:1 and then followed it with his comment: "'Lord, Thou art our dwelling place from generation to generation (Ps 90:1)'. . . Who would call God a Dwelling Place of the dead? Who would think Him to be a tomb or a cross? He is Life."[48] Evidently, the writer of Psalm 90 was relaying divine information that YHWH, the God of Israel transliterated from Hebrew, was, is, and will be a dwelling place for people. Luther continued by saying, "God is our Dwelling Place, and not earth, not heaven, not Paradise, but simply God Himself. And indeed He is that 'from

---

46. Armfield, *Gradual Psalms*, 198–99.

47. Mayes and Langebartels, *LW*, 75:46n57. In his sermon titled, "First Sunday in Advent (Matt 21:1–9)," the 1540 version is shorter by omitting the quoted part ("death is also called a sleep"), but the 1522, 1528, and 1532 versions add, 'of which the psalm speaks: "In peace I will both lie down and sleep; for You have put me in good safety" (Psalm 4:8). Therefore, death is also called a sleep in Scripture.'"

48. Pelikan, *LW*, 13:83–84.

generation to generation.' This means that from the beginning of the world to the end of the world God has never deserted His own."[49]

Between the point of death and the point of our resurrection, where did Luther think the enfolded souls were actually located? Is it supposed to be in the middle of heaven or on the edge of it somewhere? Althaus described Luther's use of equating Abraham's bosom to the word of God, in the sense of where a soul/mind exists during death, as such: "The traditional doctrines said much about the various places where the souls of the dead were. Topographical maps of the intermediate state were available. Luther criticizes them very sharply and proceeds from topographical to theological discussions in the certainty that all who die in faith have their 'place' in God's word."[50]

Luther believed that this collection of unconscious minds was somehow compressed, but in a non-spatial sense and said in 1534 that "the souls of the righteous are in the hand of God."[51] In a 1521 sermon, the young Luther asked the following question, after saying where specifically souls of the deceased are presently situated: "The location is at the hand of God rather than on a sphere like earth. Do you think that God cannot preserve souls in His hand? Or do you think that He must have a physical stall, as a shepherd does for his sheep?"[52] What does at "the hand of God" actually mean from the divine perspective, rather than within the mind of Luther at a young age? Before making my claim, recall how Luther described the literal place that holds the actual contents of each deceased person's mind (i.e., their "life is hid with Christ in God" from Col 3:3).

Althaus wrote that Luther was certain "that all who die in faith have their 'place' in God's *word*."[53] In a 1522 sermon, Luther said that the deceased "went into the bosom of Abraham; they fell asleep in the words of God."[54] The soul of the deceased is located at a literal place that Luther describes as *words*. What did he mean? "Abraham's bosom is the words of God."[55] It is possible that *Sheol/Hades* or gravedom consists of the words of God. The words of God do not necessarily have to be a proclamation from God, but instead could mean a receptacle (or a storage) of words or thoughts once contained within someone's mind that God is now processing for future

---

49. Pelikan, *LW*, 13:85.
50. Althaus, *Theology of Martin Luther*, 412.
51. Althaus, *Theology of Martin Luther*, 412.
52. Mayes and Langebartels, *LW*, 75:109.
53. Althaus, *Theology of Martin Luther*, 412.
54. Mayes and Langebartels, *LW*, 75:62.
55. Mayes and Langebartels, *LW*, 75:62.

use. *Words* could have been the closest translation to data, code, digitized ideas, or something similar. The translator of Luther's German (or Latin) chose "words." However, a modern term for this thought could be "code." For some people who are familiar with computer software or with basic biology, "code" describes it perhaps much better than "words."

Hans Schwarz may be helpful in showing how he interprets the visionary Reformer on this question of where Luther would locate the souls of the dead. Schwarz writes that "Luther was especially interested in knowing where the souls of the saved would be. . . . The 'place' in which the soul of man remains and rests until judgment day is the Word of God."[56] Schwarz sees this "word" itself as "the receptacle of the souls in which they rest . . . [in] the place [of] the bosom of Christ into which the souls of believers now enter at death. . . . Luther finds another term for the 'place' of the souls of the dead in his exegesis of the Old Testament . . . the Hebrew *Sheol* . . . and interprets it as . . . the receptacle of the soul."[57] Schwarz tries to clarify this concept of Luther's by saying that "after death the soul does not rest in a spatial place but in the Word of God. One could say that, according to Luther, the abode of the soul is simply within the dimension of God."[58] So, what does this actually mean?

It is rare in books about Luther that an author describes or even mentions this "non-spatial receptacle in God for unconscious souls," as Schwarz has done. And it is even more rare when an explanation is given about this Luther idea to help make sense out of it. Schwarz is a Lutheran theologian and preacher who has been a systematic theology professor in Germany, Italy, the Czech Republic, and the United States. His special interests include the theologies of the Reformers of the sixteenth century. But, something came to me a few years ago and so I want to express it, if I may be so bold to make a suggestion on what Luther was aiming for, as follows.

My claim about death and resurrection

A description of my assertion begins here and continues until the end of this chapter with one more section on Luther's thoughts also in this chapter. I

---

56. Schwarz, "Luther's Understanding of Heaven and Hell," 90. His endnote identifies the following as his source regarding the word being where the soul of the deceased rests: "WA 10, III, 191, 13ff."

57. Schwarz, "Luther's Understanding of Heaven and Hell," 90. His endnote identifies the following as his source regarding Sheol being the receptacle for the soul: "WA 4, 23, 2–6."

58. Schwarz, "Luther's Understanding of Heaven and Hell," 91.

would claim that the scriptural writers have repeatedly referred to the idea that symbolizes the divine method God has chosen for executing the death and resurrection of those created in God's image with the use of the concept of *Sheol*. The main aspect of "Sheol/hades/gravedom" is a computer-like storage apparatus, similar to the book of life (see Revelation 20:12, "books were opened; and another . . . the book of life") and is the specific way God fulfills the promise of eternal life, the renewing of our soul for the next heavenly life, and bodily resurrection for all. The "words of God" from Luther and the Targum are descriptive of the contents of *Sheol*. I would claim there is a direct relationship between this information in *Sheol* and human beings—both living and deceased.

For a given individual who has died, the contents of their mind (consisting of memories, attitudes, etc.) may have been recorded during their life onto a divine device or media. One of the main aspects of this claim is the suggestion that it is an unconscious copy that resides in heaven rather than a neoplatonic soul being the vehicle for transporting our mind to the presence of God prior to the last day. I am suggesting that copying the data within the mind for transport using the Spirit of God is the divine method rather than a preservation of that same information within a person's own soul. The copying function can be seen in modern biology where bodily cells replicate themselves including the duplication of DNA and its massive amount of information within each cell.

The electronic copying function for documents and photos is widely familiar today with anyone who has used a personal computer or a smartphone. It is this tremendous growth in information technology and the increase in widespread knowledge of biology that improves the chances that regular people today can readily grasp this idea, compared to a half-century ago and earlier, of easily copying very large amounts of data. It is rather clear from Luther's attempts to explain the "where and how" of death and resurrection that he was at a loss for describing the particular method used by God although he seemed rather certain of what it is not. Luther had said he did not know *how* this is done, but that it just *was being done*, when he had reached the limits of his understanding regarding mind preservation in God's receptacle of souls.

After the return of Jesus, the parousia would consist of our actual physical presence with God. The reason Luther repeatedly emphasized "death as sleep" and being awakened at the last day was because he saw in Scripture an emphasis on the resurrection of the dead. The relevancy and importance of my particular claim relates to Luther's claim about "death as unconscious sleep" by interpreting *sleep* in a certain metaphorical way, rather than thinking of a neoplatonic, ghostlike soul that literally falls asleep. I found no indication that Luther held to the belief (he may have had in his youth) that the soul literally exits the body at death in the typical sense that Plato and Augustine taught. Instead, his writings show his willingness to leave those views behind him. My claim in this chapter extends Luther's understanding of death and resurrection by showing the technological difference between the sixteenth and twenty-first centuries regarding the duplication and storing of information.

Althaus noticed Luther's use of *words* (or today, *code* would better indicate the sense of it), and Althaus compared it to what actually enfolds a deceased person's mind within Luther's "receptacle" of souls in heaven. He quotes Luther as saying that "all of the fathers who lived before the birth of Christ have gone to Abraham's bosom . . . and they have all fallen asleep, are preserved and protected in this word, and sleep in it until the Last Day as though this word were a bosom."[59] Luther believed the mind of a deceased person exists unconsciously within an enclosed space of some sort and is preserved and embraced by words, or the code God uses to symbolize a person and their life.

By updating "the book of life" references that both the OT and NT writers used, one can possibly determine the various purposes for it. By supplementing the common understanding of the book of life (i.e., a record of names and deeds performed by each person) to also include a record of our thoughts and memories, their purpose for repeating it in Scripture can be better understood. Just as the young Luther developed his skill at biblical exegesis by elevating the importance and frequency of the literal/historical way of reading a particular passage (in contrast to excessive symbolism then evident), one's understanding today of the book-of-life idea can benefit from our culture and technology. My claim in this chapter suggests that a literal reading of this divinely inspired idea would be appropriate, and for seeing how God may keep track of everyone born into this world over the centuries. The relevancy of the following excursion into nature and technology can be seen in my claim here that God's book of life may contain a massive amount of information for each person's soul, or the contents of their mind over time. It would be helpful to emphasize how information has been used by both people and God as follows.

Our "genetic information, also known as our genome, can be described as the 'Book of Life.' This book can be thought of as being made up of two volumes, each volume of the book is given to a person by one of their parents."[60]

---

59. Althaus, *Theology of Martin Luther*, 412n42. Althaus cites WA 10, III, 191 in his footnote.

60. Centre for Genetics Education, "Fact Sheet 1,"

A human being has forty-six chromosomes which consist of long strings of genes, or twisted DNA chains. Each of the 22,000 genes (on average) in a single chromosome within the microscopic cell of a body contains genetic information in the form of a chemical code, which is like an instruction or recipe book. The code is made up of four "letters" and each "word" is a combination of these letters. This allows for billions of different combinations when combining various words. "If all the DNA compacted into a cell were stretched out, it would be about seven feet long."[61] There may be hundreds of three-letter words (or even thousands) in the information in a gene coding. There are 3.2 billion sets of genetic letters, or base pairs, that make up the human genome.[62] "If you took the DNA from all the cells in your body [35–100 trillion of them] and lined it up, end to end, it would form a strand 6,000 million miles long [or 60 billion miles]."[63] Through the progress of science, we can point to examples that clearly show that the Creator God has the actual ability to store massive amounts of information that is directly related to a human being's life.

Consider the methodology people have developed in information technology over the last two thousand years and then apply this situation to Sheol/gravedom in the divine realm. The codex replaced the scroll and wax tablet, the book was an improvement on the first codex, and then other technologies advanced the storage capability of various media. Decades ago microcard and microfiche storage led the way eventually to the computer with hard disk drive (HDD) storage, which then led to the widespread use of solid-state drive (SSD), or small flash drives (or "thumb drives"), for even higher density of information storage.

This advance in computing capability can also be seen in the power of supercomputers. Consider the increase in performance of various types of supercomputers worldwide and a rethinking of the concept of Sheol/gravedom, as being a mass-storage apparatus of data or words, of God. The Cray-1 supercomputer, first delivered in 1976 (and prior to the first personal computer), was one of the most successful supercomputers (having sold about 100 units), and it had a performance rating of 160 megaflops, or MFLOPS. The fastest US supercomputer in 2012, from Cray, is rated at 18 PFLOPS; but the fastest in 2016, from China, is rated at 93 PFLOPS. There is a huge difference between one megaflop and one petaflop.

---

61. Science Clarified, "Genes and DNA."

62. See the National Institute of General Medical Sciences, National Institutes of Health, U.S. Dept. of Health and Human Services, "Genetics by the Numbers." Posted online by Chelsea Toledo and Kirstie Saltsman on June 12, 2012.

63. University of Leicester (in England), "DNA, Genes and Chromosomes."

The increase in less than fifty years in the computing speed of supercomputers equates to a factor of about one billion ([1 PFLOP, 10^{15}] − [1 MFLOP, 10^6] = 10^9 or one billion). In the world of personal computers, today's highest capacity HDD can hold about ten terabytes of information. However, the storage capacity of God's computer, if you will, may be upwards of 100 brazillion terabytes. A brazillion is so much bigger than a trillion that nobody has defined it yet, but it probably is bigger than a billion Brazils. It likely is an infinitude with no limit.

The point of all this computer and DNA discussion is to remind us that God has the ability to remember us in great detail, and that it is more believable today due to our technological culture. Additionally, Luther did not have the ability to imagine a supercomputer rating or three billion letters in the human genome that could make sense to him in the context of a *Sheol* receptacle containing sleeping souls and the contents of their minds. Recall that the scriptural writers had asserted that God knows the number of hairs on anyone's head, at any point in time (Matt 10:30 and Luke 12:7) through the Holy Spirit. A further implication of these biblical texts can relate to God having access within heaven to everyone's unique genetic information in their genes for the purpose of bodily resurrection.

The divine technique established prior to Adam and Eve for uploading the current number of hairs on your head, or the lovingkindness displayed to a friend, likely involves the Spirit of God and a functional spirit-material interface inside the brain. One aspect of a possible meaning of "being made in the image of God" (from the very first chapter of the Bible) is that, unlike animals or even Neanderthals, all humans today have the literal capability within their brain of talking to their Creator, and being heard, through the indwelling Spirit for the possibility of establishing a real relationship with the One who loves each individual ever born.

The prophets of the OT have referred to the book of life either directly or indirectly multiple times, along with Philippians 4:3 and the book of Revelation. This particular record of information has been known since the days of King David 3,000 years ago to contain not just the names of people, but also their deeds; and this data can be blotted out or completely deleted with a tap, click, or swipe in heaven today. To make this particular thesis claim involves a challenge to the Hellenized assumptions of Socrates and Plato, and then, Augustine and other philosophical theologians of the last five hundred years regarding innate immortality of the soul as a natural characteristic of everyone born in the world. To object to the scheme of information centralization by the Creator God, compared to a neoplatonic method of decentralization of the mind of an escaped soul at bodily death, would need further clarification in our twenty-first-century age of computer technology and smartphones everywhere.

The purpose of God having an unconscious copy of the soul/mind within our head includes bodily resurrection, divine forgiveness of sins, and judgment at the throne of God. Although God would not need to have all this information written down somewhere, being God, and being able to remember everyone, there are advantages to sharing this information. For example, Scripture repeatedly tells us about who specifically will be expected to carry out the process of judgment of people. This task has been delegated from the Father to the Son. Therefore, the deeds of people are not solely retained in the vast mind of the Father, but instead, may have been recorded in the famous book of life for use at judgment day as the Bible clearly teaches us (e.g., Rev 20:12). Recall that Jesus tells his followers that his heavenly Father holds certain information (such as the timing of the last day) that the Son did not know. It also is quite likely the case that a person's DNA information is also recorded for the purpose of bodily resurrection by the Son of God, who is described as the person of the trinity who carried out creation at his Father's direction. Therefore, it also seems likely that the contents of a person's mind, subject to some removal due to divine forgiveness, is also stored safely in heaven for the purpose of the resurrection of their soul/mind, and then joining this software to the hardware of the newly recreated body. The resurrection likely follows our DNA blueprint, but with some adjustments, so that everyone can recognize those in their community and social circles.

To summarize, this process could entail the following (in inverse order):

1. A bodily resurrection that seems like waking up from sleep;
2. Preceded by a downloading of information gathered throughout a person's life from Sheol into a newly reconstituted adult brain;
3. Preceded by a divine editing process within Sheol of removing irrelevant memories and attitudes according to the plan of God (similar to a Microsoft Word document);
4. Preceded by divine forgiveness of sin consisting of a complete removal of the offending details from God's record of us; and
5. Preceded by an uploading of data from the living brain to the book of life within Sheol after a translation into a divine language (consisting of code or words) from the brain's neural impulses.

If someone objects to the shareable record of the contents of everyone's mind over the last 6,000 years or so, this information may instead be kept only inside the mind of God. It is possible that God's remembrance of everyone's life in great detail may be within God's vast mind, rather than outside it. However, it may be necessary for this data to be recorded outside it to allow other divine beings in the unseen realm easy access to it for whatever purpose.

It seems *soul* is an ambiguous term in today's usage that in some contexts refers to our eternal identity, while in other contexts, it refers to that which is deep inside our head or our heart, symbolically speaking. Therefore, a human being has, what I call, an interior soul, which provides identity and uniqueness, and is the mind of the person. Additionally, the same person has an exterior soul—a copy of the interior soul—but it is not a person. The exterior soul in Sheol is unconscious bits of data that mirror the mind in somebody's head except for the memories that have been divinely forgiven and completely removed. Furthermore, with humans being higher animals at just a basic level (in the sense of quite similar DNA) that were selected by the Creator God to be specially made in the image of God, people have a potentiality of communication and relationship with God that animals do not have.

The likely method God has chosen, for purposes of full control forever throughout the entire universe, and guaranteed sovereignty over evil, is one of complete centralization in God the triune, and not one outside of heaven and subject to the forces of evil. The traditional belief, following neoplatonism, is that a person's mind is based within a ghostlike spirit that yearns to be freed from its bodily cocoon, either through a dream in natural sleep or at death. If Plato was wrong about the indestructability of the soul within us and its independence from the crown jewel of creation—the human brain—and Aristotle was instead closer to the truth as God sees it, then Luther's use of sleep in its metaphorical sense would make sense.

The other side of the coin, regarding a redefinition of soul, is that all human beings also have their own external soul (again, which is an unconscious copy of their internal soul). In combining Luther's description of Sheol with Rashi's observation of the grammar in the Hebrew Bible that there may be a double creation of Adam, and Paul's emphasis of a bodily resurrection, we can imagine this word-based, external soul living within the pages of the book of life. It is held securely with Christ, and previously with Abraham as Luther saw it, in a close relationship between this information and God, similar to the bosom embrace many people provide for their smartphone and its data. We are dependent on God for our very existence after our death, yet we can be assured of the security and functionality of

God's plan for bodily resurrection since the process has been successfully tested on the God-man named Jesus Christ.

Letting Luther speak more on death

Let's return now to Luther for an assessment of his further statements on this matter. God prepares for the last day by "making the person altogether new."[64] A person's growth, consisting of an "increase of grace and righteousness,"[65] continues beyond death into the intermediate state between the point of death and "the Last Day. Only at the bodily resurrection will this be finished."[66] Therefore, said Luther, "we must conclude that he holds in his hand the life of those who have died for if this power did not belong to him, he could not restore life."[67] Since restoring life was meant to be a literal expression by him, Luther may also have used the phrase "holds in his hand the life" in a literal way since the two ideas are contiguous in the same sentence. The enhancement of a person's character—even after death during a deep sleep—that Luther discussed is attained not by experience in the afterlife prior to resurrection, but through an act of God. "We do not yet see the life which we attain through godliness."[68]

"When we die, this does not really mean death but seed sown for the coming summer. And the cemetery or burial ground does not indicate a heap of the dead, but a field full of kernels, known as God's kernels, which will verdantly blossom forth again and grow more beautifully than can be imagined."[69] Luther continues:

> And note well that Paul refrains from calling those "dead" who will rise after Christ. No, he says that Christ is "the Firstfruits of those who have fallen asleep." [Luther is quoting Paul there] And yet he says that Christ arose, not from sleep but "from the dead." For what was a true and eternal death prior to this and without Christ is now, since Christ has passed from death to life and has arisen, no longer death; now it has become merely a sleep. And so the Christians who lie in the ground are no longer called dead, but sleepers, people who will surely also arise again.[70]

64. Jacobs and Spaeth, *Works of Martin Luther*, 1:58.
65. Jacobs and Spaeth, *Works of Martin Luther*, 1:58.
66. Jacobs and Spaeth, *Works of Martin Luther*, 1:58.
67. Lenker, *Luther's Church Postil Gospels*, 5:358.
68. Pelikan and Hansen, *LW*, 29:10.
69. Oswald, *LW*, 28:178.
70. Oswald, *LW*, 28:109–10.

Luther imagined this situation as a major part of the plan of God for restoration and he said that "it is not difficult for Christ, in the hour when body and soul are separated to hold in his hand the soul and spirit of man, even though we ourselves neither feel nor see anything, yea, even though the body be entirely consumed."[71] Did Luther understand a large collection of souls being held in the hand of Christ in the literal sense of miniature representations of people's uniqueness? Regarding Luther's use of "spirit" in the quote above, he quickly showed in this sermon (and on the same page) that he understood this literal spirit to be God's life-giving "breath of life." "Christ can preserve the breath of life and spirit apart from the body."[72] Regarding Luther's use of "when body and soul are separated," it is necessary to keep this phrase in the context that Luther intended it. Recall that while the body goes to the grave, the soul/mind seems to go, or to put it more precisely, it becomes present exclusively in heaven according to Luther (who placed Sheol in heaven). Once the reader sees this distinction in Luther, the above quote does not indicate his adherence to a neoplatonic, or a traditionally dualistic, belief. Luther is saying here that however a person exists in Sheol, the soul/mind can be preserved without the body present. The effect of God's work there on the unconscious person (who has lost normal personhood) is that there is "no possession of any capacity of feeling."[73] Luther described this holding place as consisting of a divine maintenance activity, and he was "assured that we shall not lose it ['our life'], but be truly and carefully preserved in his hand, maintained and again restored."[74] When we die, "this does not really mean death but seed sown for the coming summer."[75]

Usually *death* is taken to mean by Luther a total death with no life remaining (like for an insect or fish) for example, when he states the following: "You seem to die, but indeed it is not so, because your life . . . lives. . . . The Lord shall preserve your life . . . and keep you."[76] Here is another example of this: "As you and I see it, Abraham is dead, but Christ says: 'He is not dead to Me, for I have grasped him in such a way that I am his God.'"[77] Luther has provided several examples throughout his writings that could appear as contradictions to the "death as sleep" concept. However, he simultaneously held to an understanding of Sheol or gravedom that consists of operational

---

71. Lenker, *Luther's Church Postil Gospels*, 5:358.
72. Lenker, *Luther's Church Postil Gospels*, 5:358.
73. Luther, "Letter 111," 360.
74. Lenker, *Luther's Church Postil Gospels*, 5:359.
75. Oswald, *LW*, 28:178.
76. Vautroullier, *Commentary on the Psalms*, 156–57.
77. Brown and Mayes, *LW*, 68:26.

activity of some sort within the mind of the deceased. "Souls hear, think, see after death, but how they do it we do not understand. . . . If we think of it in terms of this life, we are fools. Christ has nicely solved it."[78] It would be foolish to ascribe to Luther the belief that the senses of a deceased person operate the same way they do in normal life during waking hours (including conscious "thinking" right after death). "There is a difference between the sleep or rest of this life and that of the future life . . . the soul does not sleep in the same manner."[79] Luther's use of this symbolic reference to sleep is not to be taken by the reader as indicating they are mostly similar. For Luther, the only similarities between sleep during death and natural sleep in our world is the lack of consciousness and being awakened from it. The main difference is that death's sleep is so much deeper than someone's sleep at night that it is like the difference between an unborn fetus's life in the womb and the life of a typical adult in the world, to use Luther's analogy. "The sleep in the future life is deeper than it is in this life."[80]

Another example of this is seen in the next quote from Luther's lectures on Genesis 26 in 1542. "Abraham is living, serving God, and ruling with Him. But what the nature of that life is, whether he is asleep or awake, is another question. We do not have to know how the soul rests. It is certain that it is alive."[81] To explain this statement above to his students, Luther immediately used the example of dreaming during natural sleep to illustrate the apparent contradiction. "When I am sleeping, I am not aware of being alive; for my senses and even reason itself do not perform their functions. . . . If we were alive while sleeping, we would be able to think in our sleep: 'I am in this house, in this bedroom.' . . . Accordingly, this is an important sign that I am alive and yet am not alive."[82] The "Luther paradox on death" is alive and well today partly because people have not been sufficiently exposed to Luther's own explanations of his claim in the quote above regarding a deceased soul being "alive" in some sense.

When Luther said that Abraham is living and serving God, he meant *living* in the sense used in the previous quote ("If we were [normally] alive while sleeping"). It is a very different kind of life, is the main point. Luther used the example of the huge difference between the life of an unborn baby and an adult. Similarly, the difference between life in this world and life in Sheol is drastic in its basic nature. Luther continued as follows: "What,

---

78. Plass, *What Luther Says*, 384.
79. Plass, *What Luther Says*, 384.
80. Plass, *What Luther Says*, 384.
81. Pelikan and Hansen, *LW*, 5:74.
82. Pelikan and Hansen, *LW*, 5:74.

then, shall we suppose is the way in which the soul rests or lives? It undoubtedly has some way of its own in which it sleeps."[83] Luther had showed that the unconscious soul of the deceased was serving a divine purpose in Sheol, but Luther was at the limits of his understanding. "We understand far less what the nature of that life after death is. Nevertheless, it is sure that we are living."[84] I would suggest that through the divine editing process of the words that symbolize our very soul, we are still interacting with God, still functioning in a sense, even though there is not true consciousness as provided by the neuron network of a brain.

For Luther, discussion of death often accompanied a reminder of the general resurrection. "The dead can be awakened upon a single word of Christ. They sleep much more lightly than natural sleep."[85] This may seem like a contradiction where a light sleeper is sleeping deeply. However, Luther was the type of teacher who enjoyed explaining the conundrums he had created. "For since we call it a sleep, we know that we shall not remain in it but be again awakened and live."[86] Although Luther occasionally made statements—or hinted with a single word—he usually chose to be ambiguous (but not always) on unusual conceptions of soul immortality probably due to the larger social-religious context as related to the public reaction to the even-more radical reformers (i.e., the Anabaptists).[87] Christ "leads us out of the death and grave of sin to the resurrection of spirit and body."[88] Here we see that Luther told the assembled church that it was probably not just the physical body that will be resurrected, but the *spirit* too. His specific meaning here is unclear regarding his use of *spirit*, but I assume he had recognized Scripture's occasional distinction between *soul* and *spirit* (i.e., when both are used in the literal and anthropological sense). The life-giving spirit of God, the breath of life, the power of God literally supports a human's life and animates its bodily cells. It is this type of *spirit* that Ecclesiastes 12:7

83. Pelikan and Hansen, *LW*, 5:74.
84. Pelikan and Hansen, *LW*, 5:75.
85. Luther, *House-Postil*, 277.
86. Lenker, *Luther's Church Postil Gospels*, 5:359.

87. Both the Calvinists and the Lutherans (not to mention the Catholics) strongly objected to the radical reformers (e.g., Menno Simons) who had spread throughout much of Europe. The strength of the objections by these many Protestants is reflected by the lengths they took, which included death by drowning and by fire for the radicals (Calvin and Zwingli themselves were complicit), against the despised Anabaptist Christians. One of the offending beliefs held near-universally by them as a result of the widespread radical reformation of the sixteenth century included the unconscious sleep of the soul during death, or more specifically, the nonexistent soul/mind (as a person) except as it is held in God until the resurrection of the dead back to conscious life.

88. Lenker, *Luther's Epistle Sermons*, 3:153.

refers to when it says the spirit "returns" to heaven at death after separating from its body. The Hebrew word for *spirit* is used in this passage rather than the one used for *soul*.

It could be the case this Luther quote above on the *spirit* may have referred to the heavenly resurrection of the spirit-copy of our mind. I suppose it is possible that Luther used "spirit and body" in the sense of "soul and body" since the neoplatonic view of the spirit-soul was common then. However, his use of *spirit* above does not typically reflect back on a traditionally dualistic soul because Luther very rarely spoke this way throughout his adult life. The next chapter examines Luther's several brief forays that challenged Plato's view of the soul's innate immortality.

The next quote of Luther supports his view of death as oftentimes for Luther meaning permanence or complete death. "He [Paul] says that Christ arose, not from sleep but 'from the dead.' For what was a true and eternal death prior to this and without Christ is now, since Christ has passed from death to life and has arisen, no longer death; now it has become merely a sleep. And so the Christians who lie in the ground are no longer called dead, but sleepers, people who will surely also arise again."[89] It was important to Luther to urge people to believe, or just to remind others, that the general resurrection involves physical bodies. "Since Christ can preserve us, so he can again bring the body together out of dust and ashes."[90]

"Our bodies become new and become alive again";[91] so at our resurrection, a person is "completely born . . . [and] only then will they put on the clothes of immortal life."[92] In determining the meaning of this proposition, it is especially necessary to know how Luther spoke or wrote about this subject of immortal bodies and immortal souls (which appears in the next chapter). By saying "only then" in his reference to Paul's use of finally putting on immortality, it appears Luther was possibly ruling out the belief that everyone is born with a spirit-soul within them that is indestructible and immortal. Luther described Sheol as "a field full of kernels, known as God's kernels, which will verdantly blossom forth again and grow."[93] Luther rarely spoke in terms of a neoplatonic description of a ghostlike entity (i.e., the soul) leaving the body at death. His conception of the soul in Sheol was quite different than the usual view of death as Plato, Augustine, Aquinas, and others had put it. Pomponazzi pointed out when Luther was very young that Aquinas

89. Oswald, *LW*, 28:109–10.
90. Lenker, *Luther's Church Postil Gospels*, 5:358.
91. Mayes and Langebartels, *LW*, 75:109.
92. Jacobs and Spaeth, *Works of Martin Luther*, 1:58.
93. Oswald, *LW*, 28:178.

disagreed with Aristotle on this point, who was opposed to Plato's conception of a soul that is indestructible and naturally immortal from birth.

Luther wrote the following, "After leaving this life the godly enter their chamber or bed, in which they sleep and rest until body and soul are again united in the future."[94] Nevertheless, the reunification of body and soul did not mean for Luther that when they separated at death, this involved an aware and functioning soul leaving its shell. Chapter 9 will explore whether Luther believed the transitional period of Sheol may be described not as just unawareness by the soul but that the mind (or internal soul) ceases to exist as a real-life person until resurrection stands them on their feet again and returns to normal life. The last chapter will attempt to show the reader that Luther rejected the view of innate immortality of the soul as Plato saw it and as many people do today.

Returning to my claim

We know from Scripture, such as John 3:16, that Jesus Christ promised "*life*" for whoever believes in him. A believer's status following their death, regarding actually receiving this gift of eternal life in a literal way would be dependent on God's action. I doubt that Scripture is telling us that everyone born already has the characteristic of eternal life for their soul and regardless of whether they believe. Check out my website, John-3-16.org, for a discussion on why Jesus used the word "*perish*" in that passage. I believe that the soul/mind, or interior soul (as I call it), of everyone who tastes physical death actually perishes when the body dies. What remains of us, though, is our exterior soul located in God which is an unconscious copy of our mind over our lifetime for divine use at the last day, I would claim. Did Luther interpret "*sleep*" as being used metaphorically by the writers of Scripture to describe death? The next chapter answers this question. According to this view, a biblical claim in a quote of Jesus of "she is not dead (i.e., in a complete sense of being dead), but is only sleeping," prior to bringing a deceased person's soul/mind back to life, and back into existence, would be an example of using natural sleep as a metaphor for describing death and subsequent resurrection. For someone who objects to this "exterior soul" idea of mine, and who has already rejected Plato's view, neoplatonism, and substance dualism, then consider the following question. If it is true that the soul/mind inside someone's body, and the body itself, both perish at death, then how would God recreate that person such that identity is sustained in the next stage of heavenly existence? This question is relevant for critical

---

94. Pelikan and Hansen, *LW*, 7:293.

analysis given the long-established, alternative view of the soul being the vehicle for transporting our uniqueness or personality across death's doorway.

If the human mind, apart from the body, was divinely created to eventually relinquish its functionality (i.e., literal death) as payment for sinful choices (recall from Scripture that the wage "for sin is death"), then a resurrection of that redeemed person who chose to sin is based on some particular method. If it is the plan of God to enact total death of sinners, rather than partial death (just the body), then Scripture may be helpful in seeing that such an illogical idea (philosophically speaking) of bodily resurrection (as seen from Paul's experience with the church in Corinth) can actually make sense. It is likely that if personal memory is not a continuous function after death (i.e., the soul/mind also dies), then God has centralized it by having our significant life experiences either copied onto something or just held within God's mind.

Consider for a moment how divine forgiveness of sin is described in Scripture. As far as the east is from the west, and washed as white as snow, paints a picture of complete forgiveness and a total elimination of certain transgressions. From what specifically is this erasing of information happening? Does it necessarily have to be the mind of God? A common phrase seen in Scripture regarding the removal of names and deeds is "blotting out" the ink on the scroll or the book. Today's description of this process could include a computer reference where a special delete key is pressed involving both the surface removal of the data and the backup storage of it hidden within the computer components.

When God hears a prayer of repentance through the Spirit, one analogy of forgiveness is that God hits the delete button and totally removes any thought of the particulars of that sin, or on the other hand, perhaps these offending thoughts reside in the mind of God. A question can then be raised about whether God intentionally forgets that which is divinely forgiven, or alternatively, if that sin which is completely deleted actually existed outside the mind of God, that is, in a book or computer file of some sort. Holding onto the assumption that the Almighty Creator of everything routinely forgets things everyday—due to requests for forgiveness of particular sins committed—can appear as inconsistent with the attribute of omniscience, meaning all-knowing, since God is perfect, not forgetful.

Therefore, it seems appropriate to utilize the many references in both the OT and NT to the "book of life," which includes King David in his psalms where he referred to deeds, and not just names, being in this record of life.[95]

---

95. See Exod 32:32–33; Deut 29:20; Pss 69:28; 51:9; Phil 4:3; Rev 3:5; 13:8; 17:8; 20:12, 15; 21:27. There are additional direct references in Scripture that do not use the phrase *book of life* (e.g., God blotting out one's name [erasing from the book], etc.).

Recall that the book of life *and other records* are used to judge people according to their works at the throne of God (Rev 20:12). It seems likely that these records of the lives of people do not just contain the names of people and their works (as we know from the Bible), but that perhaps it is even more than that. What would be the reason for God to disclose to various prophets the existence of a mega-scroll maintained in heaven, beyond judgment of the creation? Since Moses and the prophets repeatedly described death using the concept of Sheol as the place of the dead, which may consist of a copy of the mind of everyone, could there have been a dual purpose for the ubiquitous "book of life" idea? Since these people passed along messages from God and recorded them, much of ancient Israel knew about this destination of the dead being Sheol. On occasion, prior to the appearance of the Messiah, a biblical prophet would quote an oracle that alludes to a restoration of life from the grave. Perhaps some of them wondered if this divine scroll of life's deeds, minus the iniquities, also contained a person's thoughts as well. At any rate, it seems possible that a few of them pondered the use of God's detailed record of a person's life.

In the context of the OT era (regarding death being generally seen as the final end), why would an OT prophet regard God as preferring to utterly destroy people (i.e., the *heart* of a person perishing, that is, their mind) when God obviously had the option in the beginning of not doing this between death and resurrection? The probable reason God told some of his prophets about Sheol, or gravedom in heaven, is because another life had been planned by the Creator God. Another heavenly life awaited and probably would consist of physical bodies. Therefore, the Gospel message 2,000 years ago confirmed to the generation of Jesus the promise of another life to be lived, but without the permanent type of death occurring to them (as John 3:16 probably suggests with its "shall not perish").

It seems likely to me this divine promise was referring to a *literal* gift of eternal life. However, to those that believe the Gospel (and possibly others) God is offering a gift of actual, literal life beyond this world through his sheol-supercomputer, or "book of life." Consequently, this more protective and centralized method would not require our minds as being the vehicle to transport our uniqueness and identity to this other world. When this record of our lives is opened, as Revelation describes, its purpose may not only be for judgment but also for resurrection. This would be an immortality of the soul that is conditional on an act of God instead of everyone getting it naturally at birth.

What are the implications of Luther's "death as sleep" observation? What is the ramification to our resurrection being that point in time when a person (particularly their mind) finally obtains actual immortal status and eternal life, rather than it being obtained around birth? Could this sleep idea—and awakening from it—be possibly symbolizing a resurrection that returns a person (i.e., their mind) back into literal existence as a real-life person? Would it matter to God if the wicked could not be completely destroyed, but only held in prison for all eternity? It makes sense to me that God could prefer to use a literal "second death" (which may be a parallel to an obviously literal first death) within the confines of hell. The descriptions of "second death" seen in "the Revelation of Jesus Christ" (Rev 1:1) at both the beginning of the book at Revelation 2:11, and also near the end of the book at Revelation 20:6,14 and Revelation 21:8, is an emphasis that deserves pondering in the context of many real threats of destruction throughout Scripture. If the reader prefers to interpret "second death" as being only a spiritual death, rather than one that mirrors a literal first death that everyone must face, then consider what God had told Moses. If one were to read Deuteronomy and its pleas that urged the Israelites at the end of their long journey to make a choice for themselves ("life" or "death"), then due to individual accountability and fairness in divine judgment, this option of having a life even after dying could be convincing.

If the option of Christian physicalism is not excluded from an examination of the constitutional nature of humanity, then an extended analysis (including the nature of hell) may result in practical benefits for followers of Christ including the re-assessment of the perceived character of God. It can be comforting, sooner or later, to find out that our God is not a torturer that never stops tormenting the person who sinned too much. It is possible that by studying ourselves, as humans created by God, we also thereby can eventually know God more fully in terms of how God treats those who choose to finally reject God's grace and love. One of the effects of studying Luther on death is that it can eventually lead to challenging our common assumption that Scripture describes a God who would appear forever angry and unlovingly vindictive with those who exercised their apparent ability to make decisions and choices—a free will—to finally accept or reject God.

The rethinking of the nature of hell (in the context of rethinking the literal nature of a human being) by starting with the rethinking of death can arrive to the point where a determined reader of Scripture can more fully understand that "God *is* love."[96] Just showing divine love to some—but not to others eternally—is very different from *being* love. God could forever appear as the type of God that fully loves every single individual without the uneasiness of an unending torture chamber. The often-repeated divine threat seen throughout both the OT and NT regarding death and destruction to some or

---

96. See First John, chapter 4, verses 8 and 16 which both say, "God is love."

perhaps even to most could actually be carried out (in a literal hell). Because *eternal life* and *not perish* undoubtedly appear in John 3:16, the description of God's love in this passage probably is a real alternative to actual perishing occurring, given the context of many other passages.[97]

The foreknowledge by an evil person that their soul/mind will literally perish with their body again, due to an irreversible judgment—an eternal punishment—due to sinful choices would be quite excruciating, to the point of angry "weeping and gnashing of teeth" (as this exact phrase in this context of hell is found six times in just Matthew). The divine judgment that leads directly to the punishment of hell is described in Scripture as being everlasting because it is a final judgment that cannot be overturned. The punishment of hell seems to not just be "a separation from God" because many unbelievers had already lived their lives completely separated from God. Where is the justice in that kind of hell? How could that lame description of a terrible hell (as Jesus described it repeatedly) scare an atheist into reconsidering their denial of God (and thus their being already separated from God)?

Followers of the divine Christ may choose to continue holding on to the traditional view of hell and of the soul, or they may prefer to consider an alternative such as conditional immortality of the soul. Whether someone prefers to adhere to the traditional view of hell, or some other alternative, the most important thing to remember is (1) they are a brother in Christ or a sister in Christ who should be shown love and much patience, and (2) that Jesus instructed his followers to remember that the first commandment is to love God. To love God means to respect God, which leads to listening to God (through the prophets and the apostles) as the final authority, which can mean to read—and to carefully study—the Holy Scriptures themselves using various translations when needed. Even in disagreement about whether death consists of unconscious sleep, or whether God created the type of hell that may have been developed in the Middle Ages, the bottom line is whether or not only a few Christians are reviewing what all our holy book actually says about the subject. If these issues seen in my book prompt people to read the Bible more, then at least something valuable has been done.

---

97. "For God so loved the world that he gave his only Son, so that whoever believes in him may not perish but have eternal life." This is one of the Bible's most famous verses.

CHAPTER 9

Was Luther a Physicalist Regarding the Soul?

*Did Luther use sleep literally or symbolically
in the sense of mortality?*

The goal of this chapter is to provide the grounds, based mostly on quotes of Luther, for characterizing him as a type of physicalist, or mortalist, regarding theological anthropology of the Bible. We know Luther's constant assertion that death is like a sleep meant, for him, that the deceased person is without consciousness. But what exactly did he mean by that? We know that he meant more by it because in his sermons he occasionally went a couple steps beyond it—and sometimes much further in his lectures with his students.

When a Christian is described as a physicalist or a mortalist, that person disagrees with the dualistic view of body and soul where the soul is independent of the body. Rather, the belief is held that the capability and nature of the soul is fundamentally different such that the soul, or the soul/mind (as a biochemical product of the brain), is *not* independent of the body prior to the dissolution of the physical body (i.e., death). That is, the interior soul of a person perishes and actually dies with the death of the body. In a book published in the eighteenth century, Francis Blackburne, who was an archdeacon in the English Anglican church, wrote the following about the visionary Reformer: "Luther, says Cardinal Du Perron, held that the soul died with the body, and that God would hereafter raise both, the one and the other."[1] Cardinal Jacques Du Perron (1556-1618) was sent to Rome in 1604 as Charge d'affaires of France.

Luther had to be careful in his discussions of God creating a person such that they are mortal—both body and soul—and then capable of becoming immortal. It is understandable that we find relatively few quotes of Luther that

---

1. Blackburne, *Separate Existence of the Soul between Death and Resurrection*, 109.

discuss this mortality topic in explicit detail because of the cultural situation of sixteenth-century Europe regarding both Catholics and Protestants. Recall that a formal proclamation was issued near the start of Luther's career stating that the pope and the Western Church "condemn and reject all those who insist that the intellectual soul is mortal. . . . it is also immortal."[2] This 1513 papal bull from Rome commanded that university professors throughout the empire "make every effort to teach the truth of the Christian religion and to refute any philosophical arguments that challenged it, subject to punishment as a heretic."[3] This threat of death is an important point to remember when evaluating the nuance often seen within Luther's sermons and university lectures that touch on immortality and the nature of the soul.

Also recall from chapter 4 that Luther's persistent adversary, Eck (seen at *Luther in 1521*), employed a strategy "to put all non-Catholics into one heretical basket by arguing that the beliefs of Anabaptists [e.g., mortalism of the soul, adult baptism, etc.], whom both Lutherans and Catholics opposed, originated with Luther."[4] Consequently, the situation for Luther amounted to tremendous pressure from within the Lutheran Church, including from Melanchthon, his chief co-reformer, on Luther to consequently pick his battles astutely and choose his words wisely.

Although several published experts have put the label, *soul-sleep*, onto Luther's belief, I would say that may be a mistake because it is likely Luther would have objected. It should be emphasized that Luther rarely, if ever, wrote "soul sleep" or "sleep of the soul," as translated into English. Instead, he usually referred to it more generally by saying the deceased person fell asleep or that "death is like unconscious sleep." This may have been done to avoid association with Calvin's book in which he used the term, *soul-sleep*, at the beginning of his preface. Additionally, prior to this first theological book of Calvin's (published in 1534), it may have been because Luther's understanding of death was the soul/mind *perishes* with the body—rather than literally *sleeping*—based on what he said repeatedly.

Luther probably used this analogy of natural sleep in the metaphorical sense instead of using *sleep* in the literal sense. Clearly, Luther was not referring to the body (separate from the soul from a dualist perspective), nor was his interpretation of Scripture's use of *sleep*, in the context of literal death, also referring to the body alone. Obviously, Luther's explanations clearly demonstrate that when he says a person sleeps in death, he's

2. Roman Catholic Church, *Decrees of the Ecumenical Councils*, 605. See also Papal Encyclicals Online, http://www.papalencyclicals.net/Councils/ecum18.htm (at session eight). For a more full quote, see footnote 53 in chapter 3.

3. Roman Catholic Church, *Decrees of the Ecumenical Councils*, 605.

4. Hendrix, *Martin Luther: Visionary Reformer*, 163, 214.

referring to their soul, or their mind, that is unconscious until resurrection. He clearly made a distinction between the body and soul, related to their initial destination at death saying that the body goes to the grave, but the soul goes to Sheol instead.

The concept of potentially living forever can be seen at the beginning of the Bible regarding the reason Adam and Eve were banished from the garden of Eden such that they could no longer have access to the fruit of the tree of life (Gen 3:22–23). Then, at the end of the Bible (for example, at Revelation 2:7 in a message to the church located in Ephesus), we read that "to him who overcomes, I will grant access to eat of the Tree of Life which is in the Paradise of God." Combining the several references, including their contexts, in Revelation and in Genesis to this life-tree, it is likely that it and its life-giving fruit was originally meant to be taken literally because, for one reason, it was a literal banishment from the garden with this tree being identified in the biblical text as the reason.

It is critical to see the difference between a literal use of *sleep* and a metaphorical use. An example of a literal understanding of a sleeping soul is a ghost taking a long nap. Another example of a literal use (for someone who does not believe in ghosts) is a spirit-soul who has escaped its body at death but remains in an unconscious state for quite a while. However, a metaphorical use of *sleep* during literal death can suggest that the soul/mind dies with the body (while rejecting dualism's assumption of a spirit-soul). A metaphorical understanding of a sleeping soul uses the conception of unconsciousness during natural sleep to point to, as a metaphor, a complete lack of consciousness through non-existence as a person. Most of Christianity since Augustine sixteen centuries ago seems to have believed that a person's soul is innately immortal from birth. The opposite of innate immortality of the soul is the view that the soul is mortal and subject to disappearing when the body dies (except in God's memory). The mind may be completely dependent on brain neurons, and the traditional understanding of an independent spirit-soul may be unnecessary to account for fully functional persons in this world. A weakness in the argument in favor of the soul within a person being of an immaterial nature (i.e., the traditional view) is that observations of a brain-damaged person seem to complicate the dualistic theory that the invisible brain overrides the physical brain.

Now, let's see how the visionary Reformer explained "sleep during death" and what this meant to him in his reading of Scripture. Although only a portion of the writings of Luther were surveyed, I have found the following instances in primary sources that seem to suggest that Luther rejected traditional dualism of body and soul when these quotes are taken together. Based on my research, only two of the following sixteen quotes presently can be easily found in secondary sources (i.e., books and articles that are about Luther, rather than written directly by him), or online.

1 of 16: Luther pointed out (in the Promotion Disputation of Petrus Hegemon of 1545) that "it is another question whether the body and the mind are separate things." An alternate translation follows and includes its immediate context: "The entire church teaches . . . that in death the soul is separated from the body. But it is another question whether the body and soul are separate things."[5] What Luther is saying is that he does not uncritically accept the very common assumption that the literal essence of the soul within us is of a spirit nature or composed of a spirit-substance. Luther may be proposing the possibility that the soul/mind and the body/brain are not separate things (i.e., in contrasting a physical nature versus an immaterial nature within the person).

This probably means, for Luther, the soul is not separable at death in the same way the church taught. The Reformer may have been challenging the widely accepted view that the soul's nature allows it to function separately from its body (i.e., similar to a ghost) even during death because that could only happen if these two aspects of a person are not both physical. If Luther saw them as both being physical, that is, not "separate things," then he was implying with this question that the church teaching of traditional dualism could be false. Just questioning this ontology of a person shows that for Luther it is conceivable that the immediate fate of the soul/mind is similar to the body at death.

Luther was pushing back on the belief that "in death [an indestructible and aware] soul is separated from the body" which then needs an explanation to account for Luther's description of an unconscious soul of a deceased person being within the bosom embrace of Christ (since the soul is separated from the body there according to Luther). See chapter 8 for this explanation.

2 of 16: Luther preached a sermon in 1545 and said the following: "There he ['Isaiah' in Isa 26:19] says: 'Your dead shall live and rise with their bodies. You who lie beneath the earth, awake and shout!'. . . He speaks to the dead as if they were already *alive*. By this he wants to show that the resurrection from the dead is certain."[6] Luther's interpretation of this passage involves seeing that the writer understood death to not consist of consciousness or even normal life. Luther read the word *awake* in Isaiah to refer to awakening from the sleep of death. Also, we read there *shall live*, and Luther probably read it to mean that the deceased person—including their soul/

---

5. Lohse, *Martin Luther's Theology*, 326. See WA 39/2:354.
6. Brown, *LW*, 58:154.

mind (which is the relevant part of the whole person)—was dead. The basis for saying this is that Luther told his congregants at the time that it is "as if they were already alive." The mind of a deceased person could be dead, nonfunctional, and nonexistent, yet from the divine perspective that person could be already alive to God due to God knowing of their certain resurrection and becoming alive. Saying that the mind of the deceased was being spoken to by Isaiah as if resurrection had already happened shows us that Luther may have interpreted Isaiah 26:19 in a mortalist way.

Luther did not say "as if they were already *awake*" but instead used a word similar to *alive*. Therefore, this indicates he thought the deceased were dead until they become alive. The context of this quote of Luther (that is, Luther's quoting of Isaiah) shows that Luther was referring to the mind of the person which is that part that is capable of causing a person to "shout."

3 of 16: On the question of the timing of divine judgment of the unsaved, Luther pushed back against the belief that they are sent to hell immediately after dying. "Whether the souls of the ungodly are tortured immediately after death I am unable to affirm . . . In 2 Cor. 5:10 Paul says: 'For we must all appear before the judgment seat of Christ.' . . . It seems that they ['the ungodly'], too, are sleeping and resting; but I am making no positive statement."[7] This objection is, at least, noteworthy because he was questioning the traditional teaching that there was a judgment before Judgment Day. This is significant in the context of a mortality investigation because immediate torment in hell would usually necessarily presume consciousness. On the other hand, for someone who leans toward the view that the soul of the deceased is no longer alive (in the normal sense of the word), being sent to hell immediately upon death would be illogical.

4 of 16: In a university lecture on Psalm 7 very early in his teaching career, Luther asked his students, "Where does a man who hopes in God end up except in his own nothingness? But when a man goes into nothingness, does he not merely return to that from which he came? Since he comes from God and his own non-being, it is to God that he returns when he returns to nothingness."[8] Perhaps Luther had been reading Athanasius. Bishop Athanasius provided his view on the nature of human death as follows: "For the transgression of the [Gen 2] commandment was making them [Adam and Eve] turn back again according to their nature; and as they had at the beginning come into being out of non-existence, so were they now on the way to returning, through corruption, to non-existence

---

7. Pelikan and Hansen, *LW*, 4:314–15. See WA 43:361.
8. Althaus, *Theology of Martin Luther*, 111. See WA 5:168.

again."⁹ In the quote of Luther above, he twice refers to "a man" in addition to using "he" and "his" seven times. In not one of these nine opportunities does Luther suggest that he was referring to "his body" rather than to the man's soul/mind. Luther taught that the soul returns to nothingness, or oblivion, at death because the origin of the soul is in a state of nonexistence. Christianity today rejects the idea that the soul of a person lived life in heaven, or on earth, prior to being born into this world. Thus, the soul of an individual did not exist before birth.

5 of 16: The next quote of Luther suggests that, regarding a definition of death, when a person perishes, the thinking part of the deceased (i.e., the soul/mind) may be actually destroyed. Regarding the righteous souls who had lived prior to the appearance of the Messiah, Luther pointed out that the heart/mind of those in the OT went somewhere that consisted of a gathering of other deceased person's souls. "Those who believed in the Seed of the woman did not perish and were not consigned to oblivion but were gathered to their people. But (who knows) what the nature of that place is."[10] Luther considered it a possibility, at least, that a person's soul could be "consigned to oblivion" rather than continuing to live in the spirit world in the normal sense of living. It also indicates that Luther defined death differently than the traditional understanding of death. That is, he immediately follows *death* with "and were not consigned to oblivion," or nonexistence. In today's context among OT scholars, Luther's typical view of the completeness of death would not be so unusual due to their observation that it emphasizes the ontological unity of a person.

6 of 16: At the Heidelberg Disputation in 1518, Luther said the following at his defense explanation of thesis number twenty-four: "He knows that it is sufficient if he [Jesus] suffers and is brought low by the cross in order to be annihilated all the more. It is this that Christ says in John 3:7, 'You must be born anew.' To be born anew [of the Spirit], one must consequently first die and then be raised up with the Son of Man. To die, I say, means to feel death at hand."[11] Luther is not referring just to one's body since it is what is inside a person that "having your mind renewed" is pointing to. Being born of the Spirit in heaven at the last day, as opposed to being born of the water in this world, is one way how a person can have their mind renewed. The aspect of the mortality of a person's soul/mind is brought out in this quote of Luther where he says, "one must first die" a literal death.

---

9. Athanasius of Alexandria, *On the Incarnation*, 13. First published c. AD 318; an alternate title is *Incarnation of the Word of God*.

10. Pelikan and Hansen, *LW*, 4:316.

11. Lehmann and Grimm, *LW*, 31:55.

Obviously, a symbolic interpretation of "born again" in John 3:7 is predominant today, and it may be correct. However, the context of this account spoken by Jesus appears to not exclude a literal interpretation of being "born" a new child of God at our resurrection. Luther referred to a literal "death" in the last sentence above because if he meant a metaphorical death there instead, the sentence makes little sense. Therefore, in his previous sentence, "first die and then be raised up" is also meant in the literal sense. This means that Luther meant "to be born anew" in the literal sense. Of course, it is possible that both Jesus and Luther understood that these terms can be seen in both a symbolic and literal sense simultaneously, depending on whether the context is before or after death's doorway.

This literal characterization of death also opens the possibility that early in his career as a Reformer, Luther had considered the possibility that the human soul/mind of Jesus may have been "annihilated." If Luther was referring just to the body suffering and dying, the extremity of this term would have been replaced since the corpse was not burned but rather placed in a tomb. Since it appears right before the John 3 quote and explanation involving a literal death and a bodily resurrection of human beings, *annihilation* is not used in a metaphorical sense. Every phrase in the two paragraphs explaining thesis number twenty-four is presented in the literal sense. This includes the following: a holy law, God's gifts, everything created is very good, takes credit for works and wisdom, does not give credit to God, and misuses and defiles the gifts of God. If it was the case that Luther was, at least, leaning toward a mortalist/physicalist view, then it is not required that his interpretation of "brought low by the cross in order to be annihilated all the more" must be seen in the metaphorical sense. And, it can make sense if it is understood in the literal sense.

7 of 16: The next quote is a short and rather explicit one. Luther preached a sermon in 1535 that described death repeatedly and was based on Romans 6:3–11. Luther said Christ "leads us out of the death and grave of sin to the resurrection of spirit and body."[12] The traditional teaching of the church has been that only the body is to be resurrected, not the immaterial spirit-soul. Yet Luther told the assembled church that the general resurrection of the dead consists of not just the body. Luther could not have been referring to an indestructible spirit-soul since, by definition, it could not be annihilated or go out of existence at death. The object of this quote above is followers of Christ (i.e., "us"), which refers to that part of us that makes you, you (i.e., your mind). Therefore, the word translated as "spirit" in this quote of Luther must have been referring to the mind, or that essence

---

12. Lenker, *Luther's Epistle Sermons*, 3:153.

which is mainly dependent on a functioning brain while in this world. This assertion of mine must include the other fifteen quotes of Luther in this chapter as context. So, this reinforces the claim (at this point in this chapter) that it is very likely Luther interpreted these passages in a mortalist or physicalist way.

8 of 16: At the Coburg Castle, Luther wrote a commentary on Psalm 118 in June 1530, in addition to his extensive Bible translation work there. In this commentary, he defines death based on his interpretation of the Bible. He makes three points in this definition. First, a deceased believer cannot continue to enjoy life as in this world. Second, a deceased believer is literally nothing (if it were not for our Savior). And third, because of the saving goodness of the Lord, and even though the psalmist asserts that he shall not die, Luther understands *"die"* to mean in a way that is permanent and complete (i.e., including the heart/mind). Luther said the following regarding verse 17 ("I shall not die, but I shall live"): "It is impossible that they [the 'saints'] can die, or not enjoy eternal life . . . because, God cannot be the God of those who are dead or who are nothing, but must be the God of the living . . . hence death is not death to the saints, but a sleep."[13] This characterization of death Luther made, regarding how the psalmist understood the nature of death, shows Luther's willingness to define death as possibly being "nothing," but then his point is that they instead will become alive again after a period of sleep in the metaphorical sense of *sleep* where they are not alive.

A comparison between two English translations of this quote of Luther above is notable because 132 years elapsed between them (1826 vs. 1958). The 1958 translation in *Luther's Works* of this last phrase is: "Therefore, death remains no more than a sleep."[14] However, in the 1826 translation, the distinction is seen in this last phrase between a normative understanding of death within Christianity today and the OT view of death (i.e., a death that is more complete and affecting the whole person) as in "death is not death to the saints." As a second example within this quote above, seen at the first phrase ("It is impossible that they can die, or not enjoy eternal life"), the *LW* volume 14 translation instead says: "It is not possible that they should totally die and not live again in eternity."

This qualification above of *die* (by using "totally" with it) seems to be defined here by Luther in both senses of death: a temporary situation until resurrection, and that both the body and the soul/mind perish at death (i.e., a total death), based on the immediate context. Since Luther described death as being that situation where the person becomes nothing (i.e., "those

13. Cole, *Select Works of Martin Luther*, 1:349.
14. Pelikan and Poellot, *LW*, 14:87.

who are dead or who are nothing") based on the meaning of death being more explicit in the OT (i.e., the whole person dies), it seems appropriate to translate it as *LW* does (i.e., "totally die"). This particular psalm "was Luther's favorite among all the psalms."[15] It is telling that Luther, who as a young man chose the Psalms (due to his great familiarity with them) as the subject of his very first lecture series at the university, would pick the one pushing back on the church's view of death.

9 of 16: In the following quote of Luther from 1521, we see that he questioned the typical understanding regarding the spatial dimensions that a person occupies in death by suggesting that the size of the soul of a deceased person is not like this physical world. He also shows that early in his understanding of "death as sleep" Luther was reaching for a view of how God could gather the many souls in heaven and have them located "in" his hand for the purpose of preservation. "Where do our souls remain when all of creation is on fire and there is nothing to stand on? Do you think that God cannot preserve souls in His hand? Or do you think that He must have a physical stall, as a shepherd does for his sheep? . . . Heaven and earth become new, and our bodies also and become alive again."[16]

On another day, Luther again spoke of the soul of the deceased by saying that we can be "assured that we shall not lose it, but be truly and carefully preserved in his hand, maintained and again restored."[17] It should be noted that the translation into English does not say, "preserved by his hand," since it is not warranted, instead of "preserved in his hand" (which is closer to the meaning Luther intended). The consequence of these three leading questions is that after we combine them with some of these other quotes here, we can conclude that Luther rejected the description of *soul* he found in the 1513 papal bull on the immortality of the soul. This formal proclamation by Pope Leo X repeated the view given by Pope Clement V that the soul is "essentially as the form of the human body" and then went a step further to declare for the first time in a bull that the soul is not mortal. See footnote 53 of chapter 3.

10 of 16: Luther said the following at an informal gathering of friends or family: "He Himself will provide a place where my soul may continue to exist . . . Nor am I the first on whom He begins to learn how to preserve the souls of His believers. . . . Nor do I want my soul placed into my own hands and care, for in that case it would be devoured in a moment by the

---

15. Pelikan, "Introduction to Volume 14," x.
16. Mayes and Langebartels, *LW*, 75:109.
17. Lenker, *Luther's Church Postil Gospels*, 5:359.

devil. But He has it in hand, and no one can tear it from Him."[18] First, the clarification here is that the souls are located in a place such that no occupant of heaven at the time could breach the protection Christ is providing the many souls in hand. Notice that Luther described this state between death and resurrection as a place of some sort. Furthermore, he describes this thing as being a soul that exists yet is without any consciousness. Since it is very rare, if at all, that Luther described the soul in a traditionally neoplatonic way (as was common then as it is now), whenever he refers to a *soul* it cannot be presumed that he was thinking in a traditionally dualistic way. In this quote of Luther above, when God provides "a place where my soul may continue to exist," it is known from Luther's other discussions of death that when he says, "my soul," he does not mean a fully aware soul that exists exactly the same way it exists in this world we now live. See chapter 8 for an explanation that shows that he is departing from the typical view then of a spirit-soul waiting in heaven, when he refers to God knowing how to preserve the soul using "words" or code that symbolize the contents of a person's soul/mind.

11 of 16: In the next quote of Luther from one of his more notable sermons, we see him discuss life and immortality in the context of both this world and the next. The key phrase begins with "all life comes from him" at the end of the following quote: "He holds their lives in his hands that you may not remain blind . . . concerning the dead and putrefying body, but rather perceive that this is the Lord of all creatures, whether to us they be dead or alive, and that all life comes from him and is maintained in and by him, so that if he would not maintain life no one could live a single moment."[19] Not only is Christ the source of all life, Luther says here, but also he may be saying that life is maintained in him alone, rather than it being an immortal life with each soul, as an attribute within a person or their soul. The end of this quote shows that Luther saw a person's soul as not having the characteristic of deathlessness on its own, separate from the source of life.

12 of 16: If Luther had instead taken the traditional view of the soul, this next quote seems odd to ask about soul preservation during death. "Since sometimes there is nothing we feel less than life while we are living in this world, and God preserves life for those who sleep and are devoid of all actions, why shall we not attribute to Him such wisdom and power that He can also preserve the soul in death? While the soul still lives in the body,

---

18. Plass, *What Luther Says*, 377. See WA-T 4, #4833. Plass's heading here reads: "1109–'Into thy hands I commend my spirit' (Luke 23:46)."

19. Lenker, *Luther's Church Postil Gospels*, 5:358.

it is deceived in various ways during sleep."[20] The point Luther is making here is that *life* right after death for a waiting soul is a very different kind of existence. If Luther believed in an immaterial spirit-soul as the church teaches, why would he ask the question about the hesitancy in attributing to Christ the capability of preserving a deceased person's soul? Luther's point here is that God is preserving the deceased person's soul in a different way than the church assumes.

13 of 16: The next quote of Luther is especially telling since his interpretation of a Bible verse shows that he was thinking differently about the soul compared to orthodoxy. "Luther's theology of death is expressed particularly clearly in his powerful interpretation of Psalm 90 . . . Rorer took notes and reconstructed them . . . We still have Rorer's notes of these [1534] lectures as well as the printed text [from 1541]."[21] Franz Delitzsch wrote that Luther's "exposition of the Psalms, especially of the [seven] penitential Psalms and of Psalm 90, are superior to all previous works on the subject."[22]

Luther said the following: "'Lord, Thou art our dwelling place from generation to generation (Ps 90:1)'. . . Who would call God a Dwelling Place of the dead? Who would think Him to be a tomb or a cross? He is Life. And so also those will live whose Dwelling Place He is."[23] It is not obvious that this "place in which one dwells" must not be read in a literal sense, at least to Luther and perhaps to others as well. Luther's protracted exegesis of this psalm purportedly written by Moses demonstrates that there is a good possibility that he was right to explore the literal sense of this Hebrew word related to *dwelling place*. As he began his explanation, Luther noted that "it is, to be sure, a surprising manner of speech, the like of which is found nowhere else in the Sacred Scriptures, that God is called a 'Dwelling Place.' Yes, in other passages Scripture says the opposite. It calls men 'temples of God' in which God dwells. 'The temple of God,' Paul says, 'is within you' (1 Cor 6:19). But in this psalm Moses inverts the thought."[24]

Luther grouped together this unusual reference to deceased people dwelling, in some sense, in God with that found in Colossians. "Paul employs almost the same language when he writes: 'Your life is hid with Christ in God' (Col 3:3). It is a much clearer and more intelligible statement if I say that believers dwell in God than if I say that God dwells in them."[25]

---

20. Pelikan, "Introduction to Volume 14," x.
21. Althaus, *Theology of Martin Luther*, 405.
22. Delitzsch, source unknown, quoted in Lenker, *First Twenty-Two Psalms*, 7–8.
23. Pelikan, *LW*, 13:83–84. See WA 40/3:476–594.
24. Pelikan, *LW*, 13:84.
25. Pelikan, *LW*, 13:84.

Luther acknowledged that the much more common idea of "God exists inside a person" can make less sense to someone who does not have a clear understanding of the role of the Holy Spirit. Luther interpreted this passage in Colossians as saying that it is our soul that is literally in God. That is, it is the events of our life as represented by our memories and attitudes—the contents of our mind—that is being securely held in God during death until our resurrection from the state of being dead (see chapter 8). Notice that Paul's point includes the idea that it does not just inhabit heaven but that it is kept hidden. This critical NT clue relates to Luther's interpretation of the claim by Moses that God is literally a dwelling place for the souls awaiting resurrection. For a neoplatonist who imagines the soul as some kind of ghost, this literal sense is obviously objectionable. But Luther shows he understood it in a literal sense as seen next:

> God is our Dwelling Place, and not earth, not heaven, not Paradise, but simply God Himself. And indeed He is that "from generation to generation." This means that from the beginning of the world to the end of the world God has never deserted His own. Adam, Eve, patriarchs, prophets, pious kings are asleep in this Dwelling Place. If, as I believe, they have not as yet risen with Christ, their bodies are indeed at rest in the grave, but their life is hidden with Christ in God and will be revealed in glory on the Last Day. In this way Moses calls attention to the resurrection of the dead and the hope of life over death.[26]

Notice in the quote above that Luther made a distinction between the two literal destinations of a person. The body typically goes to the grave, while the other part of us, our "life," is hidden with Christ in heaven. The accumulation of memories and attitudes in one's life can be represented by this unconscious, exterior soul hidden in God. Althaus pointed out that Paul's emphasis was on the whole person, when discussing the hope of resurrection back to life. "The hope of the early church centered on the resurrection on the Last Day.... This resurrection happens to the total man and not only to the body. Paul speaks of the resurrection not of 'the body' but of 'the dead'.... Luther therefore says nothing about souls without their bodies enjoying true life and blessedness before the resurrection. They sleep in 'the peace of Christ.'"[27]

14 of 16: The following is another example where Luther's interpretation of Psalm 90 suggests that he had entertained, at least, the possibility that "a sprouting at the beginning," which signified the life of a person in

---

26. Pelikan, *LW*, 13:85.
27. Althaus, *Theology of Martin Luther*, 413–15.

this world, could involve a total death including both the body and the interior soul/mind (as opposed to a person's exterior soul held securely in an unconscious state). Luther made the following comments on Psalm 90:6: "The Hebrew word *chalaph* means 'to be changed,' as garments are changed or transformed.[28] . . . The verb *chalaph* denotes a twofold kind of change: a change from being into nonbeing [e.g., fallen leaves decomposing], or a change from nonbeing into being [e.g., a sprouted flower where none existed]. . . . He [Moses] meant to give indirect expression to the *hope* that after death *we* will again be made alive and that this physical death will terminate in true and eternal life."[29] Notice that Luther used *we* with *hope*, which is a thought initiated only from the mind and not just from the body, and therefore emphasizes that the word *we* refers to the soul/mind.

Luther puts life in perspective in the following quote: "So, then, the life of a Christian, from baptism to the grave, is nothing else than the beginning of a blessed death, for at the Last Day God will make him altogether new. In like manner the lifting up out of baptism is quickly done, but the thing it signifies, the spiritual birth, the increase of grace and righteousness, though it begins indeed in baptism, lasts until death, nay, even until the Last Day. *Only then* will that be finished which the lifting up out of baptism signifies. *Then* shall we arise from death . . . *Then* shall we be truly lifted up out of baptism and completely born, and we shall *put on* the true baptismal garment of immortal life in heaven."[30] It is remarkable that Luther emphasizes immortality being similar to putting on clothes (as Paul also did), as opposed to already having this characteristic. This is seen here in Luther's quote above by his repetition of "only then . . . then . . . then." It is only then, at our resurrection from the condition of being truly dead, that we (i.e., both body and soul) receive from God the actualization of the promise of eternal life, soul immortality, and deathlessness.

Luther called the period between death and resurrection a blessed death in which a person continues to increase in righteousness that began at birth. Since Luther clearly believed the person remains in a deep sleep during death, this improvement of their character cannot be obtained through experience. The exterior soul during death is alive, but in a very different

---

28. The most common translation in the KJV for the Hebrew verb *chalaph*, which appears twenty-eight times in the OT, is "change" (ten times) and "renew" (three times), with several others of less frequent usage, according to blueletterbible.org. The most common translation in other versions (at Ps 90:6) is "fades" according to biblegateway.com with its fifty-two English versions. The *LW* translator selected "transformed" for the Latin word seen in Luther's lectures.

29. Pelikan, *LW*, 13:103–4.

30. Jacobs and Spaeth, *Works of Martin Luther*, 1:58.

sense. Luther used the example of the difference between a fetus and an adult to show the magnitude of the difference between life in this world and a deceased person's so-called life awaiting resurrection.

If the process of "washing someone as white as snow" is a divine editing process during death, then it may involve deleting the memories of sins committed and other irrelevant details from the record in heaven of that person's life, then that exterior soul (consisting of code or data) changes from being a copy of the interior soul-mind (as lived on earth) to an enhanced child of God ready for paradise in the kingdom of God. "Nevertheless, the life is one hoped for rather than one already possessed. . . . And because of Christ, when we die we keep this *hope* . . . yet we who believe in Christ have the hope that on the Last Day *we* shall be *revived* for eternal life."[31] If it is the case that the reader has not yet been convinced that these fourteen quotes of Luther, when taken together, fail to persuade, then the next two quotes should do it.

15 and 16: The next quote of Luther on soul immortality is probably his most famous one among physicalists today. The reader may recall that Luther's response to the pope's pronouncement threatening excommunication from the church was analyzed already in some depth in chapter 4 (at *Luther in 1521*). At the twenty-seventh article in the first version (dated November 29, 1520) in his reply to the pope, Luther wrote the following: "I permit the pope to make articles of faith for himself and his faithful, such as . . . the soul is immortal, with all those monstrous opinions to be found in the Roman dunghill of decretals."[32] Clearly, Luther objected to the belief in soul immortality for all (defined as an innate characteristic of people) as being based on the Bible since he says that it is an article of faith or unreasonable conjecture.

However, this quote above did not appear in Luther's final version sent to Rome (completed in March 1521). Remember the pope's 1513 threat of death for even professors who teach that a person's soul is mortal. Consequently, it is likely that Luther remembered this too (from seven years earlier) and then toned down his explicitness in his revision. That which does appear in his *Defense and Explanation* is as follows: "The experts in Rome have recently pronounced a holy decree which establishes that the soul of man is immortal . . . and, with the assistance of the mastermind Aristotle, they decreed further that the soul is "essentially the form of the

31. Pelikan, *LW*, 1:196–97.

32. Blackburne, *Separate Existence of the Soul between Death and Resurrection*, 12–13. Luther's preliminary defense was completed in November 1520 and subsequently published with the title *Assertion of All the Articles Wrongly Condemned in the Roman Bull*.

human body," and many other splendid articles of a similar nature. These decrees are, indeed, most appropriate to the papal church, for they make it possible for them to hold fast to human dreams and the doctrines of devils while they trample upon and destroy faith and the teaching of Christ."[33]

A footnote on this quote above references a book by Carl Stange, *Studien zur Theologie Luthers*, in which he makes the claim that Luther was not criticizing the Roman Church by disagreeing with the 1513 bull concerning soul immortality. Stange proposes that instead the criticism was only due to Luther objecting "to the substitution of philosophical ideas concerning immortality of the soul for the biblical teaching of the resurrection and the life everlasting."[34]

A more reasonable interpretation of Luther's description of his own views of the 1513 bull on soul immortality would include both versions of his *Explanation* (the November 1520 and the March 1521 publications of the twenty-seventh article). Froom characterizes Luther's first version of this article as follows:

> "Immortal soul" included among pope's "monstrous opinions": ... He lists five in the series including the "immortality of the soul" as the fifth, all and each of which Luther expressly rejects. The significance of including "the soul is immortal" ... in what he denominates "monstrous opinions" and "Roman corruptions," is, of course, obvious. And he added immediately that these "all" came out of the "Roman dunghill of decretals"— thus harking back to the pope's bull of December 19, 1513, wherein he declared the natural immortality of the soul to be a doctrine of the Catholic Church.[35]

This concludes my list of sixteen quotes of Luther related to the soul's nature being mortal. Were there more instances of this beyond these sixteen? It seems likely that Luther was heard repeating something similar to the last two quotes above that was also quite unambiguous on his disagreement with innate immortality of the soul. There are probably more instances to be found in the voluminous Weimar Edition of Luther's works.

The first section of the main part of his life (1518–22) contains five examples on this subject; the middle third of it (1523–36) contains seven instances; and the final third (1537–46) contains four more examples (which total sixteen). Even though these last two quotes were written early in his public career, the collection of eleven instances between 1523 and 1546

33. Lehmann and Forell, *LW*, 32:77-78.
34. Lehmann and Forell, *LW*, 32:78n.
35. Froom, *Conditionalist Faith of Our Fathers*, 2:73.

shows that he did not change his mind on mortality. To quickly review: the following are excerpts of these sixteen quotes of Luther with keywords and phrases in italics:

1. "The entire church teaches . . . that in death the soul is separated from the body. *But it is another question* whether the body and soul/mind are *separate things*."[36]

2. "'Your dead shall live and rise with their bodies. You who lie beneath the earth, *awake and shout!*'. . . He speaks to the dead *as if they were already alive*."[37]

3. "Whether the souls of the ungodly are tortured *immediately after death* I am *unable to affirm* . . . In 2 Cor 5:10 Paul says: 'For we must all appear before the judgment seat of Christ.'"[38]

4. "Where does a man who hopes in God end up except in his *own nothingness*? But when a man goes into *nothingness*, does he not merely return to that from which he came? Since he comes from God and his *own non-being*, it is to God that he returns when he *returns to nothingness*."[39]

5. "Those who believed in the Seed of the woman did not *perish* and were not consigned to *oblivion* but were gathered to their people. But [who knows] what the nature of that place is."[40]

6. "He knows that it is sufficient if he [Jesus] suffers and is brought low by the cross in order to *be annihilated all the more*. It is this that Christ says in John 3:7, 'You must *be born anew*.' To be born anew [of the Spirit], one *must consequently first die* and then be raised up with the Son of Man."[41]

7. Christ "leads us out of the death and grave of sin to *the resurrection of spirit and body*."[42]

8. "It is impossible that they [the 'saints'] can die, or not enjoy eternal life . . . because, God cannot be the God of those *who are dead or who are*

---

36. Lohse, *Martin Luther's Theology*, 326. See WA 39/2:354.
37. Brown, *LW*, 58:154.
38. Pelikan and Hansen, *LW*, 4:314–15. See WA 43:361.
39. Althaus, *Theology of Martin Luther*, 111. See WA 5:168.
40. Pelikan and Hansen, *LW*, 4:316.
41. Lehmann and Grimm, *LW*, 31:55.
42. Lenker, *Luther's Epistle Sermons*, 3:153.

nothing, but must be the God of the living . . . hence death is not death to the saints, but a sleep."[43]

9. "Where do our souls remain when all of creation is on fire and there is nothing to stand on? Do you think that God cannot *preserve souls in His hand*? Or do you think that He must have *a physical stall*, as a shepherd does for his sheep?"[44]

10. "Nor am I the first on whom He begins to learn *how to preserve the souls* of His believers. . . . But He *has it in hand*, and no one can *tear it* from Him."[45]

11. "That *all life* comes from him and is *maintained in and by him*, so that if he would not maintain life no one could live a single moment."[46]

12. "God preserves life for those who sleep and are devoid of all actions, why shall we not attribute to Him such wisdom and power that He can also *preserve the soul in death*?"[47]

13. "'Lord, Thou art our dwelling place from generation to generation (Ps 90:1)'. . . Who would *call God a Dwelling Place* of the dead? Who would think Him *to be a tomb or a cross*? He is Life."[48]

14. The verb *chalaph* denotes a twofold kind of change: a change from being *into nonbeing*, or a change from *nonbeing* into being."[49]

15. "I permit the pope to make articles of faith for himself and his faithful, such as . . . the soul is immortal, with *all those monstrous opinions* to be found in the Roman *dunghill* of decretals."[50]

16. "The experts in Rome have recently pronounced a holy decree which establishes that *the soul of man is immortal*. . . . These decrees are, indeed, most appropriate to the papal church, for they make it possible for them to hold fast *to human dreams and the doctrines of devils* while they *trample* upon and *destroy* faith and the teaching of Christ."[51]

---

43. Cole, *Select Works of Martin Luther*, 1:349.
44. Mayes and Langebartels, *LW*, 75:109.
45. Plass, What Luther Says, 377. See WA-T 4, #4833. Plass's heading here reads: "1109–'Into thy hands I commend my spirit' (Luke 23:46)."
46. Lenker, *Luther's Church Postil Gospels*, 5:358.
47. Pelikan, *LW*, 14:x.
48. Pelikan, *LW*, 13:83–84. See WA 40/3:476–594.
49. Pelikan, *LW*, 13:103–4.
50. Blackburne, *Separate Existence of the Soul between Death and Resurrection*, 12–13.
51. Lehmann and Forell, *LW*, 32:77–78.

Luther's belief that the resurrection of a deceased person from true death (e.g., non-being, nothingness, and oblivion) involving the whole person, both body and soul, is not only contrary to the belief that the human soul is naturally immortal, but it was described by Luther as a monstrous opinion. Luther went further than just saying the pope's decision was "monstrous" since he wrote that it (which includes the "soul is immortal" statement) can be symbolically found on a large pile of dung in Rome. Furthermore, Luther said this doctrine is being promoted by devils that has had the effect of being destructive to the faith of many persons and to the teaching of Jesus.

Consequently, Luther clearly rejected the notion that Plato and his followers within Christianity had espoused for centuries, and in its place, Luther accepted the belief that soon became known, although somewhat differently, as mortalism, or today as physicalism. Luther believed that both the body and the soul were created to first be mortal, and then have the possibility of literally becoming immortal upon our resurrection, although he may have supplemented this mortality doctrine with his own style of unconscious dualism. However, not everyone agrees that this rejection of innate immortality is what he actually thought, as would be expected in several other Luther studies where there are contradictions.

Which top theologians knew what Luther believed about soul immortality?

Among the eight writers (plus two more leaders in the Lutheran Church) described in chapter 2 who mischaracterized Luther's view of death—as demonstrated by this book— it seems only one of them, Lohse (1928–97), has asserted in a publication that Luther did not ever hold to mortality of the soul. He has been described by some people as "without doubt the leading Luther scholar."[52] Lohse writes that Luther held to the natural immortality of the soul instead of it being naturally mortal. In his book titled *Martin Luther's Theology: Its Historical and Systematic Development*, which was first published near the end of his life, in 1995 (in German), Lohse writes that "this leaves no doubt that Luther held to the immortality of the soul."[53] This claim by Lohse that there was no doubt is debatable.

---

52. Edwards's online endorsement reads in full: "Lohse was without doubt the leading Luther scholar. He was better able to deal with both the historical and the systematic better than anyone I know."

53. Lohse, *Martin Luther's Theology*, 326.

Lohse's explanation around this quote above is entirely insufficient based on a lack of stated grounds in his book. It is an odd claim to make because there are no reasons or grounds that he could have provided to build this assertion upon. Lohse gave his opinion but did not even try to show in his book why he believed it. Since one's assessment of Luther's view of death is theologically related to Luther's view of the soul's nature, as indicated at death, any judgment made by Lohse on either of these two topics must take both into account. Since *Death until Resurrection* has clearly demonstrated that Luther held tightly to "death as an unconscious sleep" throughout his life, Lohse's opinion on this related topic of the soul, regarding Luther, can be held as suspicious and possibly also wrong. After reviewing this set of sixteen quotes of Luther on soul mortality, it becomes easier to completely disregard Lohse's judgment on Luther's view of both of these subjects.

Lohse wrote the following regarding Luther on death: "This utterance renders it doubtful that words concerning soul sleep, which are certainly more numerous, can really be promoted to the rank of a 'doctrine of Luther' . . . We should not attempt to regard the one or the other idea as his true opinion." This book verifiably demonstrates it was, in fact, Luther's true opinion. This was done in three ways: First, by presenting Luther's actual words to various groups of people in their social context such that the forcefulness and clarity of his position is evident. Second, it has attempted to present all of the examples of this effort throughout his career, and in historical sequence, to show the value of his repetition and various trends over time, as seen in various series on the works of Luther translated into English. Third, my book has also collected numerous quotes of Luther in his attempt to reconcile two seemingly opposing views of death that can be used to show theologically how Luther's scattered explanations of the "Luther paradox on death" can be understood. My conclusion is that there should be no longer any doubt that this view was Luther's true opinion on the nature of death.

In order to confirm the reader's possible assessment of these sixteen quotes as supporting the view that Luther believed in soul mortality, the views of the following writers begin with Althaus (1888–66). He was a theology professor in Germany and also served for thirty years as president of the International Luther Society. Althaus was described in 2013 as being "probably the most significant Luther scholar in the world in the 1930s and 1940s."[54] In addition to him, this chapter closes with similar views by Taito Kantonen and Karl Heim. So, the question now is, what did some

---

54. Ericksen, "German Churches and the Holocaust," 4. See footnote 12 in chapter 2 and its cited quote.

scholars write regarding what it is that Luther believed about the soul's nature and why does it matter?

Althaus provides the following assessment of Luther, including the observation that the resurrection affects the total person (body and soul). He begins here with the nature of death, and then shows how to determine the significance of Luther's views on both the soul and death.

> They "rest" and "sleep" in the bosom of Christ. This is Luther's definitive statement about the condition of the departed. In order to understand its significance completely, we must view it against the background of the development of eschatology since the time of the New Testament.... The original biblical concepts have been replaced by ideas from Hellenistic gnostic dualism. The New Testament idea of the resurrection which affects the total man has had to give way to the immortality of the soul. The Last Day also loses its significance, for souls have received all that is decisively important long before this. Eschatological tension is no longer strongly directed to the day of Jesus' coming. The difference between this and the hope of the New Testament is very great. Against this background, we can measure the significance of Luther's Reformation for eschatology.... Luther generally understands the condition between death and the resurrection as a deep and dreamless sleep without consciousness.[55]

Althaus also describes it as "this resurrection happens to the total man and not only to the body. Paul speaks of the resurrection not of 'the body' but of 'the dead.' This understanding of the resurrection implicitly understands death as also affecting the total man."[56] Althaus asserts that Luther's understanding of our resurrection held to this kind of raising both body and soul from the condition of a real death (as opposed to a "living death"). "Some Bible passages do compel Luther to make certain exceptions to the rule that the dead sleep. God can also awaken them for a time ... and yet, all of this changes nothing in the decisive factor that the full significance of the biblical concept of resurrection appears in Luther's thought. The Last Day has decisive significance also for the individual. Christ awakens a man— not only his body— from the sleep of death and only then gives him blessedness."[57]

---

55. Althaus, *Theology of Martin Luther*, 412–14.
56. Althaus, *Theology of Martin Luther*, 413.
57. Althaus, *Theology of Martin Luther*, 415.

Althaus also observed that "Luther always bases his expectation of a life beyond death on the resurrection of Christ—even though he frequently does not explicitly refer to it."[58] In order to highlight that it *is* Luther's view that it is our resurrection that actually makes us immortal (rather than it being granted at birth), he describes the logic Luther used as follows: "Luther therefore considers it self-understood that Christ is implicitly included in such words of God. Luther applies this syllogism when he says . . . If God speaks to you, then you are involved in an immortal relationship; for God speaks only to those who are alive. It must follow that God raises the dead. This makes them 'immortal.'"[59] It wasn't birth or death that literally brings the characteristic of soul immortality to a person, but rather, it is when God raises the dead and judges their lives to show who will receive the gift of eternal life.

Althaus also points out that "the Christian faith knows nothing about an immortality of the person. That would mean a denial of death, not recognizing it as judgment of God. It knows only an awakening from real death through the power of God. There is existence after death only by way of awakening, resurrection."[60]

Taito Kantonen explains Althaus's interpretation of Luther well in his 1954 book titled *The Christian Hope*. Kantonen was the American member of the Lutheran World Federation's Commission on Theology and was recognized in the 1950s "as one of today's outstanding theologians."[61] Regarding Luther's view of the nature of death, Kantonen observed the following: "Luther, with a greater emphasis on the resurrection, preferred to concentrate on the scriptural metaphor of sleep. . . . In Luther's view, so far as the dead person himself is concerned, the intermediate state is reduced to an unconscious moment. . . . Althaus claims that the old orthodoxy does not do full justice to the meaning of death, resurrection, and judgment. If death means entrance into heaven, then resurrection and judgment lose their significance."[62] It is because most of Christianity today seems to believe that "death means entrance into heaven" that added importance can be placed on teaching people today about the relevancy of our resurrection. So, "death as sleep" then leads to a discussion of what exactly happens when someone is resurrected from total death, and why

---

58. Althaus, *Theology of Martin Luther*, 411.

59. Althaus, *Theology of Martin Luther*, 411. See WA 31, I, 155 and Pelikan and Poellot, *LW*, 14:68 (as shown in Althaus's footnote on page 411, including this quote of Luther: "Therefore, they may live forever; otherwise he would not be their God").

60. Althaus, *Die letzten Dinge*, 126.

61. Kantonen, *Christian Hope*, back cover.

62. Kantonen, *Christian Hope*, 37–38.

the divine promise of eternal life after resurrection means so much more than getting toes and a nose.

Kantonen referred to Althaus's 1933 book on "the last things," a translation of its title, where he describes the following "line of thought . . . [having been] developed uncompromisingly by Paul Althaus":[63]

> Death is more than a departure of the soul from the body. The whole person, body and soul, is involved in death. . . . Not only is the flesh, the bodily structure, destroyed but also the heart, which in biblical usage means personality. Death is the judgment of righteous God over sinful man. . . . There is no immortality of the soul but a resurrection of the whole person, body and soul, from death. . . . "Who shall separate us from the love of Christ?" (Rom 8:35) This relationship transforms death into a privilege and a victory. "To live is Christ and to die is gain." (Phil 1:21) "Death is swallowed up in victory." (1 Cor 15:54) It makes death an act of worship and sacrifice. . . . It enables us to meet death in the spirit of reverent obedience to God, even when he asks us to surrender to him our whole existence, following the example of our Lord, who was obedient unto death, even the death of the cross.[64]

Kantonen also writes that Karl Heim, who was a German theologian during the early twentieth century, "is in substantial agreement with Althaus. . . . When we die, we really die, we pass into nothingness. There is nothing in man that is capable of resisting the destructive power of death. The Christian hope is, however, that we do not fall into nothingness but into the hands of God. It is only when we are annihilated that we can be truly resurrected."[65] Kantonen adds the following personal observation on the nature of the soul, death, and eternal life:

> The Bible does not distinguish between man and the beasts on the ground that man has an immortal soul while the beasts do not. . . . Life makes no sense and holds no hope except in terms of Christ's victory over death and the assurance that we share in that victory. There is considerable support in Scripture for the view that the soul as well as the body is destructible. This evidence has been obscured because the Greek conception of the inherent immortality of the soul has supplanted the teaching

---

63. Kantonen, *Christian Hope*, 32–33.

64. Kantonen, *Christian Hope*, 33–34.

65. Kantonen, *Christian Hope*, 34. See Heim, *Die Gemeinde der Auferstandenen*, 215–46.

of Scripture. . . . The basic text for the theology of death must therefore be: "The wage of sin is death, but the free gift of God is eternal life" (Rom 6:23).[66]

Before concluding, I would like to add to this passage by Paul in Romans a very well-known Bible verse written by John in his quote of Jesus, John 3:16b: "Whoever believes in Him shall not perish but have eternal life." That is the good news that Christ wishes to share to all individuals of his creation; it is the Gospel encapsulated in a nutshell at John 3:16. And, as Peter said in his monumental Pentecost sermon in Acts 2:27 with his quote of David (from Psalm 16:10): God will not abandon our souls to gravedom. David also wrote in Psalm 68:20 that "our God is a God who saves . . . who rescues us from death" (GNT).

Therefore, this is a situation where we all would have remained in a state of unending death—which means our soul/mind would actually perish, as John 3:16 probably is referring given the generally recognized view among scholars today that the OT, at least, usually pictures death as being a total death for the whole individual as a unity.[67] And, the NT never actually says that a human being is born with the trait of immortality of the soul (see 1 Tim 6:16 where it says only God possesses the characteristic of immortality).

God offers a literal gift of eternal life to "whoever that believes" (John 3:16) following the resurrection of both "the righteous and the wicked" (Acts 24:15) who have been "awakened" from the "sleep" of death. The Christian hope can be centered on the bodily resurrection on the last day when Christ returns. This is when we recover our consciousness as a renewed child of God. Therefore, God's plan for people is death *until* resurrection.

---

66. Kantonen, *Christian Hope*, 34.
67. See my website, John-3-16.org for further explanation.

Conclusion

An often referenced, unpublished study of the works of Luther previously claimed there existed only about a hundred occurrences of "death as sleep" in them, and consequently, that this amount was insufficient to overtake Luther's supposedly contradictory description of a soul between death and resurrection. It is probably the only time someone has tried to count up them all, until I did it too. From his first mention to his last mention of "death as unconscious sleep," Luther actually brought up this idea—based on a search of only legitimate keywords—about twice as many times as this previous study from 1946 claimed. *Death until Resurrection* demonstrates there exists 210 legitimate occurrences of "death as unconscious sleep" in Luther's writings, which increases the ratio regarding its dominance over those instances when Luther seemed to say a deceased person is not asleep. This book also shows that Luther repeatedly explained the perceived inconsistency (i.e., "death is *not* a sleep"—which is not quoting Luther but instead his interpreters—versus "death *is* a sleep") as being not a contradiction at all after these explanations by Luther are brought together and understood.

When counting the five relevant sermons that Luther personally revised fifteen to twenty years after first writing them (for publishing a new edition), there was a total of at least sixty-one days over his lifetime where he brought up "death as unconscious sleep" again and again. Luther would go five months, on average, before he would again mention "death as unconscious sleep" another three or four times to his hearers and readers that day [{(24 years) x (365 days/yr) / (30 days/mo) / (61 days)} = 4.8 months] and [210 / 61 = 3.4]. However, keep in mind that Luther did this every year for twenty-four years, as an average, until his death.

To accurately characterize Luther on this topic, this analysis provides a breakdown of his last twenty-four years into the following four (roughly equal in length) time periods to see its trends: early (1522 to 1526), early-middle

(1527 to 1533), late-middle (1534 to mid-1540), and late (mid-1540 to early-1546). The distribution of mentions (or the amount of repetition of the "death as sleep" idea) for each of these four time periods follows: early (71), early-middle (46), late-middle (36), and late (67). This means that during the first five years, Luther had a high level of confidence in his interpretation of Scripture on this topic (i.e., 71 exceeds 46, 36, and 67). Additionally, the effect on the last period of his life, from his previous nineteen years, was a positive one where neither his environment nor his own further study of Scripture would change his mind. Clearly, during the last five to six years of his life, the amount of repetition (being measured as 67 instances) far exceeded both of the previous periods, with each of these three periods being roughly equal in length (67 > 46 and 67 > 36). The method I use to demonstrate Luther's actual belief about the nature of death is twofold. First, the emphasis Luther placed on the idea is reflected by both the quantity and the timing of its occurrences. Second, his sincerity and meaning of "death as sleep" is reflected by providing many quotes of Luther in their social/historical context.

It is helpful to assess Luther's dedication to this subject by including a year-to-year comparison of high-volume years. The calendar year with the most mentions is 1532 with 26 instances. The next two high-volume years are as follows: 1540 (with 24) and 1522 (with 20 instances of mentioning "death as unconscious sleep"). The obvious observation from this distribution data is that Luther hit this subject hard in the early 1520s, the early 1530s, and the early 1540s. The average of annual mentions is only nine times per year [(210 mentions) / (24 years) = 8.8] meaning these three particular years (1522, 1532, and 1540) were outstanding examples far above a typical year (e.g., three times as much). The most emphasis in a single day was 23 instances in a lecture on Genesis 25:7–10 in late 1540. Believing that he probably was going to die soon (due to much illness), Luther kept talking about this subject nonstop, and like never before that particular day in the classroom, when he was halfway through his Genesis lecture series. My strict criteria for treating a reference to "death as unconscious sleep" by Luther (and thus being part of the running total) includes the exclusion of quotes of Scripture and its commentators.

It is most relevant to one of my main claims (seen in chapter 2) that Luther's comments on the last four chapters of Genesis in mid-to-late 1545, only a few months before he died, consisted of 11 distinct mentions of "death as unconscious sleep." Throughout the last 24 years of his life, Luther would consistently tell everyone who would listen—whether in public sermons or in more private lectures at the university—that death should be understood as being similar to sleep. And for those Christians who were interested, the implications of this deduction go beyond purgatory and prayers to saints.

And for all Christians, it even goes beyond alleviating our common fear of death for ourselves and our loved ones. The several ramifications of Luther's "death as unconscious sleep" claim has the potential of showing why his assertions are relevant and even important today to both individuals and to the church in practical and helpful ways.

The best approach when explaining Luther's theology of death is to include a characterization that clearly says he held to an unwavering belief lasting 24 years until he died that Scripture teaches us that death is like an unconscious sleep and the event of our bodily resurrection will bring back our consciousness. He was not vague or inconsistent about the nature of death as some have claimed. Luther never once reverted back to his previous belief. It was not just a "young Luther" who believed it "for a while." Throughout this period (from mid-to-late 1522 until his death in 1546), he did not ever advocate contradictory positions on this subject when his explanations are fully considered. "Death is like an unconscious sleep" was his true opinion for more than a temporary stage of his life, contrary to the relatively recent observations of eight published authors who characterized Luther's writings mistakenly—as identified in chapter 2.

Furthermore, Luther intended to use *sleep* symbolically as opposed to the soul of the deceased literally sleeping. The best evidence of this claim is the several indications Luther gave early in his teaching career, in addition to mid-career and also near the end, that all point in the direction of a symbolic use of *sleep* during death. What this specifically means, for Luther, is that it was in the sense of a soul/mind that no longer exists when the body dies (except in God). Therefore, I have concluded from my search of primary sources of Luther's writings that he undoubtedly held consistently to a physicalist view of the soul's nature with some minor modifications. Clearly, Luther was described by some people centuries ago to have held to mortalism regarding the soul within a person. The factor that can be confusing to some people relates to divine interactions with the soul of the deceased, as well as just overlooking Luther's scattered explanations for how it is understandable. As seen in chapters 8 and 9, Luther made many comments that would place his view of death in the mortalist or physicalist category (with a different nuance, though) after considering his whole understanding of the process that occurs in heaven to prepare an unconscious person, and the contents of their mind, for the next stage of life.

Moses, David, Daniel, Matthew, Luke, and Paul are examples of biblical writers who described death as being like sleep in some sense. Additionally, the prophet Jeremiah repeatedly wrote "sleep" in the context of literal death in his quotes of God. When the divine Son of God said "sleep" too— regarding the death and reversal of death of his friend, Lazarus, in addition to using this word for the deceased daughter of the synagogue official, Jesus himself was purposely describing the nature of death, and was not just referring to it with a worldly euphemism as many suggest.

Why did the apostles of Jesus misunderstand him, just days before he was crucified, regarding Lazarus "falling asleep in death" if this euphemism of *sleep* was actually common then? Perhaps they missed Jesus' use of *sleep* for the death of Lazarus because it wasn't common then. Today, it is a typical refrain that this euphemism of "sleep = death" in the Bible didn't mean anything. Additionally, as seen in the OT: why would God use a meaningless euphemism with his prophet, Jeremiah? Since this prophet of God wrote the phrase similarly in two different passages that God spoke, this repetition was probably important. And why do some Christian authors today say that references to "death as sleep" are rare in Scripture when Paul wrote it nine times in just two of his letters (to the church in Corinth and in Thessalonica)? Plus, we see it another five times in Matthew, John, and Acts, in addition to six more times in the OT (not counting another thirty-five verses that say, "fell asleep with his fathers and was buried")? Who benefits when Christians continue the tradition that God's promised gift of eternal life for the person actually applies to *everyone* throughout the world *at birth* as opposed to sometime after death when we actually obtain this literal gift?[1] How can we be sure this biblical repetition means nothing in particular? No scholar can be certain that these uses by God in the OT, and by Jesus in the NT, of *sleep* as describing death meant nothing important regarding the deceased person's consciousness or their soul.

Understanding what the prophets and apostles of God have said about human death and resurrection has the potential of causing a faithful believer to trust God even more. A belief in death being like a sleep—in which people are awakened from it—can eventually be comforting, or at least helpful in dealing with the feeling of God's wrath near death, as a God-fearing person tries to overcome the common fear of death. Althaus suggests that "everything depends on the fact that the Christian acknowledges the gracious meaning of dying by dying willingly."[2] This was based on Luther claiming that "the best that can happen in death is that our will accepts it."[3]

---

1. The NT has fifteen "death as sleep" verses (Matt 9:24; 27:52; John 11:11; Acts 7:60; 13:36; 1 Cor 11:30; 15:6, 18, 20, 51; Eph 5:14; 1 Thess 4:13–15; 5:10). The OT has forty-one "death as sleep" verses (Jer 51:39, 57; Dan 12:2; Pss 13:3, 90:5; 1 Kgs 11:43; plus another thirty-five verses in the OT very similar to this one which says, "Solomon slept with his fathers, and was buried").

2. Althaus, *Theology of Martin Luther*, 407.

3. Luther, quoted in Althaus, *Theology of Martin Luther*, 407. See WA 10, III, 76. This portion of WA is in German, and this book by Althaus was translated by Robert

In another sermon, Luther said the following: "Therefore, such a believer is so filled with joy and happiness that he does not allow himself to be terrified . . . he is afraid only of God, his Lord, who is in heaven—otherwise he is afraid of nothing that might happen to him."[4] Althaus describes the following quotes of Luther as follows:

> Since God uses a man's death to set him free from himself and from death, the Christian desires death. Luther prays, "Help us not to fear but to desire death."[5] And he confesses, "We should be happy to be dead and desire to die."[6] . . . He understands Christian perfection specifically in terms of the desire for death. The final sanctification in the Christian's life "is that he becomes perfect and gladly gives his life into death; with Paul (Phil 1:23), he desires to depart so that all sin will cease and that God's will may be fully accomplished in him."[7] . . . "Death, then, which previously was a punishment of sin is now a remedy for sin."[8] . . . Death, freed of the wrath of God in this way, is now really a sleep.[9]

It is relevant and important to discuss the relationship of "death as sleep" to "complete mortality" of a person (i.e., the perishing of both the body and the soul/mind when the life-giving force of God, the spirit, "returns" to God, as Ecclesiastes 12:7 describes what happens to God's "breath of life" at that moment). A debate on the timing of obtaining the characteristic of immortality of the soul, as a fundamental feature of human beings (e.g., around birth versus after death), then leads to a discussion, and perhaps a rethinking, of the nature of hell. Is God the type of Creator and loving sustainer to have set up a system consisting of nonstop torture for those who disobey and finally reject God's offer of redemptive love?[10] If the reader has

---

C. Schultz. It was published in 1966 in which Althaus wrote that his translation was "competent and accurate" (on page viii). The Latin parts of WA were frequently paraphrased by Althaus, and Schultz writes that these quotes of Luther are indicated in the translated version.

4. Luther, quoted in Althaus, *Theology of Martin Luther*, 111. See WA 12, 442.

5. Luther, quoted in Althaus, *Theology of Martin Luther*, 408. See WA 6, 14.

6. Luther, quoted in Althaus, *Theology of Martin Luther*, 408. See WA 12, 410 and WA 39, I, 512.

7. Luther, quoted in Althaus, *Theology of Martin Luther*, 408. See WA 17, II, 13.

8. Luther, quoted in Althaus, *Theology of Martin Luther*, 408. See WA 10, III, 76.

9. Althaus, *Theology of Martin Luther*, 408.

10. If you're interested in different interpretations of Scripture's many indirect references to hell, perhaps you may want to check out rethinkinghell.com or the Facebook group named "Rethinking Hell."

already rejected literal torment, or the traditional view of hell, then does our God honor his numerous prophecies of death and destruction for those who disobey or finally reject God's love?

Consider the example of a wicked person who chooses to remain separated from God's forgiveness: why do some believers define hell as being a "separation from God" when that's mainly just a continuation of their situation in this world? How is this view of hell (i.e., separation from God) different from a wicked person's own life of rejecting God, and how is this a display of justice when they are already used to it? Perhaps the threat/promise of real punishment for evil people seen throughout Scripture should not be diluted with this *separation* idea—which may be a response to the odd characterization of a loving God that tortures people endlessly. Obtaining a fuller understanding of the attributes of God—to know God better—in the area of perfect love versus complete justice over the very long term relates to reconsidering the nature of hell that God created.

In the beginning when God decided exactly when human beings would obtain immortality for their soul, and whether only a portion of humanity would receive the literal gift of eternal life, God thus determined whether the life actually lived should be a factor in a person existing forever or not. When God decided to banish Adam and Eve from having further access to the tree of life (which would have provided them immortality even though they had already sinned, according to Genesis 3:22–23), having this characteristic of deathlessness necessarily depended on their choice to obey a simple rule. The repeated references to this same tree of life in Revelation 2:7; 22:2, 14, and 19 make this idea important. It is relevant today because in Jesus' message to the church located in Ephesus, he described the location of the tree of life to be found "in the Paradise of God" which is our hopeful destination and one's right of access to it (e.g., "I will grant to eat of the tree of life").

It seems likely the literal banishment from Eden's life-tree, thus making it a literal tree in that garden, parallels this life-tree in Revelation and its contextual hints of it being meant literally (particularly in Rev 2:1–7). Hence, it also may be a future literal tree in paradise, which implies some similarity between the distant past and the future right around the corner regarding the process of obtaining, or "putting on" (as Paul put it) the *clothes* of immortality. Paul reminded his good friend, Timothy, that humans have been excluded from having immortality of the soul *within* themselves because "only God possesses immortality" (1 Tim 6:16).

In conclusion, this book shows that Luther was surprisingly convinced from his intense study of the Holy Bible that death is very different from what the church taught. Instead of the deceased being still conscious, they generally remain without consciousness until our resurrection from the dead. Luther believed that a new understanding of death was important to followers of Christ, and that Christianity's reconsideration of the scriptural descriptions and definition of *death*, based on the teaching of Jesus Christ, should begin with the "unconscious sleep of death" since its ramifications can be quite helpful in understanding much of Scripture better, including its major doctrines, and in knowing God better.

Epilogue

The Reformer who was named after Saint Martin of Tours, who famously gave part of his cape to some shivering beggar in real need, had one final assertion to write before dying. Luther said it is true that "we are beggars."[1] To care for others—to show love—was Luther's response after clearly denying the selfish motivation of doing good works to earn salvation. Also, perhaps, it is because of the undeserved favor that God gives—the grace of God—that Luther selected this closing phrase using his pen. Going back to his mid-thirties while confronting the authorities over his refusal to recant over indulgences (and also over divine forgiveness of one's sins being available through faith instead of purchase), Luther probably chose his last word to the world to be about the error of pride.

His point about who we are, and who the church is, still applies today, of course. We should not feel prideful, Luther is saying, about earning our own salvation—since that is not how God sees it, according to Paul. More specifically, the traditional and institutional pride that once inflated the price of God's forgiveness should serve as a reminder about the dangers of pride in mistaken tradition. The ocean of writings from this most-religious Reformer can also serve as a guide today for how to distinguish between traditional beliefs that are truthful as God sees it, and those that are inaccurate.

Ω

We read the following from *Table Talk* entry #797: "The 7th of August 1538, Luther discoursed concerning the life to come, and said: In my late sickness I lay very weak, and committed myself to God, when many things fell into

---

1. See WA-TR 5:168, WA-TR 5:317–318, and WA 48:241. He wrote this in February 1546. See footnote 83 in chapter 7 for more detail, including who lost this valuable piece of paper on which Luther penned his final thoughts.

my mind, concerning the everlasting life, what it is, what joys we there shall have . . . But how [come] . . . we cannot believe God's Word?"[2] And from #796, Luther said the following: "When Adam lived, that is, when he sinned, death devoured life; when Christ died, that is, was justified, then life, which is Christ, swallowed up and devoured death; therefore God be praised, that Christ died, and has got the victory."[3] And from #790, Luther stated: "It is written in the history of St. Martin, that being near his death . . . these were right words of faith. Such and the like ought we to cull out of the legends of the saints, wholly omitting the fooleries that the papists have stuffed therein."[4] And from #789, he said: "I know I have not long to live . . . now, loving Lord God, I hope my time is not far hence; God help me . . . I desire to live no longer."[5] And finally, from #791, Luther offered the following advice to his hearers and readers: "Comfort yourself against death . . . be not afraid."[6]

Martinus Luther

---

2. See the 1848 edition of Luther, *Table Talk*, s.v. "DCCXCVII [#797]," 323. From page x: "The contents of the book . . . were gathered from the mouth of Luther, by his friends . . . who were very much with the great Reformer towards the close of his life."
3. See the 1848 edition of Luther, *Table Talk*, s.v. "DCCXCVI [#796]," 322.
4. See the 1848 edition of Luther, *Table Talk*, s.v. "DCCXC [#790]," 320.
5. See the 1848 edition of Luther, *Table Talk*, s.v. "DCCLXXXIX [#789]," 319.
6. See the 2004 edition of Luther, *Table Talk*, s.v. "DCCXCI [#791]," 430.

APPENDIX

Analysis Tables and Outlines

Analysis tables on Luther's claim about the nature of death

Each of the following tables was created from my original research as described in the previous chapters and forms the basis of my conclusion above.

Table 1. Comparison of periods that Luther discussed death as unconsciousness

Time Period (inclusive)	Length (years)	Number of Instances
1483/84–1504	21–22	0
1505–21	17	0
1522–26	5	72
1527–33	7	46
1534–mid-1540	6.5	36
mid-1540–early-1546	6	56
TOTAL		210 instances

Table 2. Relevant works (by type and number of distinct daily events) A "distinct daily event" is a day that Luther published on the topic, or talked about, "death as unconscious sleep" after exclusions—which totals sixty-one days throughout his life (see column E description from Table 7).

Days	Type of Work	Days	Type of Work
29	Sermon	2	Funeral speech
14	University lecture	2	Unknown
4	Personal letter	1	Academic disputation
3	Sermon/explanation	1	Hymnal preface
2	Biblical commentary	1	Hymn lyrics
2	Table talk (informal)	61	**TOTAL DAYS**

Table 3. Genesis chapters with the most instances in the Genesis lecture series.

Chapter	Instances	Year
2	3	1535
5	3	1536
15	1	1538
22	1	1539
25	24	1540
26	6	1542
42	9	1544
47	1	1545
48	2	1545
49	6	1545
50	1	1545
Total	57 instances	

Table 4. Most instances ranked by type of work.

Rank	Instances	Type of Work (Subject)	Years
1	57	Lecture series (Genesis)	1535–45
2	18	Sermon series (1 Cor 15)	1532–33
3	16	Funeral speech (Duke John)	1532

Table 5. Sermons and lectures on books of the Bible with death as unconsciousness.

Biblical Book (chapter)	Years
Ecclesiastes (9)	1526
Titus (1)	1527
Psalms (3, 90, and 118)	1530–34
1 Corinthians (15)	1532–33
Matthew (9, 16, 19, and 23)	1523–40
Genesis (2, 5, 15, 22, 24–26, 42, 47–50)	1535–45

Table 6. Years ranked by highest incidence of "death as unconscious sleep" mentions.

Rank	Year	Instances
1	1532	26
2	1540	24
3	1522	21

NOTE: The year 1532 would be the exact mid-point of Luther's career speaking about the nature of death—if one started with *The Fourteen of Consolation* in 1519 (with Luther's assertion that death is a "rest in peace" to them that believe—in the context of purgatory—and not just to honored saints) until his last mention within the Genesis lecture series in November 1545. $[\{(1545-1519) / 2\} + 1519 = 1532]$.

Table 7. Measuring Luther's emphasis in his works containing "death as sleep"

The grand total of legitimate expressions of "death as unconscious sleep" was discovered by this author in various series of English translations of the works of Luther to total 210 instances of repetition, as described as follows:

Column Description:

A. Running total of days Luther mentioned "death as unconscious sleep"

B. Year of composition, or delivery of sermon, lecture, etc. ("<1532>" means it was likely written in 1532; "<1532?>" means it was likely written before 1532)

C. Number of distinct instances of "death as unconscious sleep" within the particular item

D. Running total of instances of "death as unconscious sleep"

E. Distinct daily events; excludes sermons handled by editors of revised editions (such as Cruziger and Roth) which were usually not closely reviewed by Luther (e.g., published in 1544)

F. Type of published work

G. Title of work, shortened (AT means after Trinity Sunday; AE means after Easter Sunday)

A	B	C	D	E	F	G
1	1522 (Jan)	9	9	1	Letter	To Amsdorf
2	1522	4	13	1	Sermon	1st Sunday AT
3	1522, 1540	2	15	2	Sermon/Exp.	1st Sunday Advent
4	1522	1	16	1	Sermon	1 Pet 1:4
5	1522	3	19	1	Sermon	2 Pet 3:8–11
6	1522, 1540	2	21	2	Sermon	St. Stephen's Day
7	1523–24	1	22	1	Sermon	3rd Sunday AE
8	1523–24	3	25	1	Sermon	Pentecost Wed.
9	1523–24	1	26	1	Sermon	2nd Sun. in Lent
10	1523–24	1	27	1	Sermon	Epiphany

APPENDIX: ANALYSIS TABLES AND OUTLINES

A	B	C	D	E	F	G
11	1524, 1542	1	28	2	Hymn	In Peace and Joy
12	1523–24	9	37	1	Sermon	16th Sunday AT
13	1523–25	1	38	1	Sermon	Easter Tuesday
14	1525, 1540	5	43	2	Sermon	5th Sun. in Lent
15	1523–25	17	60	1	Sermon	24th Sun. AT, 2nd version
16	1523–25	1	61	1	Sermon	24th Sun. AT, 1st version
17	1526	11	72	1	Lecture	Eccl 9:5–6,10
18	1527	1	73	1	Lecture	Titus 1:1–2
19	1530	3	76	1	Letter	To Hans Luther
20	1530	1	77	1	Letter	To Melanchthon
21	1530	1	78	1	Commentary	Ps 118
22	<1532?	2	80	1	Commentary	Ps 3
23	?	2	82	1	Table-talk	#742
24	?	1	83	1	Table-talk	#98
25	1532	16	99	2	Funeral	Duke John
26	<1532>	10	109	2?	Sermon	1 Cor 15
27	<1533>	8	117	1	Sermon	1 Cor 15
28	1533	1	118	1	Sermon	Michaelmas
29	1534–36	7	125	1	Sermon/Exp	Annotations on Matthew
30	?	2	127	1	?	(in Althaus footnote)
31	?	1	128	1	?	(in Althaus footnote)
32	1534	1	129	1	Lecture	Ps 90:1
33	1535	7	136	1	Sermon	6th Sunday AT
34	1531–45	1	137	1	Sermon	Luke 21
35	1536	1	138	1	Disputation	Concerning Man
36	1538	1	139	1	Sermon	Matt 19:13–15
37	1539–40	2	141	1	Sermon	Matt 23:3
38	1539–40	1	142	1	Sermon	Matt 23:29–30
39	1535	3	145	1	Lecture	Gen 2:21
40	1536	3	148	1	Lecture	Gen 5:21–24

A	B	C	D	E	F	G
41	1540	1	149	0	Lecture	Gen 25:7–10
42	1538	1	150	1	Lecture	Gen 15:13–16
43	1538	3	153	1	Sermon	Luke 1:68–79
44	1539	1	154	1	Lecture	Gen 22:11
45	1540	1	155	1	Sermon	Matt 24:29
46	1540	23	178	1	Lecture	Gen 25:7–10
47	1541	1	179	1	Letter	To Myconius
48	1542	4	183	1	Preface	Funeral Songs
49	1542	2	185	1	Letter	To Amsdorf
50	1542	6	191	1	Lecture	Gen 26:2–5
51	1544	9	200	1	Lecture	Gen 42:38
52	1545	1	201	1	Sermon	1 Cor 15:54–57
53	1545	1	202	1	Lecture	Gen 47:29–30
54	1545	1	203	1	Lecture	Gen 48:21
55	1545	6	209	1	Lecture	Gen 49:33
56	1545 (Nov)	1	210	1	Lecture	Gen 50:24–26

The grand total of mentions of "death as unconscious sleep" is 210 instances from January 1522 to November 1545. Luther raised this idea (excluding the unapproved 1544 revised editions) on, at least, 61 days total (56 plus 5 days from column E for revisions closely handled by Luther and republished).

Outlines

Outline 1. Description of a lecture by Luther on Romans 6:3 in the winter of 1515/1516: "Death as sleep" discussed in some unspecified sense (but probably not as *unconsciousness*)

i. Death is very often called *a sleep* in Scripture

ii. The most proper sense of *death* is that in which people see it as eternal death with no hope of resurrection

Outline 2. Description of Luther's unusual discussions of death: 1517 to 1521

i. Hebrews lecture series (delivered in 1517, Heb 2:14)

   a. Luther quoted Chrysostom on the nature of death

ii. *The Fourteen of Consolation* (written in Sept. 1519)

   a. Death is a rest in peace to them that believe, and not just to honored saints

iii. *Treatise on Baptism* (published in Nov. 1519)

   a. Our increase in righteousness does not end at death, but instead continues until the last day

   b. Only then will that be finished which the lifting up out of baptism signifies. Then shall we arise from death

iv. "Second Sunday in Advent: Luke 21" (delivered in Jan. 1521)

   a. Luther raises questions about the whereabouts of the soul, or the mind, of the deceased

   b. "Do you think that God must have a physical stall, as a shepherd has for his sheep?"

v. *Explanations* (written in March 1521, in response to the papal bull threatening excommunication)

   a. It is not clear that Luther was discussing the nature of literal death (at the often-referred to 27th article) since he also wrote there that the 1513 bull on immortality of the soul acted as if the common belief "in the life everlasting" in the Apostles' Creed was not already well-known and accepted.

   b. This ambiguity on his actual beliefs can be clarified by later comments he made over his life to his university students, for example.

Outline 3. Summary quotes of Luther when he discussed literal death as consisting of unconsciousness: 1522 to 1546

i. 1522: 20 instances of "death as sleep" for the year

   a. January: personal letter to Amsdorf ("I am inclined to agree with your opinion that the souls of the just are *asleep* and that they do not know where they are up to the Day of Judgment. . . . with few exceptions all ['departed souls'] *sleep* without possessing any capacity of feeling")—9 instances in the letter.

b. June: sermon titled, "First Sunday after Trinity" on Luke 16:19–31 ("All the fathers before Christ's birth . . . at death . . . fell *asleep* . . . and still *sleep* there until the Last Day.")

c. July to December: sermon/explanation titled, "First Sunday in Advent" on Matthew 21:1–9 ("Hence the death of the believer in Christ is not death but a *sleep*, for he neither sees nor tastes death.")

d. July to December: sermon on 1 Peter 1:4 ("So will it be with us when we are raised from the dead and have been a thousand years or more under the ground, we will think it is a short time that we *slept* in the grave.")

e. July to December: sermon on 2 Peter 3:8–11 ("So when man dies the body is buried and wastes away, lies in the earth and *knows nothing*; but when the first man rises at the Last Day, he will think he has lain there *scarcely an hour*.")

f. July to December: sermon/explanation titled, "St. Stephen's Day" on Acts 6:8–15 and Acts 7:54–60 ("It not only teaches but also excites and stimulates by calling death a '*sleep*,' at which all the world is horrified. . . . The Christian's death is a *sleep*.")

ii. 1523 to 1526: 51 instances of "death as unconscious sleep" during this period

   a. 1523/1524/1525: 40 instances

   b. 1526: 11 instances

iii. 1527 to 1531: 11 instances of "death as unconscious sleep"

   a. 1527: 1 instance

   b. 1530: 5 instances

   c. 1531/year unknown: 5 instances

iv. 1532: 26 instances of "death as unconscious sleep" (the record for one calendar year)

   a. August: funeral speeches for Duke John (16 instances)

   b. August to December: lectures on 1 Corinthians 15 (likely 10 instances for this calendar year)

v. 1533 to 1534: 20 instances of "death as unconscious sleep"

   a. 1533: likely 9 instances for this calendar year (8 of them from lectures on 1 Corinthians, ending in April)

   b. 1534/year unknown: 11 instances

vi. 1535 to mid-1540: 25 instances of "death as unconscious sleep"

   a. 1535: 10 instances

b. 1536: 4 instances

c. 1537–1539/year unknown: 5 instances

d. 1538: 5 instances

e. January to June 1540: 1 instance

vii. Mid-1540 to early 1546: 57 instances of "death as unconscious sleep"

   a. July to December 1540: 24 total, but 23 instances in one day (23 instances is a record)

   b. 1541: 1 instance

   c. 1542: 12 instances

      1. Preface to a burial hymnal (4 instances)

      2. Letter to Amsdorf (2 instances)

      3. Lecture on Genesis 26:2–5 (6 instances)

   d. 1544: 9 instances

   e. mid-to-late 1545: 11 instances

      1. Genesis 47:29–30: "He falls *asleep* most pleasantly with a calm and collected mind as he passes from this world."

      2. Genesis 48:21: "This is the theology we teach. It is altogether different from the theology which the blind and foolish scholastics and papists retain. . . . I shall die and fall asleep in peace."

      3. Genesis 49:33 (6 instances) "The words 'was gathered to his people' are truly splendid and full of meaning. . . . This way of speaking should be pleasing to us for it testifies that ever since the beginning of the world the saints fell *asleep* in faith and in the hope of the resurrection . . . Where, then, did he go? God has a receptacle in which the saints and the elect *rest* without death, without pain and hell. . . . Those who believed in the Seed of the woman did not perish and were not consigned to oblivion but were gathered to their people. . . . Thus the place of the dead has no torments; but, as we say, they *rest* in peace [RIP] . . . We depart, and we return on the Last Day, *before we are aware* of it . . . [We sleep] in most peaceful *sleep* and *rest*."

      4. Genesis 50:26: "He wants that tomb to be before the eyes of all his descendants, in order that his children and grandchildren . . . may persevere in the same faith and promise in which he had fallen *asleep* with his fathers. This is now the dear Genesis. . . . I can do no more."

   f. 1546: unknown (Luther died on February 18, 1546).

Bibliography

Cited Writings of Luther

The *Luther's Works* Series

Brown, Christopher Boyd, ed. *Luther's Works*. Vol. 67, *Annotations on Matthew*. St. Louis: Concordia, 2015.
———. "General Introduction." In *Luther's Works: Church Postil IV*, edited by Benjamin T. G. Mayes and James L. Langebartels, 78:vii–viii. St. Louis: Concordia, 2015.
———. *Luther's Works*. Vol. 58, *Sermons V*. St. Louis: Concordia, 2010.
Brown, Christopher Boyd, and Benjamin T. G. Mayes, eds. *Luther's Works*. Vol. 68, *Sermons on the Gospel of St. Matthew; Chapters 19–24*. St. Louis: Concordia, 2014.
Forell, George W. "Introduction to Volume 32." In *Luther's Works: Career of the Reformer II*, edited by Helmut T. Lehmann and George W. Forell, 32:ix–xx. Philadelphia: Muhlenberg, 1958.
Krodel, Gottfried G. "Letter 111 Introduction." In *Luther's Works: Letters I*, edited by Helmut T. Lehmann and translated by Gottfried G. Krodel, 48:360. Philadelphia: Fortress, 1963.
Lehmann, Helmut T., and E. Theodore Bachmann, eds. *Luther's Works*. Vol. 35, *Word and Sacrament I*. Philadelphia: Muhlenberg, 1960.
Lehmann, Helmut T., and Franklin Sherman, eds. *Luther's Works*. Vol. 47, *The Christian in Society IV*. Philadelphia: Fortress, 1971.
Lehmann, Helmut T., and George W. Forell, eds. *Luther's Works*. Vol. 32, *Career of the Reformer II*. Philadelphia: Muhlenberg, 1958.
Lehmann, Helmut T., and Gottfried G. Krodel, eds. *Luther's Works*. Vol. 48, *Letters I*. Philadelphia: Fortress, 1963.
———. *Luther's Works*. Vol. 49, *Letters II*. Philadelphia: Fortress, 1972.
Lehmann, Helmut T., and Harold J. Grimm, eds. *Luther's Works*. Vol. 31, *Career of the Reformer I*. Philadelphia: Fortress, 1957.
Lehmann, Helmut T., and John W. Doberstein, eds. *Luther's Works*. Vol. 51, *Sermons I*. Philadelphia: Muhlenberg, 1959.
Lehmann, Helmut T., and Lewis W. Spitz, eds. *Luther's Works*. Vol. 34, *Career of the Reformer IV*. Philadelphia: Muhlenberg, 1960.

Lehmann, Helmut T., and Ulrich S. Leupold, eds. *Luther's Works*. Vol. 53, *Liturgy and Hymns*. Philadelphia: Fortress, 1965.

Luther, Martin. "Letter 111: To Nicholas von Amsdorf, Wartburg, January 13, 1522." In *Luther's Works: Letters I*, edited by Helmut T. Lehmann and translated by Gottfried G. Krodel, 48:360–64. Philadelphia: Fortress, 1963.

Mayes, Benjamin T. G., and James L. Langebartels, eds. *Luther's Works*. Vol. 75, *Church Postil I*. St. Louis: Concordia, 2013.

———. *Luther's Works*. Vol. 76, *Church Postil II*. St. Louis: Concordia, 2013.

Oswald, Hilton C., ed. *Luther's Works*. Vol. 25, *Lectures on Romans*. St. Louis: Concordia, 1972.

———. *Luther's Works*. Vol. 28, *Commentary on 1 Corinthians 7, 1 Corinthians 15, Lectures on 1 Timothy*. St. Louis: Concordia, 1973.

———. "Introduction to Volume 25." In *Luther's Works: Lectures on Romans*, edited by Hilton C. Oswald, 25:ix–xiv. St. Louis: Concordia, 1972.

Pelikan, Jaroslav, ed. "Introduction to Volume 14." In *Luther's Works: Selected Psalms III*, edited by Jaroslav Pelikan and Daniel E. Poellot, 14:ix–xii. St. Louis: Concordia, 1958.

———. "Introduction to Volume 29." In *Luther's Works: Lectures on Titus, Philemon, and Hebrews*, edited by Jaroslav Pelikan and Walter A. Hansen, 29:ix–xii. St. Louis: Concordia, 1968.

———. *Luther's Works*. Vol. 1, *Lectures on Genesis: Chapters 1–5*. St. Louis: Concordia, 1958.

———. *Luther's Works*. Vol. 3, *Lectures on Genesis: Chapters 15–20*. St. Louis: Concordia, 1961.

———. *Luther's Works*. Vol. 13, *Selected Psalms II*. St. Louis: Concordia, 1956.

Pelikan, Jaroslav, and Daniel E. Poellot, eds. *Luther's Works*. Vol. 2, *Lectures on Genesis: Chapters 6–14*. St. Louis: Concordia, 1960.

———. *Luther's Works*. Vol. 14, *Selected Psalms III*. St. Louis: Concordia, 1958.

Pelikan, Jaroslav, and Hilton C. Oswald, eds. *Luther's Works*. Vol. 15, *Notes on Ecclesiastes, Lectures on the Song of Solomon, Treatise on the Last Words of David*. St. Louis: Concordia, 1972.

Pelikan, Jaroslav, and Walter A. Hansen, eds. *Luther's Works*. Vol. 4, *Lectures on Genesis; Chapters 21–25*. St. Louis: Concordia, 1964.

———. *Luther's Works*. Vol. 5, *Lectures on Genesis; Chapters 26–30*. St. Louis: Concordia, 1968.

———. *Luther's Works*. Vol. 7, *Lectures on Genesis; Chapters 38–44*. St. Louis: Concordia, 1965.

———. *Luther's Works*. Vol. 8, *Lectures on Genesis; Chapters 45–50*. St. Louis: Concordia, 1966.

———. *Luther's Works*. Vol. 29, *Lectures on Titus, Philemon, and Hebrews*. St. Louis: Concordia, 1968.

Spitz, Lewis W. "Introduction to Volume 34." In *Luther's Works: Career of the Reformer IV*, edited by Helmut T. Lehmann and Lewis W. Spitz, 34:xi–xvii. Philadelphia: Muhlenberg, 1960.

Other than *Luther's Works* Series

Cameron, Bruce A. *Luther's Summaries of the Psalms: A Model for Contemporary Psalm Interpretation*. Master's thesis, Concordia Seminary, 1991.

Cole, Henry. "Translator's Preface." In *The Creation: A Commentary on the First Five Chapters of the Book of Genesis . . . and Now First Translated into English*, translated by Henry Cole, iii–xxxvi. Edinburgh: T. & T. Clark, 1858.

Cole, Henry. "The Consolatory Tesseradecad of Martin Luther for the Weary and Heavy Laden." In *Select Works of Martin Luther: An Offering to the Church of God in the Last Days*, translated by Henry Cole, 2:123–74. London: Simpkin and Marshall, 1826.

———. *Select Works of Martin Luther: An Offering to the Church of God in the Last Days*. Vol. 1. London: Simpkin and Marshall, 1826.

———. *Select Works of Martin Luther: An Offering to the Church of God in the Last Days*. Vol. 2. London: Simpkin and Marshall, 1826.

Cole, Henry, trans. *The Creation: A Commentary on the First Five Chapters of the Book of Genesis . . . and Now First Translated into English*. Edinburgh: T. & T. Clark, 1858.

Currie, Margaret A., trans. *The Letters of Martin Luther*. London: MacMillan, 1908.

Hazlitt, William, trans. *The Table Talk, or Familiar Discourse of Martin Luther*. London: Bogue, 1848.

———. *The Table Talk of Martin Luther*. London: Bell, 1890.

———. *Table Talk*. Rev. ed. Philadelphia: Lutheran Publication Society, 2004.

Jacobs, Henry Eyster, and Adolph Spaeth. *Works of Martin Luther: with Introductions and Notes*. Vol. 1. Philadelphia: Muhlenberg, 1915.

Kellerman, James A., trans. "The Last Written Words of Luther . . . A Translation of WA-TR, 5:168 (no. 5468)." http://www.iclnet.org/pub/resources/text/wittenberg/luther/beggars.txt.

Kerr, Hugh Thomson, Jr., ed. *A Compend of Luther's Theology*. Philadelphia: Westminster, 1943.

Lenker, John Nicholas. "First Sunday in Advent." In *Luther's Church Postil Gospels: Advent, Christmas and Epiphany Sermons; Translated Now for the First Time into English*, edited by John Nicholas Lenker, 1:17–58. Minneapolis: Lutherans in All Lands, 1905.

Lenker, John Nicholas, ed. and trans. *The Epistles of St. Peter and St. Jude Preached and Explained by Martin Luther*. Minneapolis: Lutherans in All Lands, 1904.

———. *Luther's Church Postil Gospels*. Vol. 1, *Advent, Christmas and Epiphany Sermons; Translated Now for the First Time into English*. Minneapolis: Lutherans in All Lands, 1905.

———. *Luther's Church Postil Gospels*. Vol. 2, *Epiphany, Lent and Easter Sermons: Translated Now for the First Time into English*. Minneapolis: Lutherans in All Lands, 1906.

———. *Luther's Church Postil Gospels*. Vol. 3, *Pentecost or Missionary Sermons: Translated Now for the First Time into English*. Minneapolis: Lutherans in All Lands, 1907.

———. *Luther's Church Postil Gospels*. Vol. 4, *First to Twelfth Sunday after Trinity: Translated Now for the First Time into English*. Minneapolis: Lutherans in All Lands, 1904.

———. *Luther's Church Postil Gospels*. Vol. 5, *Thirteenth to Twenty-Sixth Sunday after Trinity: Translated Now for the First Time into English*. Minneapolis: Lutherans in All Lands Co., 1905.

———. *Luther's Commentary on the First Twenty-Two Psalms*. Vol. 1. Translated by Henry Cole. Sunbury, PA: Lutherans in All Lands, 1903.

———. *Luther's Epistle Sermons*. Vol. 1, *Advent and Christmas Season*. Minneapolis: Luther, 1908.

———. *Luther's Epistle Sermons*. Vol. 2, *Epiphany, Easter and Pentecost*. Minneapolis: Luther, 1909.

———. *Luther's Epistle Sermons*. Vol. 3, *Trinity Sunday to Advent*. Translated by Joseph Stump. Minneapolis: Luther, 1909.

Luther, Martin. *D. Martin Luthers Werke (Weimarer Ausgabe)*. Weimar, Germany: Bohlau, 1883–2009.

———. "The Fourteen of Consolation (Tessaradecas Consolatoria)." http://www.godrules.net/library/luther/NEW1luther_a11.htm.

———. "Sermon XVII." In *Thirty-four Sermons on the Most Interesting Doctrines of the Gospel*, 240–69. Glasgow: Bryce, 1767.

Plass, Ewald M. *What Luther Says: An Anthology*. Vol. 1. St. Louis: Concordia, 1959.

Schulze, J. A. *Dr. Martin Luther's House-Postil, or, Sermons on the Gospels for the Sundays and Principal Festivals of the Church-Year*. Vol. 3. Columbus: Schulze, 1884.

Smith, Preserved. *The Life and Letters of Martin Luther*. 2nd ed. Boston: Houghton Mifflin, 1914.

Smith, Preserved, and Charles M. Jacobs, eds. *Luther's Correspondence and Other Contemporary Letters*. Vol. 2. Philadelphia: Lutheran Publication Society, 1918.

Strodach, Paul Zeller. "Christian Songs, Latin and German, for Use at Funerals." In *Works of Martin Luther: with Introductions and Notes*, edited by Henry Eyster Jacobs and Adolph Spaeth, 6:287–92. Philadelphia: Holman, 1932.

———. "Hymn Book Prefaces: Introduction." In *Works of Martin Luther: with Introductions and Notes*, edited by Henry Eyster Jacobs and Adolph Spaeth, 6:277–82. Philadelphia: Holman, 1932.

———. *Works of Martin Luther: with Introductions and Notes*. Vol. 6. Philadelphia: Holman, 1932.

Vautroullier, Thomas, ed. *A Commentary on the Psalms Called Psalms of Degrees*. London: Simpkin and Marshall, 1819.

Cited Sources Other than Writings of Luther

The American Heritage College Dictionary. 3rd ed. Boston: Houghton Mifflin, 1993.

Althaus, Paul. *Die letzten Dinge*. Gütersloh, Germany: Bertelsmann, 1933.

———. *The Theology of Martin Luther*. Translated by Robert C. Schultz. Philadelphia: Fortress, 1966.

"Apostles' Creed." http://www.catholic.org/prayers/prayer.php?p=220.

Armfield, Henry Thomas. *The Gradual Psalms: A Treatise on the Fifteen Songs of Degrees*. London: Hayes, 1874.

Athanasius of Alexandria. *On the Incarnation*. Middletown, DE: Fig, 2013.

Baker, David W., ed. *Looking into the Future: Evangelical Studies in Eschatology*. Grand Rapids: Baker Academic, 2001.

Ball, Bryan W. *A Great Expectation: Eschatological Thought in English Protestantism to 1660.* Leiden: Brill, 1975.

———. *The Soul Sleepers: Christian Mortalism from Wycliffe to Priestley.* Cambridge: Clarke, 2008.

Barth, Hans-Martin. *The Theology of Martin Luther: A Critical Assessment.* Translated by Linda M. Maloney. Minneapolis: Fortress, 2013.

Bayer, Oswald. *Martin Luther's Theology: A Contemporary Interpretation.* Translated by Thomas H. Trapp. Grand Rapids: Eerdmans, 2008.

Blackburne, Francis. *A Short Historical View of the Controversy Concerning an Intermediate State and the Separate Existence of the Soul between Death and the General Resurrection.* London: Field, 1765.

Boehmer, Heinrich. *Der junge Luther.* Edited by Heinrich Bornkamm. Stuttgart: Koehler, 1951.

———. *Road to Reformation: Martin Luther to the Year 1521.* Translated by John W. Doberstein and Theodore G. Tappert. Philadelphia: Muhlenberg, 1946.

Bornkamm, Heinrich. *Luther's World of Thought.* Translated by Martin H. Bertram. St. Louis: Concordia, 1958.

Brecht, Martin. *Martin Luther: His Road to Reformation, 1483–1521.* Translated by James L. Schaaf. Philadelphia: Fortress, 1985.

———. *Martin Luther: The Preservation of the Church; 1532–1546.* Translated by James L. Schaaf. Minneapolis: Fortress, 1993.

Bucer, Martin. "Martin Bucer to Beatus Rhenanus, May 1, 1518." In *Luther's Correspondence and Other Contemporary Letters: 1507–1521,* edited by Preserved Smith, 1:80–83. Philadelphia: Lutheran Publication Society, 1913.

Burns, Norman T. *Christian Mortalism from Tyndale to Milton.* Cambridge: Harvard University Press, 1972.

Calvin, John. "Preface by John Calvin to a Friend." In *Calvin's Tracts Containing Antidote to the Council of Trent: German Interim with Refutation, True Method of Restoring the Church: Sinfulness of Outward Conformity to Romish Rites: and Psychopannychia, or the Soul's Imaginary Sleep between Death and Judgment,* translated from the original Latin and French by Henry Beveridge, 3:413–90. Edinburgh: Constable, 1851.

Canright, D. M. *A History of the Doctrine of the Soul, among All Races and Peoples, Ancient and Modern.* 2nd ed. Battle Creek, MI: Seventh-Day Adventist, 1882.

Catechism of the Catholic Church. Rev. ed. London: Chapman, 1999.

Centre for Genetics Education. "Fact Sheet 1: An Introduction to DNA, Genes and Chromosomes." https://www.genetics.edu.au/publications-and-resources/facts-sheets/fact-sheet-1-an-introduction-to-dna-genes-and-chromosomes.

Childs, Brevard. *Introduction to the Old Testament as Scripture.* Philadelphia: Fortress, 1979.

Chrysostom, John. "Homily VI: 1 Thess 4:9–10." In *The Homilies of S. John Chrysostom, Archbishop of Constantinople, on the Epistles of S. Paul the Apostle to the Philippians, Colossians, and Thessalonians,* 396–405. Rev. ed. Oxford: Parker, 1879.

———. "Homily VIII: 1 Thess 4:15–17." In *The Homilies of S. John Chrysostom, Archbishop of Constantinople, on the Epistles of S. Paul the Apostle to the Philippians, Colossians, and Thessalonians,* 414–25. Rev. ed. Oxford: Parker, 1879.

———. "Homily IX: 1 Thess 5:1–2." In *The Homilies of S. John Chrysostom, Archbishop of Constantinople, on the Epistles of S. Paul the Apostle to the Philippians, Colossians, and Thessalonians*, 426–39. Rev. ed. Oxford: Parker, 1879.

The Commission on Worship of The Lutheran Church–Missouri Synod, ed. *Lutheran Service Book*. St. Louis: Concordia, 2006.

Constant, Eric A. "A Reinterpretation of the Fifth Lateran Council Decree *Apostolici regiminis* (1513)." *Sixteenth Century Journal* 33.2 (2002) 353–79. http://www.jstor.org/stable/4143912.

Crisp, Thomas M., et al., eds. *Neuroscience and the Soul: The Human Person in Philosophy, Science, and Theology*. Grand Rapids: Eerdmans, 2016.

Cullmann, Oscar. *Immortality of the Soul or Resurrection of the Dead? The Witness of the New Testament*. London: Epworth, 1958.

de Lubac, Henri. *Medieval Exegesis: The Four Sense of Scripture*. Grand Rapids: Eerdmans, 1998.

Dobbs-Mickus, Kelly, et al., eds. *Gather*. 3rd ed. Chicago: GIA Publications, 2011.

Doermann, Ralph W. "Luther's Principles of Biblical Interpretation: Can We Still Use Them?" In *Interpreting Luther's Legacy*, edited by Fred W. Meuser and Stanley D. Schneider, 14–25. Minneapolis: Augsburg, 1969.

Ebeling, Gerhard. *Luther: An Introduction to his Thought*. Translated by R. A. Wilson. Philadelphia: Fortress, 1970.

Edwards, Mark U., Jr. Endorsement for Lohse, *Martin Luther's Theology: Its Historical and Systematic Development*. https://fortresspress.com/product/ martin-luthers-theology-its-historical-and-systematic-development.

Ericksen, Robert P. *German Churches and the Holocaust: Assessing the Argument for Complicity*. The Raul Hilberg Memorial Lecture, University of Vermont, April 15, 2013.

Free Methodist Church. *Free Methodist Hymnal: Published by Authority of the General Conference of the Free Methodist Church of North America*. Chicago: Free Methodist, 1915.

———. *The Hymn Book of the Free Methodist Church*. Rochester: Roberts, 1883.

———. *The Hymnal for Worship and Celebration: Hymnal of the Free Methodist Church*. Nashville: Word Music, 1986.

———. *Hymns of the Living Faith*. Winona Lake: Light and Life, 1951.

———. *Hymns of Faith and Life*. Winona Lake: Light and Life, 1976.

Froom, Le Roy Edwin. *The Conditionalist Faith of Our Fathers: The Conflict of the Ages over the Nature and Destiny of Man*. Vol. 2. Washington, DC: Review and Herald, 1965.

Gabor, Ittzes. "'The Breath Returns to God Who Gave it': The Doctrine of the Soul's Immortality in Sixteenth-Century German Lutheran Theology." ThD diss., Harvard University, 2009.

George, Timothy. "General Introduction." In *Reformation Commentary on Scripture: New Testament, Luke*, edited by Beth Kreitzer and Timothy George, 3:xxi–xliv. Downers Grove: IVP Academic, 2015.

———. "George Huntston Williams." In *The Contentious Triangle: Church, State, and University; A Festschrift in Honor of Professor George Huntston Williams*, edited by Rodney L. Petersen and Calvin Augustine Pater, 15–34. Sixteenth Century Essays and Studies 51. Kirksville: Thomas Jefferson University Press, 1999.

———. *Theology of the Reformers*. Nashville: Broadman, 1988.

Green, Joel B., ed. *What about the Soul? Neuroscience and Christian Anthropology*. Nashville: Abingdon, 2004.

Green, Joel B., and Stuart L. Palmer, eds. *In Search of the Soul: Four Views of the Mind-Body Problem*. Downers Grove: InterVarsity, 2005.

Gritsch, Eric W. *Martin—God's Court Jester: Luther in Retrospect*. Philadelphia: Fortress, 1983.

Hagen, Kenneth. "An Addition to the Letters of John Lang: Introduction and Translation." *Archiv fur Reformationsgeschichte* 60 (1969) 31.

———. *A Theology of Testament in the Young Luther: The Lectures on Hebrews*. Studies in Medieval and Reformation Thought 12. Leiden, Netherlands: Brill, 1974.

Heim, Karl. *Die Gemeinde der Auferstandenen*. Munich: Neubau-Verlag, 1949.

Heinz, Johann. "Martin Luther and His Theology in German Catholic Interpretation Before and After Vatican II." *Andrews University Seminary Studies* 26.3 (1988) 253–65.

Hendrix, Scott H. *Martin Luther: Visionary Reformer*. New Haven: Yale University Press, 2015.

Hillerbrand, Hans J., ed. *The Oxford Encyclopedia of the Reformation*. Vol. 3. New York: Oxford University Press, 1996.

Hillerbrand, Hans J., trans. "Luther's Will: 1542." In *Christian Life in the World*, edited by Hans J. Hillerbrand, 5:9–13. The Annotated Luther. Minneapolis: Augsburg Fortress, 2017.

Holder, R. Ward, "Luther, Martin." In *The Westminster Handbook to Theologies of the Reformation*, edited by R. Ward Holder, 104–5. Louisville: Westminster John Knox, 2010.

Hsia, R. Po-Chia. *The Cambridge History of Christianity*. Vol. 6, *Reform and Expansion, 1500–1660*. Cambridge: Cambridge University Press, 2007.

Hughes, Richard T. "Restoration, Historical Models of." In *The Encyclopedia of the Stone-Campbell Movement*, edited by Douglas A. Foster et al., 638. Grand Rapids: Eerdmans, 2004.

Kantonen, Taito A. *The Christian Hope*. Philadelphia: Muhlenberg, 1954.

Kellerman, James A. trans. "The Last Written Words of Luther . . . A Translation of WA-TR, 5:168 (no. 5468)." http://www.iclnet.org/pub/resources/text/wittenberg/luther/beggars.txt.

Ketola, Toivo N. "A Study of Martin Luther's Teaching Concerning the State of the Dead." Master's thesis, Seventh-day Adventist Theological Seminary, Washington, DC, 1946.

Kolb, Robert, and Carl R. Trueman. *Between Wittenberg and Geneva: Lutheran and Reformed Theology in Conversation*. Grand Rapids: Baker Academic, 2017.

Kolb, Robert, et al., eds. *The Oxford Handbook of Martin Luther's Theology*. Oxford: Oxford University Press, 2014.

Kostlin, Julius. *The Theology of Luther in its Historical Development and Inner Harmony*. Vol. 1. Translated by Charles E. Hay. Philadelphia: Lutheran Publication Society, 1897.

Lohse, Bernhard. *Martin Luther: An Introduction to His Life and Work*. Translated by Robert C. Schultz. Philadelphia: Fortress, 1986.

———. *Martin Luther's Theology: Its Historical and Systematic Development*. Translated by Roy A. Harrisville. Minneapolis: Fortress, 1999.

Lortz, Joseph. *Die Reformation in Deutschland*. Vol. 1. 4th ed. Freiburg: Herder, 1962.

Lull, Timothy F., ed. "Introduction." In *Martin Luther's Basic Theological Writings*, 1–6. Minneapolis: Fortress, 1989.

Marius, Richard. *Martin Luther: The Christian between God and Death*. Cambridge: Harvard University Press, 1999.

Martin, Craig. "Pietro Pomponazzi." *The Stanford Encyclopedia of Philosophy*. https://plato.stanford.edu/archives/win2017/entries/pomponazzi.

Marty, Martin. *Martin Luther: A Penguin Life*. New York: Penguin Group, 2004.

Matheson, Peter, ed. *Reformation Christianity*. A People's History of Christianity 5. Minneapolis: Fortress, 2007.

Maxfield, John A. *Luther's Lectures on Genesis and the Formation of Evangelical Identity*. Sixteenth Century Essays and Studies 80. Kirksville: Truman State University Press, 2008.

McDermott, Gerald R. *The Great Theologians: A Brief Guide*. Downers Grove: InterVarsity, 2010.

McGrath, Alister E., ed. "The Last Things." In *The Christian Theology Reader*, 534–66. 4th ed. Chichester: Wiley-Blackwell, 2011.

McKim, Donald K., ed. *The Cambridge Companion to Martin Luther*. Cambridge, UK: Cambridge University Press, 2003.

Methodist Episcopal Church. *Hymns for the Use of the Methodist Episcopal Church*. Rev. ed. Cincinnati: Hitchcock and Walden, 1849.

Metzger, Bruce M., and Bart D. Ehrman. *The Text of the New Testament: Its Transmission, Corruption, and Restoration*. 4th ed. New York: Oxford University Press, 2005.

Meuser, Fred W., and Stanley D. Schneider, eds. *Interpreting Luther's Legacy*. Minneapolis: Augsburg, 1969.

Michelet, M. (Jules). *The Life of Luther: Written By Himself*. Translated by William Hazlitt. London: Bogue, 1846.

Moltmann, Jurgen. *The Coming of God: Christian Eschatology*. Translated by Margaret Kohl. Minneapolis: Fortress, 1996.

———. "Is There Life after Death?" In *The End of the World and the Ends of God: Science and Theology on Eschatology*, edited by John Polkinghorne and Michael Welker, 238–55. Harrisburg: Trinity Press International, 2000.

Morey, Robert A. *Death and the Afterlife*. Minneapolis: Bethany, 1984.

Murphy, Nancey. "Human Nature: Historical, Scientific, and Religious Issues." In *Whatever Happened to the Soul? Scientific and Theological Portraits of Human Nature*, edited by Warren S. Brown et al., 1–29. Minneapolis: Fortress, 1998.

———. "Introduction." In *Neuroscience and the Person: Scientific Perspectives on Divine Action*, edited by Robert John Russell et al., i–xxxvii. Vatican City State: Vatican Observatory, 1999.

Murphy, Nancey, and Christopher C. Knight, eds.. *Human Identity at the Intersection of Science, Technology, and Religion*. Burlington: Ashgate, 2010.

Noll, Mark A. *Turning Points: Decisive Moments in the History of Christianity*. 3rd ed. Grand Rapids: Baker Academic, 2012.

Oberman, Heiko A. "Hus and Luther." In *The Contentious Triangle: Church, State, and University: A Festschrift in Honor of Professor George Huntston Williams*, edited by Rodney L. Petersen and Calvin Augustine Pater, 135–66. Sixteenth Century Essays and Studies 51. Kirksville: Thomas Jefferson University Press, 1999.

"Ordinary Time: November 10th: Memorial of St. Leo the Great, Pope and Doctor." http://www.catholicculture.org/culture/liturgicalyear/calendar/day.cfm?date=2017-11-10.

"Ordinary Time: November 11th: Memorial of St. Martin of Tours, bishop; Veterans Day (USA)." https://www.catholicculture.org/culture/liturgicalyear/calendar/day.cfm?date=2019-11-11.

O'Reggio, Trevor. "A Re-examination of Luther's View on the State of the Dead." *Journal of the Adventist Theological Society* 22.2 (2011) 154–70.

Oxford University Press. "About Us." https://global.oup.com/academic/aboutus/?lang=en&cc=us.

———. "Oxford Encyclopedia of the Reformation." https://global.oup.com/academic/product/the-oxford-encyclopedia-of-the-reformation-9780195064933?cc=us&lang=en&#.

Papal Encyclicals Online. "Fifth Lateran Council 1512–17 A.D." http://www.papalencyclicals.net/Councils/ecum18.htm.

Paulson, Steven. *Luther for Armchair Theologians*. Armchair Theologians. Louisville: Westminster John Knox, 2004.

Pelikan, Jaroslav. *From Luther to Kierkegaard: A Study in the History of Theology*. St. Louis: Concordia, 1950.

Pernoud, Regine. *Martin of Tours: Soldier, Bishop, Saint*. Translated by Michael J. Miller. San Francisco: Ignatius, 2006.

Peters, Ted, et al., eds. *Resurrection: Theological and Scientific Assessments*. Grand Rapids: Eerdmans, 2002.

Piper, John. *Martin Luther: Lessons from His Life and Labor*. Minneapolis: Desiring God Foundation, 2012.

Plass, Ewald M. *This is Luther: A Character Study*. St. Louis: Concordia, 1948.

Plass, Ewald M., ed. *What Luther Says: An Anthology*. Vol. 1. St. Louis: Concordia, 1959.

Quistorp, Heinrich. *Calvin's Doctrine of the Last Things*. Translated by Harold Knight. London: Lutterworth, 1955.

Rathel, Mark. "Theories of Death." In *The Popular Encyclopedia of Apologetics*, edited by Edward E. Hindson and Ergun M. Caner, 164–67. Eugene, OR: Harvest, 2008.

Roman Catholic Church. *Decrees of the Ecumenical Councils*. Vol. 1, *Nicaea I to Lateran V*. Edited by Norman P. Tanner. Translated by the Trustees for Roman Catholic Purposes Registered. London: Sheed and Ward, 1990.

Rosin, Robert. *Reformer, the Preacher, and Skepticism: Luther, Brenz, Melanchthon, and Ecclesiastes*. Mainz, Germany: von Zabern, 1997.

"Saint Leo I." https://www.britannica.com/biography/Saint-Leo-I.

Science Clarified. "Genes and DNA." http://www.scienceclarified.com/scitech/Genetics/Genes-and-DNA.html.

Schwarz, Hans. *The Human Being: A Theological Anthropology*. Grand Rapids: Eerdmans, 2013.

———. "Luther's Understanding of Heaven and Hell." In *Interpreting Luther's Legacy: Essays in Honor of Edward C. Fendt*, edited by Fred W. Meuser and Stanley D. Schneider, 83–94. Minneapolis: Augsburg, 1969.

Secker, Philip J. "Martin Luther's Views on the State of the Dead." *Concordia Theological Monthly* 38.7 (July–August 1967) 422–35.

Selderhuis, Herman. *Martin Luther: A Spiritual Biography*. Wheaton: Crossway, 2017.

Smith, Preserved. "Complete List of Works of Luther in English, Compiled, Chronologically Arranged, and Annotated." *The Lutheran Quarterly* 48 (October 1918) 490–508.

Stange, Carl. *Luther's Gedanken über die Todesfurcht.* Berlin: de Gruyter, 1932.

———. *Studien zur Theologie Luthers.* Gutersloh, Germany: Bertelsmann, 1928.

Szczucki, Lech. "George H. Williams' Studies on the Radical Reformation in Central Europe." In *The Contentious Triangle: Church, State, and University; A Festschrift in Honor of Professor George Huntston Williams*, edited by Rodney L. Petersen and Calvin Augustine Pater, 129–34. Sixteenth Century Essays and Studies 51. Kirksville: Thomas Jefferson University Press, 1999.

Tavard, George H. *The Starting Point of Calvin's Theology.* Grand Rapids: Eerdmans, 2000.

Thielicke, Helmut. "Death in Luther's Theology." In *Death and Life*, translated by Edward H. Schroeder, 150–61. Philadelphia: Fortress, 1970.

Thiselton, Anthony C. *Life after Death: A New Approach to the Last Things.* Grand Rapids: Eerdmans, 2012.

Toledo, Chelsea, and Kirstie Saltsman. "Genetics by the Numbers." https://www.nigms.nih.gov/education/Inside-Life-Science/Pages/genetics-by-the-numbers.aspx.

Tregelles, Samuel P. *An Account of the Printed Text of the Greek New Testament.* London, Bagster: 1854.

University of Leicester. "DNA, Genes and Chromosomes." https://www2.le.ac.uk/projects/vgec/schoolsandcolleges/topics/dnageneschromosomes.

"What is the Apostles' Creed?" https://billygraham.org/answer/what-is-the-apostles-creed.

Whitford, David M. *Luther: A Guide for the Perplexed.* Guides for the Perplexed. London: T. & T. Clark, 2011.

Williams, George Huntston. "Radical Reformation." In the *Oxford Encyclopedia of the Reformation*, edited by Hans J. Hillerbrand, 3:375–84. New York: Oxford University Press, 1996.

———. *The Radical Reformation.* Sixteenth Century Essays and Studies 15. 3rd ed. Kirksville: Sixteenth Century Journal, 1992.

Wolff, Hans Walter. *Anthropology of the Old Testament.* Translated by Margaret Kohl. Philadelphia: Fortress, 1974.

Wriedt, Markus. "Luther's Theology." In *The Cambridge Companion to Martin Luther*, edited by Donald K. McKim and translated by Katharina Gustavs, 86–119. Cambridge: Cambridge University Press, 2003.

www.ingramcontent.com/pod-product-compliance
Lightning Source LLC
Chambersburg PA
CBHW070249230426
43664CB00014B/2468